GROW YOUR OW
ORGANIC
FRUIT &
VEGETABLES
A COMPLETE GUIDE

GROW YOUR OWN
ORGANIC
FRUIT &
VEGETABLES

A COMPLETE GUIDE

JOHN FEDOR

Consultant: Bob Sherman of Garden Organic

Photography by Steven Wooster

FRANCES LINCOLN LIMITED
PUBLISHERS

DEDICATION
For David and my mother,
who are always there when I need them,
And for Babcia,
who inspired me to garden.

Frances Lincoln Limited
4 Torriano Mews
Torriano Avenue
London NW5 2RZ
www.franceslincoln.com

Grow Your Own Organic Fruit and Vegetables
Copyright © Frances Lincoln Limited 2001
First Frances Lincoln edition published in 2001
as *Organic Gardening for the 21st Century*
This paperback edition published in 2010

Text copyright © John Fedor 2001
Photographs © Steven Wooster
Illustrations Sarah John and Kate Simunek
© Frances Lincoln Limited 2001
Designed and edited by PAGE*One*
for Frances Lincoln Limited

A catalogue record for this book is available
from the British Library.

ISBN 978 0 7112 3073 6

Printed and bound in China

1 2 3 4 5 6 7 8 9

CONTENTS

INTRODUCTION BY BOB SHERMAN
DIRECTOR OF OPERATIONS, GARDEN ORGANIC

Published by *Country Life* magazine in 1900, *The Century Book of Gardening* makes no mention of organic gardening – this term had yet to be coined. On the other hand, it mentions few pesticides. Following a century of impressive developments and innovations, the still labour-rich estates had all the technological advances of the time as well as the calloused wisdom of countless Victorian gardeners behind them. This knowledge, however, included only a few instant remedies for controlling pest and disease. Reliance was principally placed on good husbandry, observation and knowledge of what constituted healthy growing conditions for plants. *The Century Book of Gardening* makes much reference to a 'love of gardens' and 'love of gardening', a passion that is not often associated with the staid formality generally ascribed to the period. But perhaps this passion, combined with that good husbandry, should be our starting point for *Grow Your Own Organic Fruit and Vegetables.*

What gardeners have always shared, together with a fair measure of curiosity, is a deep love for plants and the process of growing. Contact with the soil is so basic, so levelling and yet uplifting – especially if our efforts are successful. We are in a situation where, while imposing some degree of control, we are not in absolute control. Luck and judgment play almost equal parts. Our attempts during the twentieth century to impose ever more control over nature have led to an unparalleled assault on the environment that sustains us. In the space of a few decades in the middle of the century the arsenal of controls employed by farmers and gardeners alike mushroomed into a poisonous cloud of toxins that rapidly led to loss of habitat and loss of wildlife, and now even threatens human health. Few of the early chemicals remain in legal use and the aggressive 'garden warfare' approach has been replaced.

Now organic gardeners, once a few die-hard desperadoes, are no longer pioneering radicals. At the start of a new millennium they quite probably form close to a majority, with many additional aspirants making just a few concessions to the now old-fashioned way of gardening.

Nothing looks or tastes quite as good as your own home-grown organic produce, harvested ready for the kitchen table.

MARRYING THE OLD WITH THE NEW

It should never be thought that organic gardening is backward looking. It is very much twenty-first century in outlook, embracing a great deal of technology and science that was not available to our forebears. We know more about soil, about plants, about the life cycles of pests and diseases, and about the relationships between pest and predator. Predators come in many sizes and are not all large-toothed felines or canines. If you are the size of a pinhead, a lacewing is a seriously dangerous creature, yet an insouciant gardener could casually crush it without noticing. A gardener able to recognize beneficial insects will carefully nurture such garden friends, finding them suitable homes and creating wildlife-friendly habitats where they can thrive. Thus gardening becomes ecology with a concern for habitats and even entomology, because insects are so fascinating and varied.

We are now able to mimic a range of infinitesimally tiny smells given off by insects to attract mates or to warn of danger. Use of these smells, or pheromones, allows us to trick misinformed pests to a sticky death on a trap or to panic them with a chaos of mixed messages, thus keeping them away from our plants. This technology is improving year by year and is of enormous benefit to organic gardeners without causing any harm to the environment. Gone are the days when decisions were based on the approach

Organic gardening embraces the gardener's love for plants and the process of growing, and combines it with a deep respect for the environment.

of 'if it moves, spray it; if it doesn't, squash it'. In an organic garden the aim is to encourage balance. There will always be pests but, if you can provide a safe haven for predatory and parasitic beneficial creatures, you will have more time to enjoy your garden and spend less time fighting it.

It is important to remember that, however keen we may be on our gardens, we only spend our leisure hours there. For other creatures it is their whole world; they live and die there. We have a responsibility to them.

EARTH MATTERS

Surely one of the greatest contributions to the future that any of us can make is to feed and nurture the soil. Faced with environmental degradation, pollution of air and water, rapidly escalating world population and loss of forest and hedgerow, the individual can feel powerless. Yet one major service that anyone can perform is to make compost – such a simple task but one that is of great value to us and our environment.

The soil is not an inert medium but buzzes soundlessly with life, perhaps even more frantically than the world above ground! What sustains this microcosm is organic matter. Our soils are bound by it and stimulated by it. It is a natural recycling process requiring little effort and only a modicum of skill for adequate success. By composting we are reducing landfill, improving soil and feeding our plants at no extra cost to the planet. It is all benefit. Why should anyone need synthetic fertilizers? Nature's own fertilizer is free and infinitely recyclable. In the 1900s a major concern was rural migration to the cities and towns in search of work in the new industries. One hundred years later the legacy of that concern is still with us but other much more pressing problems now face us, the origins of which can also be seen in those years of massive technological growth. There is much we can do to make beneficial changes to reverse the damage even in the small spaces that we tend. I am delighted to be able to add my few words to John Fedor's sound practical advice in the pages that follow. With his help you can learn to tread lightly on the land, take all you need and leave a piece of paradise for gardeners to come.

Asparagus is one of a wide range of vegetables and fruits that are high in disease-fighting phytochemicals.

CHAPTER 1

GARDENING ORGANICALLY

WHY GARDEN ORGANICALLY?

As more people are now discovering, gardening is a fun pastime that takes us away from our hectic duties. With growing concern about man-made chemicals in what we eat, gardening organically offers us the opportunity to produce tasty food that is good for us and for the environment.

GOOD FOOD FOR GOOD HEALTH

Our personal health and diet have assumed growing importance in recent times. Awareness and consideration of the relationship between our health and the food we eat is receiving more attention every day. News stories report that some vegetables have cancer-fighting properties; government campaigns urge us to eat more vegetables and fruits, and to reduce the amount of fat and sugar in our diets.

The welfare of the environment is also a key issue in the twenty-first century, and has become a common topic in political debates. The effects of global warming are evident in our changed weather patterns. Many of us are concerned about reports of toxic environmental pollutants being spilled or leaked into our rivers and drinking water, especially when these incidents happen uncomfortably close to our homes. The disregard for the environment is putting our health at risk.

WORKING AGAINST NATURE

Most commercial agricultural practices work against nature, which produces some undesirable results: topsoil is lost or is of lower quality; land becomes less fertile; and the excessive use of pesticides results in resistant insects. The natural predators of these pests are often greatly reduced in number by the pesticides, which in turn creates more pests and the need for even

stronger pesticides to be produced. In some places the problem has been still further aggravated by the introduction of non-native pests, for which there are no local predators. As the population of the world grows, cities sprawl and the amount of usable farmland decreases. At the same time, the productivity of the existing farmland decreases because of topsoil degradation and loss. To keep productivity levels the same or higher, inorganic fertilizers are often deemed necessary; however, these products create other problems. For example, inorganic fertilizers can kill off soil micro-organisms which make nutrients and trace elements available to plants.

WORKING WITH NATURE

Using synthetic chemicals in the garden is not a sustainable method of growing food. Today's organic gardeners are looking to produce fresh, tasty, nutritious food for the table. They want to enjoy food that is not tainted with chemicals; they also want what is good for the environment.

Many gardeners are choosing to use the environmentally friendly techniques offered by organic gardening. They then no longer have to worry about young children coming into contact with synthetic weedkillers and fertilizers on the lawn and shrubs, or causing unintentional harm to visiting wildlife. With organic gardening, very few commercial products are required. Kitchen and garden waste are recycled into compost, reducing the amount of rubbish sent to the incinerator or landfill, while soil fertility is increased by the organic method and helps to reverse environmental damage. Especially in the home garden, organic practices need a minimum of space to grow plants intensively and produce a large crop of vegetables.

WHY GARDEN ORGANICALLY?

FRESH PRODUCE FOR THE TABLE

If you garden organically, the food that you grow is picked fresh and used in the kitchen for the next meal or preserved for later in the year. It is also much fresher than shop-bought produce. Generally, when fruits and vegetables are harvested, they begin to lose nutrients. Vitamins and enzymes start to break down, and the more time that passes, the less nutritious the food and less delicious the flavour. When you grow vegetables in your garden, you are likely to choose the variety based on flavour, texture, scent, appearance and nutritional value. In contrast, the varieties grown for commercial production are generally chosen for good looks, the ability to be shipped long distances without spoiling or bruising, and ease of cultivation and harvesting.

The most common reason why gardeners choose to practise organic techniques is to provide pesticide- and additive-free, nutritious food for the table. However, there are many other reasons to garden organically. The environment benefits from the reduction in chemical pollution, destruction of the soil and contamination of drinking water, rivers, lakes and streams. And when trees, shrubs and flowering plants are grown organically, they provide a healthy habitat for insects and animals.

DRAWING ON TRADITION

I have been asked many times if beautiful ornamental gardens can really be grown without using synthetic chemicals. The answer is a resounding 'Yes'. The use of manufactured pesticides and other chemicals in the garden is a recent invention, dating back little more than a hundred years. Long before these chemicals were invented, beautiful gardens existed (although they were more labour-intensive).

Throughout history, people have used the land around their houses to grow food for use in the kitchen. The kitchens were virtually miniature factories where fruits and vegetables were preserved in autumn for use throughout the year. Bread was baked, not bought; food was prepared, not taken out of a tin and reheated. People were much more self-sufficient than they are today.

By gardening organically and preserving our own food using methods that retain flavour and nutrients, we are learning to become a little more self-sufficient like our forebears, providing better food for ourselves and our families, and helping to save the environment.

Successional planting helps ensure a steady supply of lettuces for use in the kitchen from spring through to autumn.

WHAT IS ORGANIC GARDENING?

The definition of organic gardening is quite elusive. It involves a complicated series of rules and regulations drawn up by governments or organic certifying organizations. But generally it boils down to a few key issues that can be explained and understood quite easily.

KEY CONCEPTS OF ORGANIC GARDENING
Organic practices avoid the use of most manufactured pesticides, herbicides and mineral or synthetic fertilizers. The soil is kept healthy, rich with nutrients and, most importantly, it is kept alive with a high content of micro-organisms. The essence of all organic techniques is to work with nature, not against it. All refuse produced in the kitchen and garden is recycled back into the soil. Organic gardening is a sustainable activity: the soil is fed by the gardener; the soil feeds the plants; the plants

By using close spacing when planting crops in beds, you will help to keep weeds at bay and prevent the loss of moisture from the soil.

WORKING WITH THE SOIL

Organic gardeners have a particularly close relationship with the soil. They do not think of soil as a largely inert medium to which mineral fertilizers and nutrients are added. Nor do they think of it as being simply the place where plants' roots reside. Organic gardeners value and respect the soil as a living ecosystem of organisms, minerals and organic matter. The organisms interact with organic and inorganic materials and water to provide nutrients that the plants need in order to survive. Organic gardeners know that healthy, vital soil is essential to grow flowering plants, shrubs and trees, and vegetables successfully. They need to understand the complexities of the soil's ecosystem in order to develop and maintain optimal conditions for soil health and plant growth.

feed the gardener. The plants also provide excess organic matter, which is composted and used to feed the soil. The entire cycle is fuelled by sunlight and water. By working with nature, you can control pests in your garden. If you create an inviting habitat for natural predators, they will be drawn to your garden where they will feed on pests. Weeds are removed by hoeing. Plants are spaced closely to conserve water by reducing evaporation from the soil. By shielding the soil from sunlight, the intensive planting helps to prevent weed seeds from germinating and growing. Soils with a high humus content will feed the plants, making them healthy, vigorous, and less prone to damage by pests and diseases.

Organic gardeners rotate crops to discourage pests and diseases – even in small gardens, crop rotation is very beneficial (see pp. 78–81). Choosing resistant varieties of plants is not a requirement of most organic standards; however, by selecting varieties that best suit your region and climate you will greatly reduce pest and disease problems in the garden. Seed-saving (see p. 24), again not a requirement by most organic standards, enables you to select a strain of a variety that particularly suits your garden. In

effect, you are producing a site-specific plant variety that will experience fewer problems.

As an organic gardener, you will be rewarded for keeping a close watch over the garden, taking note of birds and other predators, and looking out for pests and weeds. From these observations, you will learn to recognize the delicate balance in nature. For example, the presence of particular weeds in a bed may draw your attention to deficiencies in the soil, which you can take steps to remedy.

When a problem occurs, you will realize that something is out of balance. The instant 'fix' may be an organic remedy, but the long-term solution is to restore the balance in nature. If a plant begins to fail, an application of a high-nitrogen liquid organic feed may provide the immediate cure, while the long-term solution would be to rotate the crop the following year to a bed where beans or peas – valued for their ability to fix nitrogen in the soil – had grown that year.

Looking after the soil is the organic gardener's number-one task. If the soil is fertile, full of life and moist (not waterlogged or dry), plants will be healthy and vigorous, bearing an abundant crop with little damage from pests and diseases.

SUSTAINABILITY

Sustainability refers to the ability of a society or an ecosystem to function indefinitely without squandering the resources on which it relies. In terms of the organic garden, it means no net loss of nutrients or topsoil.

SUSTAINABILITY IN AGRICULTURE

Most common agricultural practices call for the use of large tractors, which consume lots of fuel. Chemicals are brought on to the field by the lorry load. Yet more fuel is used when crops are subsequently transported long distances. It is estimated that for every calorie of food produced by this form of agriculture, between three and ten calories are used, mostly in the form of non-renewable fossil fuel. Clearly this type of agriculture is not sustainable indefinitely.

The solution to the problem lies in local food production utilizing organic techniques. While it is sometimes argued that organic practices are not commercially viable, in fact these techniques can cut production costs faced by farmers. Savings on chemicals and fuel more than offset the cost of extra labour demanded by organic methods.

Local food produced using organic techniques offers many benefits for the environment:

- Global warming and pollution are not further increased by the use of fossil fuels.
- Ground water does not become polluted with agricultural chemicals.
- Topsoil is not lost or reduced because of poor soil management.
- Topsoil is created by organic techniques.
- Biological diversity is promoted.
- A natural balance between predator and pest is encouraged.

EDIBLE LANDSCAPING

Planning the landscaping around your house is an important part of organic gardening. By choosing a wide range of trees, bushes, perennials and annuals, you are encouraging biodiversity – of plant, animal and insect species – in your garden. Group together plants that have similar cultural needs and try to provide food for wildlife as well as for people when designing the landscape. The land around your house provides an opportunity not only to grow food but also to plant a variety of flowers and herbs that nourish the soul. In many developed nations around the world, natural habitats are disappearing. Organic gardeners are provided with the opportunity to care for their small plot in a way that protects and sustains wildlife. They are able to leave the land in better ecological shape than when it came under their stewardship.

THE IMPORTANCE OF BIODIVERSITY

What is biodiversity and why is it important? Biodiversity refers to all organisms on Earth, from single-cell bacteria to plants, viruses and fungi. Biodiversity often refers to the genetic variation between individuals. The evolution of a species is dependent on this genetic variation because conditions may change, making some members unable to survive, while others that have even very slightly different genes may flourish.

Biodiversity has taken on three specific meanings:
● Genetic diversity between individuals.
● Diversity of breeds within a species.
● Diversity of species existing in an ecosystem.

Diversity in all three areas is important. As an ecosystem of its own, the garden needs different species. If a single crop were planted, the monoculture could easily result in a crop failure due to pests. By planting a diversity of crops, a wide variety of wildlife can be attracted into the garden. Beneficial insects and other predators will control pests also drawn to the garden.

The diversity of breeds within a species is also vital. In commercial agriculture, very few varieties of any particular vegetable are grown, and consequently many varieties are fast being lost (for example, three open-pollinated varieties of corn are now extinct). This results in a reduction of the gene pool. When a change in growing conditions or the introduction of a disease affects commonly cultivated varieties, the food supply may be in jeopardy. Less popular varieties are often kept from extinction by the interest and efforts of home gardeners. On a few occasions these near-extinct varieties have been used to develop new strains after disaster has hit commercial varieties.

Open pollination is a means of growing a seed crop so that it is pollinated only by plants of its

Create informal areas with wild flowers and fruit-bearing shrubs to provide habitats and food for beneficial insects and wildlife.

own variety. Open-pollinated plants show greater genetic diversity between the individuals of a particular variety than Fı hybrids (see p. 67). This genetic diversity results in some individual seeds producing plants that perform better than others in the growing conditions of a particular garden. If the seeds from the better plants are saved and replanted, the beneficial traits can be repeated with a greater portion of the crop raised in the following year.

THE ORGANIC CYCLE

Organic gardening imitates the cycles found in nature, but with the addition of our help, to produce wonderfully nutritious vegetables and fruits for the table. Nothing is wasted here, everything is recycled by making compost and saving seeds. The only deviation from the cycle in nature is the deliberate rotation of crops in order to discourage pests and diseases. In the organic cycle, the compost feeds the soil; the soil feeds the plants; and the plants feed the people. The plants are used to make the compost; and this year's plants provide next year's seeds.

Saving seed

Making compost

Food to eat

HARVESTING

Harvested food is eaten fresh or stored to ensure a supply of produce throughout autumn and winter. The remains of harvested plants, together with kitchen waste, are added to the compost heap, while seeds for sowing the following year are saved from varieties that have grown successfully.

DIGGING THE SOIL

In nature, the soil is loosened by earthworms, deep-rooted plant growth, and the freeze–thaw cycle. This process is imitated in the organic garden by double digging new beds to achieve the best possible soil structure.

ADDING COMPOST

Made from garden and kitchen waste, well-rotted compost is worked into the soil to improve soil structure, drainage, and its ability to supply plants with essential minerals.

SOWING SEEDS

Seeds from the previous year's harvest are selected and sown for their suitability to the climate and location of your garden.

WATERING AND WEEDING

As the young plants grow, they need a regular supply of water and frequent weeding to reduce the competition for space and nutrients in the bed.

DIGGING THE SOIL

In nature, the soil is loosened by earthworms, rodents, deep-rooted plant growth, and by the freeze–thaw and drought–rain cycles. Walking through the woods in early spring, the effects of the freeze–thaw cycle can easily be seen. Where water has frozen in the soil, there are mounds of frozen earth loosened and pushed up from the ground. And in an unmown field, you can see where rodents have been digging the soil.

While these activities help in the organic garden, they are not equal to double digging the soil (see pp. 129–31). This is the way the organic gardener helps and improves on nature. Over time soil can become compacted, which inhibits root growth. By double digging, the soil is loosened quite deeply, promoting good root growth and allowing the plants to access water and nutrients deeper beneath the surface. These healthier plants are less susceptible to diseases, and more likely to recover quickly from pest damage. Digging also improves drainage and allows air to reach the roots of plants. When digging the soil, it is important not to mix the subsoil with the topsoil; however, a small amount of organic matter will work its way down. Ultimately this will increase the depth of the topsoil and improve fertility.

ADDING COMPOST

For the best quality and most nutritious vegetables, adding organic matter to the garden annually is essential. This mimics the cycle in nature whereby leaves fall to the ground and decompose, animals eat plants and return manure to the soil, the roots of annuals add organic matter deep into the soil when their season is over, and the bodies of dead animals decompose.

Double dig beds to loosen and break up the soil. Add compost to increase fertility and give plants the best possible start.

All of these become humus and feed the soil. As you weed and harvest your crops, you need to replenish the soil with compost – the organic gardener's fertilizer. Containing manure and decomposing vegetation, compost is very close to nature's fertilizer. Add it to the surface of the garden bed after digging; a light lifting action with a garden fork will incorporate the compost into the top layer of the soil. Using a rake to smooth the bed will further mix the compost into the soil surface.

Compost provides nutrients that are released very slowly to the plants, without any danger of the benefits being washed away by rain or watering. Compost also builds soil structure: it allows sandy soils to retain water and nutrients, and loosens clay soils so that they drain and permit better root growth.

SOWING SEEDS

In nature there are many ways that seeds are sown. Birds that eat fruit scatter seed through their droppings. Some seeds are sown by the wind, others by gravity. Some seeds have burs and attach themselves to animals. Most of these seeds never germinate because they are not sown under optimal conditions. But the gardener can improve on nature, sowing the seeds at the right times and the right depths, in prepared seedbeds.

Many gardeners regard seed sowing as a spring activity, rather than an ongoing process. While many crops can be sown in late spring, a succession of planting works better. If lettuce is planted out all at once, then it will be ready for harvesting all at once, whereas planting a small amount of fast-maturing crops each week is less work for the gardener and provides an extended harvest throughout the season. When early-season crops such as peas are harvested, the site can be replanted with an autumn crop such as spinach, or used to raise a green manure, like winter rye.

Seeds sown indoors are given a head start over outdoor seed. Sowing indoors protects seedlings from late frosts and temperature variations.

Nature does not plant crops in rows interspersed with walking paths, and neither should the organic gardener. Planting in rows leaves large areas of bare earth for you to walk on, but the soil quickly becomes compacted. Worse still, bare earth is simply an invitation for weeds to grow. A better method is to plant in beds that are narrow enough for you to reach the middle from either side. In this way, the soil that you have spent time and effort digging does not subsequently get trampled underfoot. Within the bed, plant the seeds with equal spacing, but close enough for the mature plants to touch, and leave no bare earth visible. This restricts the light that reaches the soil surface, preventing the soil from drying out and discouraging weed growth.

ROTATING CROPS

Crop rotation is the gardener's best defence against soilborne pests and diseases. In a small garden, rotating crops from one area to another makes a tremendous difference in productivity and health in the garden. Even with just two crops, such as sweetcorn and beans, your plot will benefit from alternating the site on which they are grown each year. Beans add nitrogen to the soil, and sweetcorn needs nitrogen to grow – so an annual rotation provides the corn with the nitrogen it needs (see pp. 78–81). Different insects and diseases affect sweetcorn and beans, so anything left in the soil will be kept in check.

WATERING AND WEEDING

To grow nutritious vegetables, consistent watering is essential. Nature provides rain, but to produce the best vegetables additional watering is usually necessary. Too much rain floods the garden, and there is little that you can do other than provide good drainage. If there is too little rain, plants will be stunted or die without supplementary water: aim to provide an average of 2.5cm/1in of water per week.

The sky usually clouds over during rain, so that plants are protected from the sun scorching their wet leaves. This is worth bearing in mind when watering. If you water in the midday sun, most of it will evaporate and the wet foliage may be damaged by the sun. To avoid this happening, water the soil at the roots of the plants, and try not to wet the leaves. A good way to accomplish this is with a soaker hose or drip irrigation system (see pp. 144–5). Another way is to apply the water with a hose or watering can only at the roots of plants. Water early in the day, when the sun is still low in the sky; watering in the evening

Not all weeds are bad in the garden. Nettles, for example, attract wildlife. The organic gardener learns to recognize those whose presence is beneficial.

may encourage moulds and fungi to develop as the plants stay moist in the cool night air.

Weeding the garden has no equivalent in nature, but it is necessary to reduce competition with the vegetables on your plot. In some cases, the weeds that you have pulled out can be left on the bed as a mulch; however, if the weeds have set seed or are quite large, it is better to add them to the garden compost. By composting the weeds that are 'harvested' from the garden, you can recycle their nutrients to enrich the soil.

HARVESTING

In nature, the final crop is not as abundant or large as it is in the garden. This is because of droughts, lack of good soil structure, competition from weeds, and pests. The gardener improves on nature by watering, digging, weeding and pest control.

When a gardener finds that rabbits or deer are eating the vegetables, a fence can be erected. If birds are eating the berries, netting can be installed. Nature has methods of pest control too: ladybirds eat aphids, hedgehogs eat slugs, and so on. You, too, can encourage natural predators by providing habitats for them (see pp. 121–5).

When harvesting edible crops, the remainder of the plant should be composted. If the crop was a nitrogen-fixing legume, make sure that you cut off the plant at the soil surface in order to leave some of the fixed nitrogen in the soil to fertilize next year's crop.

If the garden is planted over time with successive sowings, it is possible to harvest fresh vegetables from late spring through winter and into the following spring. The choice of variety of vegetable sown has a great effect on harvest, too. Some varieties, especially F1 hybrids, are very uniform and mature all at once. This is wonderful for the commercial grower, but not for the home gardener. There are varieties that can be harvested over a long period of time, extending fresh usage for the table. Certain varieties of bean can be picked in different forms. For example, some beans can first be harvested as young pods, then later as shell beans, and finally harvested as dried beans. Other crops can be grown in cold frames (see pp. 94–5) to produce a harvest in the winter and spring.

SAVING SEEDS

When harvesting crops, let some plants go to seed so that you can save it. It must be harvested properly, cleaned, dried and stored. There are many important reasons why you should save seed. Old varieties with unique qualities are being lost at an alarming rate, and preserving this biodiversity is important. Choosing a variety with qualities that suit your tastes and storage needs is just one element. Some varieties grow better in certain locations than others, and some are more resistant to pests. When you find the best-tasting, most vigorous and disease-resistant varieties in your garden, the resulting seed will have those qualities. If you save this seed and plant it, the following year a sub-variety that is specifically

suited to your microclimate and location will emerge. In this way, it is you not nature who selects the desirable traits in a plant; the seeds raised become customized to your site and personal preferences.

Planting only open-pollinated seeds is important in the organic garden because their seeds can be saved. Most hybrid seeds produce a very uniform first-generation crop; genetic diversity among individual plants is extremely low. Saving seed from hybrid plants tends to have very unpredictable results. Frequently the plants grown from saved seed look like the hybrid's parents rather than like the hybrid itself.

Seed-saving techniques vary widely depending on the crop. Beans can be dried on the plant then collected and stored, but beets are overwintered in a cool place and planted out the next spring to bear seed. Tomato seeds may be harvested from the fruit and dried (see p. 75), while sweetcorn

Save seeds from your favourite and most successful crops to produce plants that suit your own site, climate and tastes.

There is scarcely a more satisfying sight than a basket of freshly harvested vegetables that you have grown yourself. Just-picked produce has a taste that is immeasurably superior to food that has been transported long distances.

seed should be saved only from plants that have not been cross-pollinated with another variety.

FEEDING THE SOIL

In nature, animals leave behind their droppings on plants and other creatures. By their very design, fruiting plants rely on animals to eat their fruits in order to spread the seeds in their droppings. This interdependent cycle of feeding differs slightly in gardens, because fruit and vegetables are harvested for human consumption, and herbivore rather than human manure is usually brought in and added to the compost. The manure from herbivores, especially cattle, horses and sheep, contains few viable weed seeds, does not have a strong smell and is the perfect choice for use in the home garden.

When preparing food, save all vegetable kitchen scraps for making compost. Learn to think of apple cores, cauliflower leaves and potato skins as rich and useful additions to the compost.

Bear in mind the need to preserve some of your harvest (see pp. 276–9). Freezing is the most common choice, but there are many other methods to consider. Spinach and broccoli can be covered with cold frames, while potatoes, carrots and beets can be stored in a cool, damp place. Brussels sprouts can be left in the garden and picked as needed during winter. Parsnips are tastiest when they have been frosted and are therefore best left in the ground over winter.

After the food has been harvested and stored, it is important to think about feeding the soil.

Add lawn and garden waste to the compost heap, where they will be converted into a valuable resource for your garden.

Leaving the garden bare over the winter can result in a loss of nutrients and soil erosion during the spring thaw. The best method for preventing this is to plant a green manure that suits your climate. For example, planting winter rye in empty garden beds will provide organic matter for the garden when the soil is dug in spring, and its roots will stop erosion in winter.

MAKING COMPOST

It is essential that every organic gardener maintains a compost heap. All of the waste produced in the garden, the scraps and leftovers from the kitchen, and leaves and grass clippings can be recycled into a fertilizer for the garden. Compost feeds the soil and keeps it full of the nutrients necessary to grow successful crops.

Composting organic debris helps to kill weed seeds, pests and diseases. As the bacteria aid decomposition, the composting itself generates heat. This speeds up the process and kills pathogens and seeds. Animal manure will add extra nutrients, particularly nitrogen, which provides fuel for the decomposition process. Additional lime may be necessary to maintain the required pH. A little water needs to be added to the compost heap, but too much brings the decomposition process to a halt.

Compost heaps may be cool or hot and the advantages and disadvantages of the two systems, as well as the methods of building the different types of heap, are described in greater detail on pages 44–8. Building a hot compost heap in specific layers rather than simply adding a variety of materials at random works well and gives quicker results. Start with some woody material at the bottom to allow air into the heap, but avoid using it thereafter because woody material takes too long to decompose. Follow this with a layer of green materials such as grass clippings, weeds and kitchen waste, and then add a layer of manure. Make the following layer from brown materials, such as dried leaves, straw, or dry plant debris after harvest. This layering process is repeated until the compost bin is full.

Achieving a compost heap of approximately 1m³/1yd³ will significantly increase its ability to heat up (see p. 46). You may need to place a cover over the heap to prevent it from becoming too wet. Equally, in hot, sunny spells, you may need to water the heap from time to time if it looks likely to become too dry. Turn the heap when it begins to cool down so that the decomposition process can start again. If you have enough room in your garden, you will find it very helpful to have two compost bins side by side (see p. 44): this allows a completed heap to heat up while the second batch of compost is in the making.

GARDENING ON A SMALL SCALE

Organic techniques can be applied to all gardens, whatever their size. You can reap their benefits everywhere, so use them on the smallest of plots, and even when gardening in tubs and pots. It is essential to build soil fertility by making and using compost, and to practise crop rotation.

SMALL PLOTS

When planning the planting in small plots, scale down the numbers of plants you want to grow and choose compact varieties. It is also useful to prioritize which vegetables you plan to grow. For example, fresh organically grown tomatoes are often not available in shops and you may choose to grow them for their fantastic home-grown flavour. Even in small plots, it is important to rotate crops to help prevent diseases and pests. In the small garden, you may choose a three-year rotation plan of vegetables by setting up four small beds, using the fourth bed for perennials. Even in the smallest of gardens, making compost remains central to the organic cycle. A tumbling composter or worm composter may work best if space is limited. If managed properly, a worm composter can be kept indoors (see pp. 50–51).

CONTAINER GARDENING

It is possible to grow a good portion of your food even if you do not have a garden. Growing plants in containers on a patio or balcony can produce a bountiful harvest. When choosing plants, look for compact varieties, or vines that can be trained vertically or be allowed to tumble over the edge of the container. Many seed catalogues will identify which varieties are best suited for containers. For example, the tomato variety 'Totem' is ideal for container growing. It reaches only 25cm/10in in height and spread, but bears heavily. Choose heavy-bearing vegetables like summer squash – one plant is often capable of providing enough for a small household.

If you garden in containers, each spring rotate the crops planted in them and remove the top 10–15cm/4–6in of the soil from each. Replace the soil with compost and work it in lightly. The top layer of soil should be fertile enough to provide essential nutrients to the growing plants. In smaller pots, replace the soil completely each spring. When gardening in containers, it is often necessary to give the plants an extra boost by watering with liquid organic feeds every two to four weeks during the growing season.

Climbing beans can be grown in a container to produce beautiful flowers and a large tasty crop. They will climb up a string, occupying little space.

CHAPTER 2

SOIL & COMPOST

WHAT IS SOIL?

Soil is the thin layer of the Earth's crust in which plants grow. If the soil is healthy, it in turn can feed the plants that feed us (and the plants will grow well, with fewer pests and diseases).

THE IMPORTANCE OF SOIL

In each tablespoon of topsoil, there are more than six million living organisms – three-quarters of soilborne life exists in the top 15cm/6in. When we apply pesticides and herbicides, micro-organisms die and fewer minerals are made available by the microbiotic life. At the same time, non-beneficial micro-organisms, which typically are fast colonizers, establish a foothold in the soil. Consequently, the soil is unable to feed plants with the nutrition they need.

The very process of harvesting food removes nutrients from the soil. By returning manure to the garden, planting green manures and adding compost, we can restore the health of the soil. By testing the soil, we can check that the right elements are present to produce the best and most nutritious harvest. Even if you do not keep livestock, it should be possible for you to obtain composted manure for your plot. Rotating crops (see pp. 78–81) is also an essential part of organic gardening.

HOW SOIL BEGAN

To understand soil, it is important to know what it is and how it was created. The Earth is a large sphere that has a molten centre covered with slowly shifting plates of solidified rock. The forces of nature have broken up the outermost layer of this stone into weathered rock. Over millions of years, the remains of dead plants and animals have decomposed and added humus. Nature has slowly built up the surface of the Earth into layers of fine, nutrient-rich soil that feeds plants. Soil is the weathered rock, mixed with decaying vegetation, manure and decayed animal matter.

If you watch water flowing in a stream during floods, you will notice the movement of rocks. When the rocks hit one another, chips are broken off and fine rock powder is carried downstream. This material is often deposited in lowland fields. If you look at the forest floor, you will see how last year's leaves are decaying and adding humus to the soil. The new growth of leaves on trees depends not only on soil nutrients, but also on elements in the air. Trees consume carbon dioxide and release oxygen. The carbon that is obtained from the air is converted into wood, bark, roots and leaves, all of which become part of the soil when they decay.

KEEP THE SOIL FERTILE
HOW

1–Raise live stock*
2–Rotate the crops
3–Grow clover, alfalfa and other legumes
4–Save the barnyard manure
5–Pasture rolling lands to prevent washing
6–Add humus – don't burn the stalks
7–Supply needed elements

FARM KNOWLEDGE, VOLUME II, SOILS AND CROPS.
ED. SEYMOUR, E.L.D., DOUBLEDAY, B.S.A.,
PAGE & CO., NEW YORK, 1918

---

*For today's gardener, this means add composted manure

Farm Knowledge (1918) devotes the first hundred pages to soil, recognizing its immense importance. Its list of ways to keep soil fertile remains true today.

RECOGNIZING SOIL LAYERS

Soil types, such as clay or sand, differ according to their location and how they were formed. How the soil is formed also affects soil layers and their thickness. Although soil is made up of many layers, typically you will only see the top two or three. The topsoil is generally dark and contains plenty of organic matter. Fungus, insects, bacteria, microbiotic organisms and worms aerate the soil and release beneficial nutrients in a form that can be utilized by plants. The deeper your topsoil, the better your soil is for gardening.

Subsoil is usually lighter in colour than topsoil, because it contains little or no organic matter. To a large degree, the composition of the subsoil determines the rate of drainage and the

Earthworms help to improve drainage and air circulation around plant roots, as they tunnel through the soil feeding on organic matter.

amount of water available to plants. Gravelly subsoil drains quickly, so the topsoil may need more frequent watering, whereas clay subsoil drains slowly, and less watering is needed (however, clay soils are slower to warm up in spring, which may delay planting).

Beneath the subsoil is the substratum, which is composed of material relatively little affected by weathering. You are unlikely to reach the substratum in your garden except in areas with very shallow soil, or when digging holes for planting large trees.

Soil structure shown in cross-section

❶ *Topsoil is rich in organic matter and nutrients. It tends to be darker in colour.*

❷ *Subsoil is usually lighter in colour than topsoil, but is not as rich in organic matter.*

❸ *Substratum is unconsolidated material little affected by weathering or biological activity. Below the unconsolidated layer is bedrock or parent material.*

IMPROVING TOPSOIL

When working the soil, take care not to mix different layers of soil, especially when double digging to loosen and aerate the subsoil. Increasing the depth of the topsoil raises the fertility of the beds and will produce better plants. To do this, add organic matter, or convert subsoil to topsoil by growing deep-rooted plants, known as green manure or cover crops. Some vegetables and green manures, such as clover, have very deep roots that reach down into the subsoil. When the plant tops are turned under and mixed into the topsoil, the roots remain in the subsoil and begin to decay. This decomposition helps to break up clay subsoil.

CHOOSING SOIL CONDITIONERS

Some gardeners advocate the addition of soil conditioners to improve soil structure. These are bulk organic materials that are worked into the topsoil (or used as a mulch). In the organic garden, it is important to keep a careful check on what you add to the soil. For example, recycling centres often claim that shredded newspaper is an ideal soil additive that complies with organic gardening principles. However, many newspapers are printed with inks that may leach undesirable chemicals into the soil when added as a conditioner.

Well-rotted sawdust and wood shavings are a good choice if you can be sure they do not come from wood that has been treated with a chemical preservative. Any sort of organic matter that has not been treated with chemicals can be used. Grape pomace, spent hops, spent mushroom compost and composted bracken make good soil conditioners. Matted or manure-coated wool (wool dags) can also be used, although it may sometimes contain the residues of petroleum-based soaps. Very often this sort of industrial waste is free for the asking if you are willing to cart it away.

IDENTIFYING SOIL TYPES

When gardening, it is very useful to know what type of soil you have. There are six types of soil: clay, sand, silt, loam, peat and limestone. It is also important to test your soil to determine whether it is deficient in nutrients so that you can assess what improvements are needed.

GETTING TO KNOW YOUR SOIL

Without a soil test, you will not know if your soil is deficient until problems occur. A good approach is to have a newly established bed tested using a professional testing service. You can then add soil amendments to resolve any deficiencies. Later on, you can carry out your own soil tests, with a home testing kit.

It is important to ask people in your area if they know of any specific soil deficiencies in the locality, because the soil might be deficient in an element that is not normally covered by standard soil tests. If there is something deficient in your area, be sure to ask the laboratory to test for it.

Soil testing kits are inexpensive and easy to use. Soil samples can be collected with a purpose-made soil sampler, made up of a simple round tube with a handle, or with a bulb planter, which works almost as well. To take a sample, drive the sampler about 15–20cm/6–8in into the ground

To support a broad range of crops, it is important that your soil remains in peak condition throughout the growing season.

KNOW YOUR SOIL pH

It is worth learning how to to tell if your soil is acidic or alkaline, because some plants have a distinct preference for one type or the other. However, most prefer a soil with a pH close to the neutral 7.0. By looking at which weeds and plants grow well in your garden, you can get a good idea of your soil's pH. For example, sorrel likes acidic soil, while forsythia thrives in alkaline soils. The best method of determining soil pH is to carry out a simple soil pH test, which is available in kit form from most garden centres.

Kale and other brassicas need a soil pH of between 6.5 and 7.0, and a feed of bonemeal for a steady supply of nutrients.

and twist it to scoop up a plug of soil. Avoid picking up any subsoil; if you do find some in the sample, remove it before adding the sample to the collection jar. Use a pocket-knife, small spoon, or gloved hands to handle the sample, as your skin pH may influence the test results, and remember to use a glass container, not a plastic or metal one. Always take more than one sample, and try to collect them from random points around the site being tested. Cover the jar that contains the sample and shake it thoroughly to mix the contents. Take out the required amount for the soil test and send it to the laboratory.

Use the remainder of the soil to test for soil type. To do this, reduce the soil level in the jar to about one-third and fill the rest of the jar with water. Shake the jar well and let the contents settle. The sand will rest at the bottom; silt will be the next layer, and clay will settle on the top. The thickness of the three layers can be measured and will indicate the relative proportions of each soil type. If your soil comprises more than 50 per cent sand, clay or silt, then the dominant one is your soil type. It might also be a loam, sandy loam, clay loam or silty loam. If your soil does not separate into clearly defined layers, add a small amount of powdered eco-friendly detergent to help break up the soil particles.

HOW TO TEST THE SOIL pH

1 *Using a pipette or spoon, add a small sample of your soil to the test chamber. Avoid touching the soil with your hands as the pH of your skin may affect the results.*

2 *Gently shake the sample so that it mixes well with the testing fluid. Then leave it to stand for a couple of minutes, to allow the contents to settle fully.*

3 *Using the pH indicator chart provided, match the colour of your sample to the chart. Green usually indicates alkaline soil; yellow or red indicates acidity.*

IDENTIFYING SOIL TYPES

CLAY
Clay soils are made up of the smallest particles. A very heavy soil, clay can become brick-hard when dry and hold water for long periods of time when it is wet. It is hard to dig and slow to warm up in spring. However, clay retains nutrients very well and can be very fertile.

SILT
Silt particles are almost as small as clay particles and silt soil is generally rather similar to clay. It can be difficult to manage as it is not improved by the addition of lime and does not shatter when exposed to frost. It feels slippery when wet.

SAND
Sandy soil is made up of particles large enough to be visible to the naked eye. They allow water – and, with it, nutrients – to drain away very quickly. Sandy soil tends to be light and dry. It is easy to dig and the first soil to warm up in spring.

IDENTIFYING SOIL TYPES

LIMESTONE

Limestone, or calcareous soils, as the names suggest, contain a lot of lime or chalk and are very alkaline; so they are unsuitable for acid-loving plants. They drain well but tend not to be very fertile. Nutrients are washed out quickly by rain or irrigation and can also be 'locked up' by the calcium in the soil.

LOAM

Loam is made up of a mix of clay, sand and silt. Loams are described as silty, clay or sandy, according to the proportions of particles present. The ideal loam has 40 per cent silt, 40 per cent sand and 20 per cent clay; it is friable, quick to drain yet moisture-retentive, and contains lots of organic matter.

PEAT

A rare soil type, very dark in colour, peat is made up almost exclusively of partly decayed organic matter. It tends to be low in minerals. Highly moisture-retentive, it is prone to waterlogging, so good drainage is essential. Peat is very acidic, which makes it unsuitable for alkaline-loving plants. It is often necessary to add lime to peat soil to raise the pH.

IMPROVING YOUR SOIL

Using the soil identification chart on pages 36–7, it should be easy for you to determine your soil type and assess what actions are needed to improve it.

The addition of compost is almost invariably part of any solution for improving soil. An analogy that suits compost is to picture it as stiff sponges that are not compressed by the weight of the soil. These sponges are able to draw moisture through the soil. Other solutions include green manures (see pp. 57–61), which will break up subsoil as well as clay and silt topsoils.

SAND

To improve the retention of moisture and nutrients in sandy soils, you need to incorporate compost into the soil to fill the areas between the particles of sand. Keep a regular check on the pH of sandy soils because lime is quickly washed out. Water plants growing in sandy soils frequently. Sandy soils need less cultivation than heavier soils; overworking the soil may result in faster nutrient loss.

Using a green manure is a quick way of adding organic matter to sandy soils. Try to keep something growing in the beds throughout the year. Erosion is swift in sandy soils, and nutrients will leach out quickly when nothing is growing in the beds.

SILT

Like clay, silt soils may have drainage problems and become compacted. By adding compost, you can improve the drainage in silt soils and prevent them from turning powdery when dry. The compost allows drainage of water by separating the soil particles. This enhances the

Some plants dislike certain soil types. By growing them in raised beds, you can create the preferred conditions for a particular crop.

soil structure and reduces the likelihood of compaction. The incorporation of compost also allows air to penetrate the soil and reach down to the roots of plants.

The best time to cultivate silt soils is when they are dry and do not feel slippery when worked between your fingers. Silt must be cultivated well and needs to be mulched to prevent an impenetrable crust forming on the surface. The pH of silt should be checked and adjusted as necessary.

CLAY

With a little work and lots of compost, clay soils are among the best for growing crops. Working in compost aggregates the particles and allows moisture to drain out of the soil, making it easier to work. This helps clay soil to warm up more quickly in the spring, and reduces the likelihood of it hardening into solid bricks during drought. As the clay becomes easier to work, more air is able to reach the roots of plants.

You will need to test the pH of clay soils and add lime if necessary. An added benefit of working lime or gypsum into clay soils is that the small penny-like particles are bound together and form larger aggregate particles. This improves soil structure. Be careful to avoid walking on clay soils, because they compact more easily than other types; use a plank if you need to stand on the bed. Cultivate clay soils when they are moist. If you work on them when they are too wet, the soil structure will be damaged; working on them when dry is difficult because of the brick-like texture.

LIMESTONE

Working compost into limestone soils improves water retention. Limestone soils, like sand, have large particles and suffer from nutrients washing out with watering. When cultivating this type of soil, do so only shallowly, as the topsoil tends not

PEAT CONSERVATION

Peat, which is promoted to improve soil structure, is harvested in England, Ireland, Scotland and Canada. In some of these areas this has caused great damage to the delicate ecosystems of the bogs. This threat to the environment is a cause for concern among organic gardeners. Look for coir and other amendments instead, and try to use peat-free planting pots and composts.

to be very deep. Aim to grow alkaline-loving plants appropriate to this soil type or consider building raised beds (see p. 99) so that acid-loving plants can be grown. Erosion takes place very quickly in limestone soils. When nothing is growing in the beds, nutrients leach out more quickly than when the bed is full, so try to keep something growing at all times.

LOAM

If the soil in your garden is loam, you are very fortunate. The widest range of crops will grow in loam with few soil additives.

PEAT

Being composed largely of organic matter, peat needs compost less than other soil types do. It is, however, short of minerals, so will benefit from the addition of organic fertilizers. Except where the plants being grown are acid-loving, lime should be added to reduce acidity. To improve drainage in peat soils, it may be necessary to install clay drainage tiles beneath the soil surface or to build raised beds (see p. 99). But if you drain your peat soils, you must be prepared to irrigate them during times of drought: if peat does dry out it takes a lot of slow irrigation to moisten it again.

WHAT IS COMPOST?

Compost is the main soil amendment used in organic gardening and every organic gardener must produce compost. In fact, compost is the most important thing produced in the garden. When you make compost, you are recycling organic matter and using it to feed the soil.

TYPES OF ORGANIC MATTER

When making compost, consider what types of organic matter should be used. For example, some contribute higher levels of nutrients than others, and some make nitrogen unavailable in compost until they have decayed completely.

FROM GARDEN AND KITCHEN

Green garden waste Weeds and plant remains after harvest are just a few examples of green garden waste; however, avoid adding weeds that are high in seeds unless your compost heap reaches a high temperature. This waste tends to be very rich in nutrients and is an excellent addition to the compost heap. When weeding, green vegetation may be left on the surface of the soil as mulch, but it is better to compost it.

Kitchen waste When preparing vegetables and fruits in the kitchen, keep a small bowl or bucket nearby in which to collect all of the peelings and scraps for the compost heap. These scraps may also be used to make worm tea (see pp. 50–51). Orange peel, carrot tops and melon rinds are some of the best additions to the compost heap. Eggshells may be added to the heap, but crush them first to speed up decomposition.

Leaves It can be a chore to rake and dispose of fallen leaves. If they are turned into leaf mould (see p. 49), they make an attractive mulch and can be worked into the soil to improve its structure and increase the level of organic matter.

Leaves have very few nutrients. Many parks and cemeteries allow gardeners to collect them. Some cities make leaf mould available, but watch out for glass, plastic and other foreign material.

Grass clippings Clippings are very nutrient rich. It is best to let them stay on the lawn where they will decompose and feed the grass. In some cases, when mowing the lawn, it is preferable to collect the clippings instead of letting them decompose on site. If the grass is too long when it is mowed or if an area needs to be kept clear for exercise or children's play, the clippings can be composted or used as a mulch in the garden.

If you collect clippings from neighbours, be sure to ask if they treat their lawns with any synthetic chemicals.

Organic poultry manure is a valuable by-product of keeping chickens. Use it as a compost additive to boost nitrogen and speed decomposition.

Many of the peelings and offcuts from harvested food can be recycled in the composting process rather than thrown away with the rubbish.

LOCALLY AVAILABLE

Hay and straw Hay is rich in nutrients but often contains viable weed seeds. With the exception of potash, straw has very few nutrients and contains few viable weed seeds, making it an ideal mulch. Straw also has thicker stems that allow air to penetrate a compost heap. When added to the compost heap, hay is like any other brown organic matter: it will compact and decompose slowly, releasing its nutrients over a long period of time. It is best to get hay and straw from organic farms if possible. You need to be particularly careful about sources of straw: cereal crops on conventional farms are often treated with growth hormones and there may be residues in the straw.

DECOMPOSED MATTER

Compost is decomposed plants and animal manure. Dark and rich, it looks a lot like healthy garden soil. Garden waste and kitchen scraps are piled in a heap, where they decay.

Humus is the material formed by the decomposition of organic matter. When mixed into the soil, humus improves its structure and ability to retain nutrients. A green manure turned into the soil forms humus. Compost breaks down to form humus.

Manure, cow Cow manure is rich in nutrients and has few viable weed seeds. Well-rotted manure can be used as a mulch, incorporated directly into the soil, or added to the compost heap. Fresh manure has a pungent smell and is high in nitrogen, which will burn plants.

Manure, horse This is rich in nutrients but tends to contain viable weed seeds. Horse manure mixed with shavings takes a long time to decompose. It is quicker if mixed with straw. Use it to build a hot compost heap to kill weed seeds.

Manure, poultry Poultry manure is rich in nutrients and does not contain viable weed seeds. It is very high in nitrogen and may burn plants if not composted thoroughly. It is also very alkaline, so is not suitable for lime-hating plants. Poultry manure is typically available mixed with the litter (often sawdust) that the poultry live on. By the time poultry manure is delivered to your garden, the chickens have scratched about in the wood shavings, and the high nitrogen levels in their manure have decomposed the wood. Very fresh manure should be added to the compost heap, where it will work to speed decomposition.

Manure, rabbit Rabbit manure does not contain viable weed seeds. It is not as rich as other manures and does not contain high levels of nitrogen that can burn plants. It can be used fresh to side-dress plants or incorporated into beds. Composting reduces its nutritional value.

Manure, sheep Sheep manure is rich in nutrients and does not contain viable weed seeds. It is very heavy and should be mixed with hay or some other organic material before use. It is the finest manure for use in the garden. Well-rotted manure, mixed with hay, can be spread directly on the garden and incorporated into the soil.

Spent mushroom compost This is a good source of organic matter. However, it will have a high pH (from the lime used in mushroom culture) so is not suitable for lime-hating plants. Moreover, unless it comes from organic mushroom production, it may well contain residues of insecticides. It should be composted for six months before use.

The effects of earthworms, micro-organisms and time produce a rich organic fertilizer from a variety of compost ingredients.

Seaweed This nutrient-rich plant provides lots of trace elements and potassium. As it decays, seaweed helps to activate the compost heap. It may also be used as a mulch or dug into the soil if the bed is not needed right away. Beware of using very salty seaweed.

Urine Human urine is rich in nitrogen and potassium. Dilute it with water and add to the compost during composting.

PRUNINGS

Soft prunings Add hedge clippings and thorn-free green prunings to the compost pile, or shred them for a mulch.

Woody prunings Shred these prunings before adding them to the heap. Unshredded, prunings can be used as the bottom layer of a compost heap to assist the flow of air. Woody prunings may be left to decay in a heap if you have the

When it reaches maturity after twelve months or so, rich compost smells sweet and is fine and crumbly in your hands.

space and time to let them rot. Add grass clippings and fresh manure to speed up their decomposition.

MULCHES AND INDUSTRIAL WASTE

Shredded bark A very popular choice for use as a decorative mulch, shredded bark has little or no nutrients and may rob the soil of nitrogen as it decays. It should be used only as a mulch, rather than incorporated into the soil as an improver. Before buying shredded bark, first ascertain that it was not treated with any chemicals.

Sawdust and wood shavings These have very few nutrients but can make a good mulch. Age them for about twelve months in the open before use or they will rob nitrogen from the soil. Do not to incorporate these into the soil.

Spent hops This is an organic waste available from breweries. Provided that the spent hops have not been treated with manmade chemicals, they are a good source of trace elements and also of nutrients. They can be used as a mulch, dug into garden beds or they can be added to the compost heap.

Wool shoddy This is the waste from the wool-cleaning process. If you can obtain shoddy that was not treated with any chemicals, it makes an excellent mulch that is high in nitrogen. Work it into the soil to increase water retention.

 ## COMPOST REJECTS

These types of organic matter should not be composted:

- Cooked kitchen waste produces a strong smell that is likely to attract dogs and vermin to forage in the compost heap.
- Never add protein in the form of meat, chicken, fish or cheese: it attracts vermin, including rats.
- Paper often has petroleum-based ink and may leach chemicals into the soil.
- Diseased plants or pest-infested plants should be destroyed, especially potato top growth because it may contain diseases.
- Manure from pigs, dogs and cats may contain diseases that affect humans.
- Weeds with a high seed content should be avoided unless your compost heap reaches quite a high temperature.
- Metal objects and plastic will not decompose.
- Roots of invasive weeds should be destroyed or they may grow in the soil when the compost is used.

METHODS OF COMPOSTING

The most fundamental part of organic gardening is to recycle nutrients and organic matter back into the soil by making compost. Fortunately, making compost is easy and inexpensive. Most of what is composted is waste that many people would arrange to have taken away with the household rubbish.

READY-MADE COMPOSTERS

Many people waste money buying extravagant wooden units or ugly plastic bins. This is largely unnecessary as a compost bin need not be ugly or expensive.

Compost tumblers are also available, but they do not produce compost any faster than a hot heap. In general, they tend to be very expensive and should only be considered where vermin are a problem or space is at a premium. Do not add any material to the tumbler during the composting process.

COMPOST BINS FROM FENCING

If you have any carpentry skills, a compost bin can be made from wood quite easily. DIY centres and local hardware shops often stock 2.5m/8ft lengths of pre-assembled fencing.

Choose fencing that is 90cm–1.2m/36in–4ft in height and check that it has not been made from pressure-treated or preserved wood. Buy four 2.5m/8ft lengths and eight L-brackets with screws. This will be enough to make two bins. Cut each of the lengths of fence in half and, using the L-brackets, re-attach the two halves at a 90° angle. You will now have four L-shaped pieces of fence that can be set up to provide the two compost bins. Do not worry about fixing the two pieces of each bin together, as this is rarely necessary. Just stand two L-shaped pieces of fencing on the ground so that they form a square.

If your material has a tendency to lose heat and dry out around the outside, you can line the

ASSEMBLING YOUR OWN PANELS

1 Take an 2.5m/8ft length of fencing and saw it in half through the struts to make two 1.2m/4ft pieces. Cut a second length of fencing in the same way.

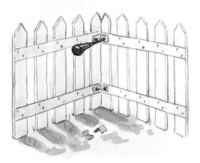

2 Position the first pair of 1.2m/4ft lengths at right angles to each other. Screw them together with two L-brackets. Repeat with a second pair.

3 Stand the two right-angled pieces of fencing together to form a square compost bin. Repeat the whole process from Step 1 to make a second bin.

bin with cardboard boxes, sheets of newspaper or hessian. Alternatively, you can make (or get someone else to make) a compost bin with solid sides, or even a double-walled bin with straw sandwiched between the two walls. Double-walling is a very effective way of retaining heat.

Site the bins in a sheltered location, for example under trees, or use covers to protect them from excessive rainfall or the heat of the sun. In areas with summer drought, sprinkle water on the compost if it shows signs of drying out. Make sure the bins are also within easy reach of the kitchen and the vegetable garden, which produce the most compost ingredients.

MAKING COMPOST

There are two ways to build compost heaps. One is to build a pile carefully in layers so that it heats up; this is called a hot compost heap. The other way is to make a cool compost heap by continually tossing whatever organic matter you have on the pile; then you just wait patiently for the compost ingredients to break down. The results are the same but the time it takes to produce useful compost differs. A carefully layered heap that heats up may be ready within two months, while a cool compost heap may take a year or more.

BUILDING A COOL COMPOST HEAP

A cool heap may or may not heat up. You add the ingredients as they become available, a little at a time. It is particularly important that the compost bins are easily accessible from the kitchen, because at the end of each day you need to add your vegetable scraps to the heap. Two bins are needed for a cool compost: one to build up slowly during the year, and one to hold the previous year's finished compost.

Start a heap by laying small woody branches and sticks at the bottom of the bin. This will assist in allowing air to infiltrate the pile. Add

---

COMPOSTING TIPS

- Add as much as possible at one time.
- Add a mix of lush green material and tough brown material.
- Keep the pile moist but not wet or waterlogged. Cover the pile if necessary.
- Build air into the heap by placing branches at the bottom and mixing straw into the middle to let air penetrate the pile.
- Avoid outside inputs; only add amendments to cure nutrient deficiencies in the soil.

---

garden debris, grass clippings and kitchen waste to the pile. If you are including lots of green materials in your compost, add in some hay or straw. The straw is rigid and will encourage air to infiltrate the pile. After collecting the garden debris, such as plant remains after harvest and autumn leaves, start building the second heap. By the following spring, the bottom of the first heap should be ready for use. The top of the heap may not be decomposed yet.

Spring is the time to turn the pile to improve decomposition. In areas with summer drought, it is often helpful to turn the pile in early winter before the rains. Remove both halves of the compost bin and set them up next to the existing heap to form another bin. Using a garden fork or shovel, turn the pile over into the bin. The bottom of the heap should be well composted and can be used immediately. Consider adding an activator, such as manure, at this stage. The combined effects of turning the pile and applying the activator will speed up the process and produce a completed compost.

Throughout the summer, continue to add organic matter to the second bin. Worms quickly tend to find their way into cool compost heaps and move in to eat the nutritious organic matter. They will help with decomposition and add their manure to the pile.

SPEEDING UP THE COOL COMPOST HEAP
The biggest complaint about cool composts is that they take too long to produce useful compost. To speed up decomposition, add as much organic matter as possible in one go. Include green and brown organic matter in equal amounts, then apply manure. Chopping up organic matter increases its surface area, which helps it to decompose more quickly. Use a spade to break up large or thick pieces and smash tough stalks. Put tree and bush prunings through a shredder or run over them with a lawnmower to break them down. Finally, to speed decomposition, turn the pile in autumn and mix in some manure to activate it.

BUILDING A HOT COMPOST HEAP
Making a hot compost heap is a little more complicated because it is usually built all at once in layers to ensure a good even mix of green and brown organic matter and manure. In order to heat up, the pile needs to be large enough in size and shape. A pile measuring about 1m³/1yd³ is

By the time your first compost heap has matured, a second pile should already be in the making to ensure a steady supply of rich organic matter.

best. It is important to keep the pile near this size, because if it becomes too large, air will have trouble penetrating the pile and reaching the middle. Equally, if it is smaller, the pile will not heat up properly.

To build the heap, begin with a layer of small woody branches and sticks at the bottom of the bin. On top of this, put a 10–15cm/4–6in layer of green, succulent organic matter, such as grass clippings, soft kitchen waste and weeds. On top of this layer, add 2.5cm/1in of fresh manure; cow, sheep or horse manure works best. Unless there is a lot of soil on the roots of weeds already on the pile, add a 2.5cm/1in layer of garden soil to introduce soil-borne organisms. The final layer is made up of 10–15cm/4–6in of brown organic matter. Straw makes an ideal choice because it allows air to infiltrate through its stems. Other semi-rigid brown organic matter also works well,

COOL VERSUS HOT COMPOSTS

METHOD	ADVANTAGES	DISADVANTAGES
Cool pile	The pile can be built slowly as materials become available. It is easier to build, because it is not necessary to add the material in layers. Resulting compost is more fertile because undecomposed material traps nutrients which are released later into the soil.	The pile takes longer to produce compost (possibly up to one year) because the decomposition process is much slower. Weed seeds and diseases may not be killed.
Hot pile	Compost is produced very quickly (in as little as two months) thanks to the high temperature reached. Weed seeds and diseases are usually killed. Roots and woody material are generally broken down thoroughly.	A lot of organic material is required all at once to build up the pile in layers. High temperatures release nutrients that may be washed out of the compost quickly. High temperatures can cause ammonia to volatilize, resulting in reduced nitrogen levels and an unpleasant smell.

but avoid any woody material. Continue adding layers to the pile in the same order: green organic matter, manure, soil, and brown organic matter.

When the pile nears the top of the bin, make brown organic matter the final layer. The purpose of layering is to ensure a good mix of compost ingredients. Mixing the material is often difficult but produces the best results.

Once the compost heap has begun the decomposition process, do not add any more material to the pile. Check the temperature of the compost regularly by using a purpose-designed thermometer. A temperature of between 54°C/130°F and 60°C/140°F will kill weed seeds. Keep an eye on the moisture content of the pile too. If the pile is getting very wet or waterlogged, use a waterproof cover or large wooden panel to protect it. If the pile is too dry, water it liberally.

FINISHING A HOT COMPOST PILE

As the decomposition process proceeds, the pile slowly heats up and eventually reaches a plateau. Once you notice that the temperature has begun to drop, it is time to turn the pile. This will incorporate air into the pile and encourage further decomposition.

Remove the two sides of the compost bin and set it up alongside the existing pile. Place a layer of woody material at the bottom of the newly set up bin. Using a garden fork or shovel, turn the pile over into the bin. Do not add any fresh organic matter. The pile will heat up again, typically to a hotter temperature than the first time. Again, check the moisture content and cover the pile to keep it dry or water the pile, as necessary.

When the temperature drops to within the soil/air temperature range, the composting process has slowed to a point where the compost is ready for use. The organic matter will continue to decompose either in the bin or in the garden where it is used.

Compost bins are used to recycle weeds, kitchen waste and garden debris into rich organic matter that can be used as a garden fertilizer.

MAKING SEED COMPOST

In order to produce compost for sowing seed in, a further step is necessary. Take a portion of the compost to make a new, small pile in the spring, and keep it covered for up to a year. Compost used for sowing seed should be two years old and thoroughly decomposed.

If you suffer from severe frosts, bag up the compost in autumn and store it in a shed or garage so that it can be used in late winter. Hessian or cloth will keep the compost moist during storage. For best results, sieve the soil through a 0.5cm/¼in mesh before using.

SOIL FEEDS

Maintaining the soil is easily accomplished by growing green manures, incorporating compost or by adding mulch, which will later rot and add nutrients to the soil. Leaf mould and worm castings are valuable additions to the soil, and liquid feeds are used to supplement container plants.

MAKING LEAF MOULD

Leaf mould is a very useful product in the garden, used as a mulch and worked into the soil later. Leaves from any deciduous trees are suitable, but avoid those that are diseased. When starting a new bed, a thick 8–10cm/3–4in layer may be spread over the surface to deter weeds. Seeds and seedlings may be planted directly in the leaf mould. It can even be used as potting mix if left to decompose for two to three years.

Begin by setting up a bin for the leaves. A section of wire fencing works best. Use canes to stake it in a circle with a diameter of between 90cm/36in and 3m/10ft, depending on how many leaves you have.

In autumn, collect the leaves from your land; it does not matter if they are damp. If you need more leaves, ask permission from neighbours and parks to collect theirs. Some gardeners use a bagging lawnmower for collection. This adds grass, which speeds decomposition and reduces the labour of raking. Fill the bin with leaves and keep the pile moist.

Leaf mould may be ready as early as spring, but can take until the following spring. The process of decomposition is unlike composting. Fungus breaks down leaves into leaf mould, whereas bacteria break down organic matter into compost. This fungal process takes longer and depends on the leaf types being composted as well as the temperature and climate.

ORGANIC TEAS

Where conventional gardeners add liquid chemical fertilizers, organic gardeners make 'manure tea'. Using liquid organic feed is not a common practice in organic gardening, except in feeding container plants. Most often, the soil is fed with compost which, in turn, feeds the plants. In some cases, certain plants need an extra boost and are fed directly by the gardener. For more information, refer to pages 50–53.

Leaf mould makes an excellent mulch and can be used to add organic matter to the soil. It is made by fungus breaking down the leaves.

MAKING LIQUID FEEDS

Making a liquid organic feed is quite easy. Choose the appropriate ingredients depending on what nutrients are needed by your plants.

Compost tea For a general, well-balanced liquid feed, make compost tea. Put a cloth bag of finished compost into a bucket or dustbin filled with water. Cover and let it sit for three to four days. Remove the bag of compost and apply it as a mulch in the garden. The liquid should be diluted with water until it has the colour of weak tea. Using it full strength may burn plants' roots.

Manure tea For a high-nitrogen feed, make fresh manure tea. Dry manure works too but it has significantly less nitrogen than fresh. Sheep manure produces the best results, but cow and horse manure make a satisfactory liquid feed. Site a dustbin away from the house where the smell will not be offensive, and fill it with water. Place a few shovels of fresh manure in a hessian sack or cloth bag, and suspend it in the water with a rope. Cover the bin and leave the manure to steep.

After several hours, a very mild feed may be obtained which can be used undiluted straightaway. Better yet, leave the bag for about two weeks. The water will heat up like a hot compost heap. While the water is hot, the tea is not ready. When the water returns to the ambient temperature, it is ready to be used. Manure tea should not be used as a foliar feed. It may be used at full strength or diluted to a weak tea colour, depending on the amount of nitrogen necessary.

Nettle or comfrey tea Nettle makes a feed containing iron, magnesium, sulphur and nitrogen; comfrey makes a high-potassium tea. Place 450–900g/1–2lb of leaves in a cloth sack and submerge it in a large bucket of water. Let the bag steep for one or two weeks before use. Nettle tea should be diluted 1:15 with water.

USING A WORMERY

Worm composting is very easy and takes little space. It is ideal for gardens where space is at a premium. Worms eat kitchen waste and other

MAKING A LIQUID FEED

1 Put the organic material in a cloth bag or hessian sack and tie it tightly at the top. Fill a large, clean plastic or metal container with water.

2 Secure the bag to an overhead batten and steep it in water for three days to two weeks depending on the organic material being used to make the tea.

3 When the water becomes dark brown in colour, it is ready to use. Always dilute the tea before applying it, as full-strength tea may burn plants.

The worms live in the lower layers of the worm composter and come to the upper layers to feed. Once established, a small wormery will house around 30,000 worms and will be able to accept 450–900g/1–2lb of kitchen scraps per day.

organic material and produce castings for use in the garden. Worm composting does not produce any nasty smells and may be done on porches, patios or even under the kitchen sink. If you want to make worm compost, I strongly recommend ready-made plastic wormeries. Typically, they come with excellent instructions. They are round bins raised on legs and fitted with a drain to remove worm tea. The best models have three or more perforated bins that stack. Wooden and other non-watertight containers rarely produce worm tea.

To start a worm composter, fill the bottom bin with compost or coir and introduce worms from your compost heap or purchase appropriate worms from a supplier. In the middle bin, add kitchen waste. When the middle bin is full, add organic matter and kitchen waste to the top bin. The worms will work their way up as they digest the scraps. When the bottom bin is fully converted, and most of the worms have moved on to the middle bin, remove the bottom bin and use the worm castings. Return this empty bin to the top of the stack. Make sure that the composter is sufficiently moist, but leave the cover on to keep out light and excessive moisture. Any excess water drains through and can be used as liquid feed. The worms need to be kept warm but not hot; they prefer a temperature of 16–21°C/60–70°F. To keep the process working in winter, bring the wormery into a garage or basement with a temperature above 10°C/50°F.

COMMERCIAL LIQUID FEEDS

Any purchased liquid feeds, such as fish emulsion, should be diluted exactly as directed. These feeds tend to be very concentrated and there is a risk of burning plants. Fish emulsion, for example, is a good general fertilizer, containing nitrogen, phosphorus and potassium (shown as NPK on labels). It is often applied with seaweed and makes a useful foliar feed if sufficiently diluted. Be sure to choose an organic fish emulsion that has no additives.

USING LIQUID FEEDS

The use of liquid feeds is a temporary solution to poor plant growth; it is not a common practice in organic gardening. Ideally, you should feed the soil with compost, and let the soil feed the plants. If plants are growing poorly, a crop can often be saved by using a liquid feed. The deficiency in the soil should be corrected for future crops.

Liquid organic feeds are most useful when growing container plants and raising vegetables in tubs or planters. Applications of liquid feed can be made by pouring it on to the soil near the roots of plants or by spraying it on to the vegetation. It should only be applied to moist soil. Plants growing in containers, tubs or planters can be watered regularly with very dilute liquid feeds, but the feeds can be used in a less diluted form when a problem is discovered in the garden.

To apply liquid feeds, create a small depression in the soil around the base of the plant and fill it with a small amount of feed. Alternatively, bury a small plant pot in the soil near the roots of the plant, and pour the feed into it; you will see it quickly penetrate the soil.

Container-grown plants like these strawberries benefit from liquid feeds which compensate for the limited amount of soil available to their roots.

The excess 'tea' produced by worms as they work through the compost can be drawn off and used as a liquid fertilizer.

APPLYING FOLIAR FEEDS

When you notice a visible deficiency in the leaves of a plant, use a foliar feed to provide an immediate boost. Pour a very dilute mixture of liquid feed into a watering can fitted with a spray rose or into a spray bottle. You might find it useful to add 1 tablespoonful of vegetable oil to help the feed adhere to the foliage. Apply it directly to the leaves in the early morning when dry weather is forecast; rain or overhead watering will wash away the benefits of a foliar feed. Make sure that the leaves are not in direct sunlight when applying a foliar feed.

SOIL & COMPOST ADDITIVES

Ideally, a good well-balanced organic compost will supply all the nourishment your soil needs. However, some soils do have specific deficiencies which should be addressed, and some plants have very specific needs. A soil test may indicate that your soil has a very high or very low pH, that it has low potassium levels, or that it is deficient in particular minerals such as phosphorus, calcium or boron.

WHAT IS A DEFICIENCY?

A plant that is lacking a much-needed nutrient will grow poorly and be subject to diseases, distortion of growth and leaf discoloration. Typically the lack of nutrients is caused by a deficiency in the soil which is remedied by supplying the necessary additive to the compost. Some plants may have specific needs. To address these, add the supplement directly to the soil near the plant. Again, a soil test is the only way to be certain that there are no soil deficiencies.

The soil additives listed below are organic. They are found mostly in a form that will be slow to decompose, so they will not act as a 'quick fix' like chemically based fertilizers. They remain in the soil and slowly release nutrients. Microbe action as well as time and moisture break down these additives. Many of them are mined from the earth, and collecting them causes some environmental damage. Before using an additive make sure that it is acceptable to your organic certifying agency. Rules vary between countries, so that additives advocated in one region may be banned in another. Please take this into consideration when choosing additives.

Garden waste that is composted will recycle some of the nutrients derived from these additives into the finished compost. With time, you will probably find that some soil deficiencies in your garden have been eliminated.

TO ADJUST pH

The optimal pH for the average soil is between 6.5 and 7.0. Some plants are acid loving and require a lower pH. Others prefer alkaline soils with a higher pH.

Lime Made from pulverized calcium carbonate, this is added to the garden to increase the pH of the soil. It also provides calcium. Limestone is the most common form of lime. Another form, oystershell, contains nutrients and micronutrients and is also used to adjust pH and add calcium. The particles are of different sizes, so they break down at different rates, providing immediate as well as long-term results. Dolomite lime provides both magnesium and calcium.

Peat Peat lowers the pH of soil. It also improves soil structure. However, the use of peat is not permitted under organic standards in some countries; elsewhere it is discouraged (see p. 39). Try using pine needles instead.

Coir Made from the husk fibre of coconuts, this additive was once popular as a peat substitute. However, environmentalists now discourage the use of this and other products

---

SUPPLYING ADDITIVES

- Supplying additives is the easiest solution for satisfying nutrient needs and correcting nutrient deficiencies in the soil.
- For a garden that is deficient in some nutrients, add the supplements to the compost heap as it is being built (see pp. 45–8).
- For plants that require higher levels of some nutrients, mix the supplement into finished compost as you add it around the plants.

SOIL & COMPOST ADDITIVES

Lime is often used to increase the pH of acidic soils. There are several forms of lime and all of them are a good source of calcium.

of tropical agriculture, since they are important for improving soil structure and stability in their country of orgin.

Pine needles These are often used as a mulch around acid-loving plants or to adjust the pH of alkaline soil. Use pine needles instead of brown organic matter to make a low-pH compost.

Most common additives

Bonemeal Made from finely ground animal bones, this is a good source of phosphorus and calcium and encourages root development if worked into holes before planting trees and bushes. It also contains many trace elements.

Blood meal Trace minerals and lots of nitrogen are released into the soil by incorporating blood meal (dried, pulverized animal blood). Even though it is high in nitrogen, blood meal does not burn plants when mixed into the soil.

Fish blood and bone This is a balanced fertilizer which is a good source of nitrogen and phosphorus. An application on a garden bed will slowly release nutrients during the entire summer.

Hoof and horn A good source of nitrogen and, to a lesser extent, phosphorus.

Animal manure Well-rotted manures are good additives to mix directly into the soil where increased nitrogen levels are necessary. For details of different manure types, see pp. 41–2.

Wood ash The nutrient content of ashes depends on the type of wood burned. Typically, ashes are high in potassium. If small woody prunings are burned, then the ashes may contain a fair amount of minerals. Ashes may be added in moderation to the compost heap.

Crushed eggshells Eggshells are a wonderful source of calcium and are especially useful around brassicas. Add them to the compost heap,

Either purchased dry or harvested fresh from the coast, seaweed is an excellent fertilizer additive, mulch and soil improver.

or work them directly into the soil, along with compost, around those vegetables that require higher calcium levels.

Gypsum Gypsum contains calcium and sulphur. It also increases pH, but to a lesser degree than lime. It is good for improving structure in clay soils, and very effective in alkaline soils that are high in salt. It can be added to the compost heap or can be spread on the beds and worked or watered in.

Seaweed or kelp Seaweed is high in potassium and an excellent source of trace elements – it contains seventy-plus minerals, vitamins and enzymes. It is also an organic fertilizer additive. Add seaweed to the compost heap, use it as a mulch, or work it into the soil. If you collect it from the beach, choose only fresh wet pieces

from the surf and rinse off the salt in fresh cold water before use – beware of high salt levels. Dried seaweed can be purchased.

Rock phosphate Also called colloidal phosphate, this is an excellent source of phosphorus and calcium. Add to the compost heap so that the acids produced by the microbes can help to break the particles down and make the phosphorus more available.

Rock dust Various companies market ground mineral rock, in soft or hard form, as a source of calcium, magnesium, iron and other elements. There is no conclusive evidence that these are of any benefit to the soil.

Epsom salts Also called magnesium sulphate, this is a good source of magnesium but is not permitted by some organic certifying agencies.

GREEN MANURES

Green manures, also known as cover crops, are grown to improve soil fertility and to protect the soil from erosion when crops are not being grown. These deep-rooted plants suppress weeds, prevent soil crusting during long, hot summers and bring nutrients to the surface from below.

USE OF GREEN MANURES

The practice of sowing green manures began more than two thousand years ago, and is still a vital way to enrich the soil. Green manures should be worked into your plant for crop rotation (see pp. 78–81). Sow a green manure whenever a crop has been harvested and you do not intend to use the bed for other crops for at least thirty days. The table on pages 58–9 lists some of the options available. In warm weather, for example, consider growing buckwheat or marigolds; in cool weather, try clover or vetch; or sow a crop of grazing rye for winter.

UNDERSOWING CROPS

Undersowing is a form of companion planting (see pp. 118–19): a green manure is sown in a bed after the main crop is well established, and remains after the main crop has been harvested. Undersowing can be very advantageous, for example when a green manure of legumes is desired for winter. Legumes are difficult to establish in cold weather, and undersowing gives them a good head start. But undersowing must be timed well, or the green manure may be in competition with the main crop. Generally it is a good idea to allow six weeks between planting the main crop and undersowing.

Before undersowing, clear the bed of weeds and loosen the surface of the soil. Broadcast the seeds by hand under the foliage of the crop. A few examples of good companions are dwarf white clover or oats sown under tomato plants, sweet clover around winter squash, and beans growing under sweetcorn.

Sow grazing rye in autumn, immediately after harvesting crops. It may be turned under in the spring or allowed to grow to maturity for the grain to be harvested.

RECOMMENDED GREEN MANURES

Name	Conditions	Comments
Rape *Brassica napus*	Cool weather	Breaks up clay soils extremely well with long taproot. Chokes out weeds.
Mustard *Brassica hirta*	Cold weather	Great for loosening heavy clay soils. Fast growing.
Buckwheat *Fagopyrum esculentum*	Warm weather	Excellent for crowding out weeds. Produces lots of organic matter quickly. Attracts bees. Provides habitat for beneficial insects. Matures in 30–40 days.
Annual rye grass *Lolium multiflorum*	Cool weather	Less bulk than grazing rye. Easier to dig in.
Agricultural lupin *Lupinus angustifolius*	Cool weather	Deep roots fix nitrogen and aerate the soil. Thrives on acid soil.
Trefoil *Medicago lupulina*	Cool weather	A biennial suitable for longer term use. For undersowing winter crops.
Alfalfa *Medicago sativa*	Cool and warm	Fixes nitrogen. Does not like acidic soils. Provides habitat for beneficial insects.
White/Sweet clover *Melilotus alba/ M. officinalis*	Cool weather	Long taproots open up soils. Fixes nitrogen, with appropriate inoculation.
Grazing rye *Secale cereale*	Cold weather	Hardy winter crop. Good for sowing in autumn. Prevents soil erosion. Chokes out weeds.
Fenugreek *Trigonella foenum-graecum*	Cool weather	Seeds germinate at very cold temperatures. Quick growing. Deep roots break up soil.

RECOMMENDED GREEN MANURES

Name	Conditions	Comments
Fodder radish *Raphanus sitivus*	Cool weather	Discourages nematodes. Long taproot penetrates subsoil.
Sparky marigold *Tagetes patula*	Warm weather	Grown for nematode control. Adds organic matter.
Alsike clover *Trifolium hybridum*	Cool weather	Excellent on poor soils. Fixes nitrogen. Dense growing. Crowds out weeds.
Crimson clover *Trifolium incarnatum*	Cool weather	Shade tolerant. Fixes nitrogen. Good cover crop in beds used to grow grains.
Kent wild white clover *Trifolium pratense*	Cool weather	Low growing. Fixes nitrogen.
Essex red clover *Trifolium pratense*	Cool weather	Attracts bees and fixes nitrogen. Requires high calcium and good drainage.
Field bean *Vicia faba*	Cool weather	Fixes nitrogen. Strong roots break up hard soil and bring up nutrients.
Common vetch (tares) *Vicia sativa*	Cool weather	Fixes nitrogen. Chokes out weeds. Feeds beneficial insects. Tolerates mowing.
Hairy vetch *Vicia villosa*	Cool weather	Fixes nitrogen. Best for cold climates. Feeds beneficial insects. Chokes out weeds.

BENEFITS OF HUMUS

Adding humus to the soil has the following results:
● Improves drainage
● Aerates the soil
● Allows water to penetrate the surface
● Retains moisture
● Loosens heavy soils
● Helps heavy soils warm up in the spring
● Prevents loss of nutrients from light soils

ADDING ORGANIC MATTER TO TOPSOIL

Planting green manure and turning it into the soil is a quick way to add organic matter. The above-ground vegetation decays and forms humus.

When the tops are turned under, the roots are left in the ground to decay, and help to deepen the topsoil. There are two ways to incorporate the vegetation into the soil. The first is to turn under green moisture-filled growth. This stimulates microbiotic activity, but adds little humus to the soil. The second is to mow the green manure and leave it to dry for a day or two before turning it under. Although it takes much longer for the dry vegetation to decay, it adds more humus to the soil and makes organic material available for a longer period of time to feed future crops grown in that area.

Which method is better? This depends on your situation. It may be difficult to try to plant a bed where dried vegetation has recently been turned under. So if you intend to plant the bed very soon, turn it under green. If you want to increase the long-term fertility of the bed, turn it under dried.

BREAKING UP THE SUBSOIL

Many green manures have deep roots that break up compacted subsoil. While topsoil is generally light and filled with lots of humus, subsoil is usually heavy and lacks organic matter. When the roots of deep-rooted cover crops spread out and penetrate the subsoil, they loosen it and break it up so that it is aerated. Future crops then find it easier to extend their roots into the subsoil to obtain minerals, nutrients and water. When the roots decay, they leave behind organic matter in the subsoil. Improved air circulation allows oxygen to reach deeply into the soil and assist the breakdown of organic matter.

NITROGEN FIXING

Some green manures extract nitrogen from the air and fix it in nodules on their roots. These nodules slowly release the nitrogen into the soil for use by future crops.

These green manures are legumes, just like beans and peas. And, again like beans and peas, in order to fix the nitrogen they require a special type of bacteria in the soil. These are bacteria of the genus *Rhizobium*. There are many strains of *Rhizobium* and specific crops require particular strains. The strains of *Rhizobium* for many crops – including, probably, peas, broad beans, field beans and at least some clovers – are likely to exist naturally in your soil.

For legumes to fix nitrogen, a pH of 6.5 to 7.0 is preferred, and there should be no deficiency in cobalt, which is a catalyst for the chemical reaction.

PREVENTING NUTRIENT LOSS

When soils are left unplanted, rain falls on the bare earth and washes away its nutrients. Sandy soils are particularly susceptible to nutrient loss; clay soils less so. Planting a green manure will help prevent nutrient loss, as nutrients that might otherwise be washed out will be used by the green manure, and then returned to the soil when the crop is turned under. Try to plant a green manure crop as soon as possible after harvesting from a bed. The deep roots of some green manures collect nutrients from deep down in the soil and bring them to the surface where they will be available to future crops raised in the bed.

STIMULATING SOIL MICRO-ORGANISMS

As mentioned above, turning under moisture-filled green vegetation stimulates microbiotic activity in the soil. This helps to break up organic matter in the soil and makes nutrients available to future crops grown in that bed. It also breaks up woody and undecomposed organic matter into rich humus that will improve the drainage of heavy, moisture-retentive soils and help retain water in light, powdery soils. Even peat soils are improved by cover crops that are turned under when lush and green, because this stimulates microbiotic activity and improves drainage.

SOWING AND TURNING UNDER

To sow a green manure, prepare the bed as you would for vegetables (see pp. 128–31). Broadcast the seeds by hand and rake to cover the seeds lightly with soil. If you are sowing a large area, you will find that a hand-held broadcast seeder (see p. 137) will make your task much easier. If you have some tree branches to hand, dragging them across the area makes quick work of lightly covering the seed. If you are sowing in a dry spell, water the area after planting. Little other care is necessary until it is time to turn the crop into the soil.

Use a garden fork or spade to turn the crop under when green. If it is possible to mow it just before turning under it will make your task easier, but this is not essential. Mowing the cover crop and letting it dry before working it in will increase the humus level in the soil. If you are working on very large areas, you may find a tiller useful. As a rule, green manure is ready to be turned under when it flowers, but before it sets seed. Do your research, choose the right cover crop for your site's needs and situation (see pp. 58–9) and incorporate it at the appropriate time.

When a green manure crop has flowered but not yet set seed, it is time to incorporate it into the soil. It can be dug in green, or mowed and allowed to dry before being incorporated.

CHAPTER 3

PLANNING THE

ORGANIC GARDEN

THE IMPORTANCE OF PLANNING

After soil fertility, planning is the most important step to a successful organic garden. Crop rotation and choosing varieties that suit your location and climate are fundamental to organic gardening. They are more help in growing healthy plants than the use of beneficial insects or organic fertilizers.

ASKING QUESTIONS

Rotating crops discourages diseases and many pests. Rotation also allows soil fertility to be maintained or improved. Heavy-feeding crops can follow crops that feed the soil. But before drawing up a plan of crop rotation, you must decide what to grow.

Which fruits and vegetables do you and your family like? And which are most nutritious? Which varieties should you choose? What will grow in your climate? These are all questions that must be answered first.

Heirloom fruits and vegetables are old varieties that are open pollinated. Unlike many modern varieties, they tend to grow very well without chemical fertilizers. Most of the old varieties were developed before the invention of pesticides, and many of the heirlooms are resistant to pests in the conditions where they were developed.

FOOD FOR THE HOME

It is important to plan your garden so that it provides for your nutritional needs and those of your family. A well-balanced diet is essential for good health. It is also worth taking into consideration the new science of functional foods. These provide phytochemicals that can lessen the risk of cancer as well as of heart disease and other serious illnesses, and are necessary for good health. Do not worry if this subject is new to you or if you find it confusing; it is explained in more detail later in this chapter (see pp. 88–9).

Planning the garden so that there is something to harvest throughout the year ensures that you have a fresh supply of organic vegetables during winter. Many plants are quite cold hardy and can be harvested from greenhouses and cold frames all winter long. You will need to assess how much you and your family are likely to consume of any particular fruit or vegetable, so that you can devote the appropriate amount of space to them in the garden.

It is also useful to consider companion

To make the most of your vegetable plot, take time to assess the quantity and variety of plants that you want to grow.

PARTS OF A FLOWER

Plants that have male and female reproductive parts on the same plant are called monoecious; those where male and female parts are borne on separate plants are called dioecious.

❶ Ovary The ovary, at the base of the flower, is where seeds form. In fruiting plants, the fruit is the mature ovary; inside the ovary are ovules.

❷ Petal Thin leaves that form the colourful blossom of the flower, which attracts pollinators. Sepals are leaf-like coverings over the unopened flowerbud.

❸ Stamen The male reproductive parts of the flower, made up of anthers and filaments. The anther is the location of the pollen, and the filament extends from the base of the flower and holds the anther.

❹ Pistil Made up of the stigma, style and ovary, this is the female reproductive part of the flower. The stigma receives the pollen and is generally quite sticky. The style is the tube that holds the stigma and transmits pollen into the ovary.

planting at the planning stage. If you grow certain vegetables and fruits in close proximity to one another, one plant can provide nutrients needed by the neighbour, or discourage pests that would otherwise be attracted to that neighbour.

ORNAMENTAL PLANTS

Finally, when considering the overall plan for your garden, take time to think about the decorative aspects. There is a wonderful selection of plants available, from which you can choose edible plants that are attractive, as well as ornamental plants that are edible, to landscape your site. Flowers are an essential part of this plan, for they attract beneficial insects and provide habitats for predators in the garden. Toads and frogs, birds and beneficial insects, all of which feed on pests, are encouraged to live in your garden.

BASIC BOTANY

Some plants have complete flowers, containing both male and female reproductive organs (highlighted in the box above). Other plants have incomplete flowers, that is to say, they possess only one set of sexual organs. All flowers are held on a stalk or stem, which usually has leaves. Alternatively, leaves form on other stalks or emerge directly from the roots.

Seed is formed when pollen from the anthers is deposited on the stigma and the style conveys this pollen to the ovary where fertilization takes place. The stigma must be at the right stage of development to accept the pollen. In self-fertile flowers, this stage is often reached before the blossom opens. If this is not the case, the plant depends on an external pollinating agent, which is usually an insect. Other plants rely on the wind to carry pollen to the stigmas.

CHOOSING PLANTS

Deciding what to grow can be very difficult, but it is easy to come up with answers if we consider what our ancestors grew and why. Our grandparents and great grandparents were much more concerned with the quality of vegetables in the garden. Quantity was of less concern.

ASSESSING SUITABILITY

Our ancestors chose to grow things that worked well together; after one crop was harvested, another could be planted in its place. They also learned to plant so that the preceding crop fertilized the following one. These are useful factors that we should bear in mind when planning the organic garden.

Another key factor when deciding which plants to grow is that some vegetables can be bought from a shop, while others are not available on the shelves or are simply unpalatable. For example, the taste of shop-bought tomatoes cannot compare to that of home-grown varieties. Lettuce or strawberries picked fresh from the garden taste much better than those offered in shops. When planning your garden, start on a small scale, growing only the vegetables that have a short lifespan or that are not commercially available. In subsequent years, you can expand your range of garden produce to match your diet and taste.

CLIMATE AND LOCATION

When choosing plants, take practical factors into consideration. You may love cucumbers, but it may not be possible to grow them if you live in a cold climate with short summers. If this is the case, search out a variety that matures more quickly or consider using a cold frame or greenhouse. Vegetable varieties often differ in their tolerance of climates and locations. For example, some varieties of dry bean are prone to mould and produce poorly in the humid

CLIMATES AND ZONES

Climate is an important consideration when planning. You should determine the date of the average last spring frost in your area, and that of the average first autumn frost. The number of days between these two dates is your growing season. When buying seed, you need to consider the number of days it takes the plant to mature. Most seed companies will list the number of days required from sowing to maturity.

Similarly, when choosing perennials, trees and bushes, it is important to consider your climate. In particular, you need to know the average minimum winter temperature for your area. In many countries, this temperature is converted to give what is called a temperature zone. Gardening books and catalogues often indicate plant hardiness by giving a range of zones in which a plant may successfully be grown.

heat of warm areas, but grow very well in temperate climates. Other varieties will not mature in the short summers of cold climates, and prefer hot climates.

For good results from your crop, choose the variety that is most appropriate to the growing conditions of your particular climate, location and soil type.

SAVING SEED

After growing an open-pollinated variety successfully, you may notice that some individual plants grew better than others. These are the ones that are likely to prefer the climate and soil conditions of your site, and so you should save their seeds for use when planting in the next year. By selecting seeds from those plants that grow best in your garden, you are choosing a sub-variety that is well suited to it. However, if you repeat the practice of seed saving year after year, that particular strain of the variety will differ slightly from the seed that you originally bought and sowed. As well as site suitability, seeds may also be chosen for their colour, form, flavour or time of harvest – the beauty of saving seed is that you set the criteria.

THE EFFECTS OF AGRIBUSINESS

In the last couple of decades, large commercial concerns have started to take over the food-growing industry, buying up most of the seed companies. They mix up chemical fertilizers in the laboratory and advertise them to farmers and home gardeners alike.

In order to make profits, these big businesses have hybridized new varieties of vegetable, then patented and promoted them. These hybrids are rarely chosen for their taste or nutrition. More often, they are selected for their uniform appearance, transportability and ease of growth under chemical control. These hybrids tend to produce a crop that is ready for harvest at the

Seedheads can be hung upside-down in the warm sun to dry. Protect the heads with paper bags to keep out light and to catch any seeds that fall.

same time – a necessary feature for commercial farmers – whereas the home gardener wants the exact opposite of this, namely a harvest over an extended time.

HYBRIDS IN THE GARDEN

Some hybrids grown for their taste still create problems for organic gardeners. Again, the plants tend to be very uniform and are ready for harvest all at the same time, rather than over an extended period. The hybrid crop rarely produces any individuals that grow better than others because it lacks diversity; hence, the benefits of saving seed from open-pollinated varieties is lost.

If you save seed from a first-generation hybrid between two true-breeding varieties (these plants are referred to as FI hybrids), the population of

Open-pollinated varieties provide diversity of colour and flavour.

plants (called the F2 generation) produced from this seed is likely to be very irregular. If succeeding generations are selected repeatedly, the hybrid can be 'stabilized' to produce plants that are very close to the parent. At this point the plant is referred to as a new open-pollinated variety.

IMPORTANCE OF GENETIC DIVERSITY

Open-pollinated seeds are usually a better choice for the organic garden than FI hybrids. They have a greater genetic diversity among individuals, which is a strength when adverse conditions occur. For example, some individual plants may be resistant to disease or able to survive pest attack. If a crop is damaged, you can still expect some harvest, albeit smaller than expected, rather than no harvest at all.

The importance of genetic diversity is well illustrated by the following tale. In 1970, most commercial farmers in the United States were growing the same hybrid variety of corn. When corn blight attacked this non-resistant variety, more than 15 per cent of the entire US crop was destroyed. Vast amounts of corn were lost because the commercial variety lacked genetic diversity. In contrast, small farmers who were growing open-pollinated varieties of corn lost little if any of their crop. Following the blight, the large-scale seed suppliers offered open-pollinated varieties to commercial farmers for the next year's planting. Sadly, little has been learned from this incident because, today, these suppliers are once again selling hybrids to commercial growers.

The founder of Seed Savers' Exchange, an organization that preserves heirloom varieties, has likened the offering of these uniform hybrids to a burglar stealing the key to a single apartment and finding that the key opens every other apartment in the building. Many commercially grown crops are of a similarly small genetic diversity. Most of the major commercially grown cash crops are hybrids, which have virtually identical genes.

GENETICALLY MODIFIED FOODS

Instead of increasing genetic diversity, large-scale seed producers opted to produce chemicals that combat pests and diseases, for which they charge the commercial growers dearly. More recently, the major chemical companies that make pesticides have come up with a new idea – genetically modified seed, commonly referred to as a genetically modified organism (GMO). Instead of hybridizing seed, these companies now inject the DNA of viruses, bacteria, fish, animals, and other vegetables into the DNA of vegetables in the hope of creating a 'better' variety.

Seed producers claim that genetically modified seed is necessary to 'feed the world'. In reality, there is no evidence that the harvests have increased in size; in fact, studies show that the harvests produced from genetically modified seeds are sometimes smaller. Why, then, is this work is being done? The answer is profits. The primary factor that is introduced in the process of genetic engineering is pesticide and herbicide resistance. For example, a soya bean has been produced that can withstand virtually unlimited doses of the most popular brand of pesticide.

With growing concerns over GMOs in wheat and other commercial crops, many organic gardeners are choosing to raise their own.

When one of these seed companies sells its seed to a commercial grower, it issues a contract to license the seed. Not only does this contract require the grower to use the company's pesticide, it also forbids them from saving seed for the next year's planting.

Besides the obvious concerns about the possible adverse effects of such huge doses of pesticide on people eating produce from these seeds, another concern exists. The genetic diversity of pests is such that when their complete eradication is attempted by using chemicals, the process inevitably results in the survival of the resistant individuals only. These individuals breed and reproduce, eventually creating a strain that is resistant to the pesticide. Given the rapid rate of reproduction in the insect world, widespread use of pesticides, such as that seen in the midwest of the United States, may result in resistant strains in as little as five years.

CREATING RESISTANCE

This concern about the rise of a resistant strain is analogous to documented medical data from Mexico. Doctors in that country in the past prescribed penicillin for every little ailment. When patients were diagnosed with a viral infection such as a cold, it was customary to prescribe penicillin as a preventative measure in order to discourage opportunistic infections. A study carried out in 1997 indicates that the overuse of penicillin has resulted in the creation of resistant bacteria; the number of cases of antibiotic-resistant pneumonia rose from 14 per cent in 1994 to 25 per cent in 1997 – compare this with a few decades ago, when there were no known resistant strains of pneumonia.

If you work with a resistant variety, you can achieve a harvest of perfect peaches and nectarines by using organic rather than chemical controls.

A recent study shows that tobacco budworm (*Heliothis virescens*) will be completely resistant to *Bacillus thuringiensis* (*Bt*) within three to four years (see p. 172),[1] because of the prevalence of *Bt* corn. When a chemical company executive was confronted with this information, he replied, 'We can handle this problem with new products. The critics don't know what we have in the pipeline. Trust us.'[2]

In the United States, the Environmental Protection Agency (EPA) has recommended that a percentage of farmland be planted with conventional corn to slow down the process of resistant pest formation. Areas of non-genetically modified corn will provide a habitat for pests.[3] It is ironic that an organic method of pest control (*Bt*) has been used to create a super-pest that is much harder to control.

UNSEEN GENES

Genetic engineering has gone far beyond the genetic manipulation of hybrids, and the safety of genetically engineered food has not yet been determined. Hybridizing involves human assistance in a natural process; genetic engineering may have unforeseen consequences. No study has proved that GMO foods are safe.

Any plants may face infection with genetically modified genes, through the natural process of insect or wind pollination. There have been several documented incidents of genetic drift, resulting in at least one court action. There is no easy solution to this problem.

[1] Gould, F., Anderson, A., Jones, A. et al. *Initial frequency of alleles for resistance to* Bacillus thuringiensis *toxins in the field populations of* Heliothis virescens, Proceedings of the National Academy of Sciences, 94, pp. 3519–23, 1997.

[2] Pollen, Michael. *Playing God in the Garden, New York Times Sunday Magazine*, 25 October, 1998.

[3] *Ibid.*

Heritage & Heirloom Varieties

Heritage and heirloom varieties of vegetables and fruits are old open-pollinated varieties that have long been in cultivation. They refer to historic and ethnic varieties or to varieties that have been passed down through generations of a family or culture.

BENEFITS OF OLD VARIETIES

Growing old and open-pollinated varieties has many advantages for the organic gardener. First and foremost, the seed from these vegetable plants can be saved and replanted. This has

Parsnips have long been common kitchen garden vegetables. They keep well if simply left in the ground over winter.

several benefits. There is no reason to go out and buy new seeds every year when they can easily be collected in the garden, and they have the advantage of being organically grown. It is often difficult to find organically grown seeds, and organic seeds are essential.

Seed companies often discontinue older varieties of vegetables and replace them with modern hybrids, which are more profitable for them to sell. You may find that your favourite tomato or bean has suddenly been discontinued or withdrawn from stock. In fact, between 1984 and 1991, 45 per cent of the open-pollinated seeds available for sale in North America were removed from seed catalogues and replaced with Fi hybrids. Many of the older varieties have been selected for traits that make them more suitable to specific locations than the current commercial varieties. The taste of the old varieties is often unique, whereas most of the vegetables sold in shops have a 'standardized' taste.

OPEN-POLLINATED VARIETIES

While all heirloom and heritage seeds are open pollinated, not all open-pollinated varieties are old. A good example is the 'Sweet 100' tomato, a hybrid that was stabilized over many years. The seed of the Fi generation was saved and grown out again. The individual plants closest to the Fi generation were chosen to be the parents of further generations. After more than six generations, the hybrid was stabilized so that the seed comes true to type.

Some hybrids have qualities that are not found in the open-pollinated varieties. You may choose to stabilize them yourself in your garden. You may consider some of the newer open-pollinated varieties, which can offer wonderful qualities for the vegetable garden.

REGIONAL VARIETIES

Among heirloom plants, regional varieties are most suited to being grown in certain areas. 'D'Arcy Spice' is an example of a regional variety of apple. Needing low rainfall and lots of sun, it thrives in its native East Anglia, but does much less well in wetter, less sunny areas of the British Isles. There are regional varieties for almost every area of the world and it is well worth seeking out varieties that are special to your area. Typically they will be resistant to the local pests and diseases and be able to produce an abundant crop in your climate.

When choosing varieties, look beyond plants that are propagated by seed. There are many perennials, trees and bushes, as well as potatoes, artichokes, asparagus and garlic, that are asexually propagated. These plants are reproduced by division or other vegetative methods rather than by fertilization. While all the arguments in favour of open-pollinated seeds do not apply to these plants, the other benefits still weigh heavily in favour of the heirloom, heritage, and regional varieties. Older vegetable varieties often grow better without the use of chemical fertilizers and pesticides, and are likely to be more pest resistant. Most important of all, they produce a harvest that is full of flavour.

Heirloom varieties of fruit are well worth growing, and, because they often have a natural resistance to disease, they tend to thrive with relatively little care.

WHAT IS AN HEIRLOOM VARIETY?

It is difficult to define an heirloom accurately, but set out below are three primary guidelines about the characteristics of heirlooms.

- Heirlooms must be open pollinated. Seed saved from one year will produce plants that are largely like their parents, or 'true to type'. The edible parts of the plant will taste basically the same as their parents. There is room for biodiversity in open-pollinated varieties; this is not so in F1 hybrids where almost all individuals are identical. Asexually propagated plants are exempt from this guideline.
- Heirlooms must have withstood the test of time. The amount of time required is rather arbitrary, but some standard expectations have developed. Plants started from seed are generally considered heirlooms if they have been cultivated for more than fifty years. Bushes and perennials require fifty to seventy-five years, and trees are considered heirloom varieties if they are still valuable after seventy to one hundred years.
- The variety should have a history. This may include its association with a particular ethnic group and its cuisine. The variety may have been an important crop for a society or a treasured fruit or vegetable passed down through one family. It may have a historical link with a particular event in a certain culture. Many varieties have been grown for a long time but their histories have been lost. Nevertheless, they are still considered to be heirlooms.

Some of the more recent varieties of asexually propagated plants are also worth considering, but choose carefully. You may find yourself raising the latest and best variety that can be harvested green, shipped over long distances, and that needs doses of pesticides to yield a decent crop – in other words, a variety bred to please commercial growers rather than organic gardeners.

GOVERNMENTAL THREAT TO BIODIVERSITY

One of the most serious threats to heirloom seed is governmental pressures for the elimination of varieties that are almost identical in appearance and taste. The Common European Catalogue removed 1,500 varieties from its lists in 1980, claiming they were identical. What governments overlook is the fact that many similar-looking varieties possess different qualities of pest and disease resistance because of their ancestry. For example, a variety that has long been grown in northern England is better suited to that climate than a variety that looks and tastes similar but has been developed and grown in southern Italy for the last fifty years. The climates, pests and diseases are not identical, so the resistance levels are bound to differ between varieties.

Some countries, including the UK, have gone so far as to make it illegal to supply varieties that are not recognized by the government. In these countries gardeners seeking specific varieties have to join a seed-saving group in order to exchange (rather than buy) restricted seeds.

BREEDING VARIETIES FOR YOUR GARDEN

Saving seed from the best plants in the garden will result in a selection that is especially well s uited to your particular location and climate. Saving seed is easy for most vegetables. The hard part is choosing the individual plants from which to harvest seed.

SELECTING THE BEST PLANTS

You need to be a constant observer in your garden. If a few individual plants bear fruit earlier than the others, you can select for that trait by saving seed only from those individuals. You get to decide what qualities constitute 'best'. For one gardener the quality might be flavour but for another it might be pest resistance or drought tolerance, depending on your location and climate, as well as on the types of pest and disease present in your area. Whatever your criteria, make sure that you save seed only from healthy, disease-free plants that are hardy or drought tolerant in your garden. Choose several plants from which to save seed – this helps to protect the genetic diversity of the variety. Always label your seed plants so that they do not get accidentally harvested for the table. It often helps to keep a journal recording your seed selection and the reasons why you chose them.

SAVING SEED

The first step is to determine if the plant is an annual, a biennial or a perennial. Perennials are most often propagated asexually; however, some are propagated from seed like annuals.

Annuals are the easiest plants from which to harvest seeds. They flower and produce seed in one season. Many of them are self-pollinating, although some require cross-pollination. Those that cross-pollinate must be isolated from different varieties and other vegetables in the

SAVING TOMATO SEEDS

1 Take several fully ripe tomatoes and slice them to expose the seeds and pulp. Squeeze the pieces and use your thumb to remove all of the pulp and seeds.

2 Smear the pulp and seed mixture on a dry paper towel. Spread them out evenly for quicker drying and leave them in a well-ventilated, dark, warm area.

3 When the seeds appear dry, place them in a paper envelope to finish drying. They can then be stored in an airtight jar. Label and date the seeds.

75

same family, otherwise the resulting seed may be an unexpected hybrid. A good way to accomplish this is to separate insect-pollinated plants in a screen enclosure and to pollinate by hand. Choose a flower from one plant, peel back its petals and brush the pollen against the stigma of the flowers of the plant you will use to harvest seed.

Wind-pollinated plants need to be separated from each other by a significant distance in the garden for successful results; alternatively, they must come into flower at different times. A greenhouse is occasionally required for growing plants for seed (see pp. 96–8).

Although garlic sets seed, it is best propagated by division. Separate out the individual cloves of a garlic bulb and plant them in the autumn.

Biennials are plants that require two growing seasons to flower and set seed. Some may be left in the ground over winter, while others must be harvested and replanted in the spring. All the above information about self-pollination and cross-pollination applies equally to biennials.

HARVESTING SEED

Timing is essential when harvesting seed: unripe seed will not germinate, and seed that is left on the plant too long is likely to become damp or damaged by pests. Typically, you should harvest seed at the end of the growing season, long after the point when the plant would normally have been harvested for the table. In some cases, the seeds need to be extracted from the fruits (see Saving tomato seeds, p. 75).

Water is the enemy of all seeds. Dry seeds thoroughly in a dark, warm area, such as a cupboard, but check that it is well ventilated so as to encourage free air circulation. Spreading seeds thinly on a fine-mesh screen works well. After the seeds are dry, store them in a glass or some similar container, and label and date them.

TESTING SEED VIABILITY

Most seeds remain viable for a long time, but others, like carrots and parsnips, germinate well only in the following spring. Test the germination rate of your seeds first before relying on them for your spring planting. To do this, plant ten seeds indoors in a flat and see how many germinate. Another method is to put the seeds on a wet paper towel inside a plastic bag and leave them in a warm spot. If you have less than 50 per cent germination, discard the seeds or grow a crop just for the purpose of producing fresh seeds.

Divide large plots into smaller beds and rotate crops from year to year. You may choose to include flowers in your rotation plan.

CROP ROTATION

Crop rotation is one of the most important factors in planning the organic garden – even in the smallest of gardens. The order of rotation should aim to have heavy feeders follow those that nourish the soil. Rotation also breaks the cycle of soilborne pests and diseases.

BASIC PRINCIPLES

Once you have a good idea of what you plan to grow in your garden, it is time to plan the order of crop rotation. Although it is more difficult to rotate crops in a small plot, you must persevere in order to discourage pests and diseases. Crop rotation is absolutely essential if you are going to achieve success when gardening organically.

Plants that feed the soil should be followed by those that take nutrients from the soil. Let us start with a simple example of a two-year plan where only sweetcorn and beans are to be grown. Beans are legumes that fix nitrogen into the soil

Sweetcorn and beans make a good choice for simple crop rotation. The beans fix nitrogen in the soil, on which the corn thrives in the next year.

THREE-YEAR ROTATION PLAN

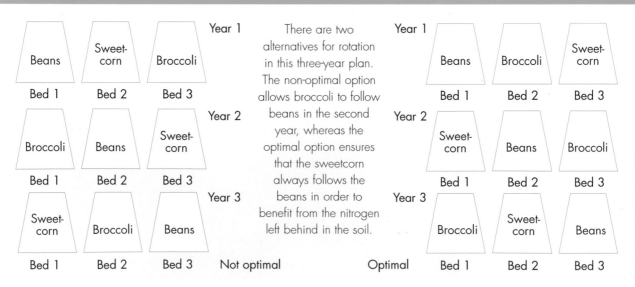

	Year 1	
Beans	Sweet-corn	Broccoli
Bed 1	Bed 2	Bed 3

	Year 2	
Broccoli	Beans	Sweet-corn
Bed 1	Bed 2	Bed 3

	Year 3	
Sweet-corn	Broccoli	Beans
Bed 1	Bed 2	Bed 3

Not optimal

There are two alternatives for rotation in this three-year plan. The non-optimal option allows broccoli to follow beans in the second year, whereas the optimal option ensures that the sweetcorn always follows the beans in order to benefit from the nitrogen left behind in the soil.

Year 1		
Beans	Broccoli	Sweet-corn
Bed 1	Bed 2	Bed 3

Year 2		
Sweet-corn	Beans	Broccoli
Bed 1	Bed 2	Bed 3

Year 3		
Broccoli	Sweet-corn	Beans
Bed 1	Bed 2	Bed 3

Optimal

and sweetcorn needs nitrogen to grow well. You can create two beds, and alternate the crop grown in each bed every year. In this way, the beans leave nitrogen behind to be used by the sweetcorn.

Now suppose that you choose to introduce a third crop, such as broccoli. This would provide you with two possible rotation plans (see three-year rotation plan, left). The real question here is which is the best order to rotate them in? One option would be for the first bed to be sown with beans, followed in the next year by broccoli, and then by sweetcorn in the third year. A second option would be for the sweetcorn to follow the beans every year. The latter option is preferable because the sweetcorn has a greater need than the broccoli for the nitrogen left behind by the beans. Also, experience has shown that brassicas are not good preceding crops for heavy feeders such as sweetcorn.

GROUPING THE CROPS

There is no crop-rotation plan guaranteed to produce perfect results because each garden has

TWELVE-YEAR ROTATION PLAN

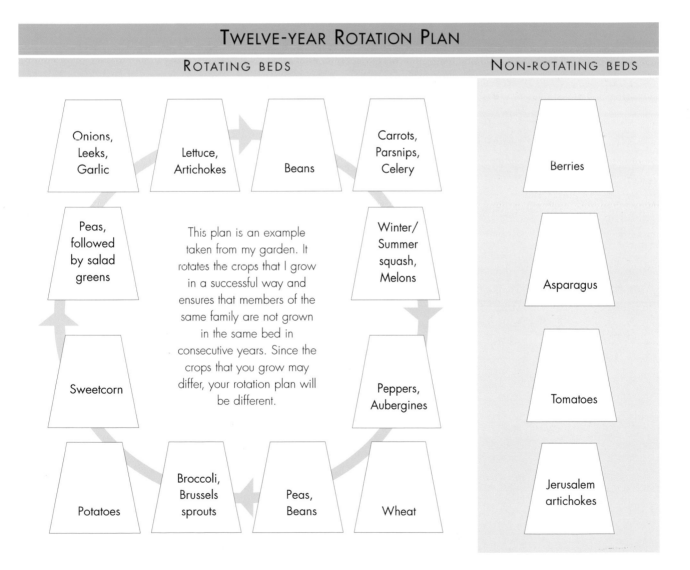

ROTATING BEDS

NON-ROTATING BEDS

Onions, Leeks, Garlic

Lettuce, Artichokes

Beans

Carrots, Parsnips, Celery

Berries

Peas, followed by salad greens

This plan is an example taken from my garden. It rotates the crops that I grow in a successful way and ensures that members of the same family are not grown in the same bed in consecutive years. Since the crops that you grow may differ, your rotation plan will be different.

Winter/ Summer squash, Melons

Asparagus

Sweetcorn

Peppers, Aubergines

Tomatoes

Potatoes

Broccoli, Brussels sprouts

Peas, Beans

Wheat

Jerusalem artichokes

Plant broad beans as a green manure or as a crop to harvest for use in the kitchen. They are an ideal preceding crop to heavy feeders.

- *Brassicaceae*/Mustard family: kale, radishes, cabbages, Brussels sprouts, kohlrabi, broccoli, swedes, turnips, cauliflowers
- *Cucurbitaceae*/Gourd family: watermelons, melons, cucumber, summer squash, winter squash
- *Poaceae*/Grass family: wheat, corn, rye
- *Papilionaceae*/Pea and bean family: beans, peas
- *Alliaceae*/Onion family: onions, leeks, garlic
- *Polygonaceae*/Buckwheat family: buckwheat
- *Solanaceae*/Nightshade family: peppers, aubergines, potatoes
- *Apiaceae*/Carrot family: celery, carrots, parsnips

Many gardeners group their vegetables based on how they are grown, rather than by their botanical family. On this basis, a grouping of root crops would comprise potatoes (*Solanaceae*), radishes (*Brassicaceae*), carrots (*Apiaceae*), and beets (*Chenopodiaceae*). The drawback here is that although it may aid in cultivation and harvesting, it does not assist with the prevention of pests and diseases. For example, you might choose to have root crops (including swedes) followed by greens (including kale), and then cabbages; this would result in brassicas being grown in the same bed for three consecutive years and would allow diseases that plague brassicas to flourish. For this reason, the better method is to group vegetables based on their botanical family and to rotate the families.

a different selection of crops. It is up to you to work out one that really suits your garden and the crops that you want to grow. The easiest way to accomplish this is to use slips of paper labelled with the names of the vegetables and fruits. Cut the pieces of paper in proportion to each other so that the size of each slip roughly reflects how much you want to grow of that particular crop.

Arrange the slips of paper on a table in front of you, with similar vegetables grouped together by family (shown below):
- *Chenopodiaceae*/Goosefoot family: beets, spinach, Swiss chard
- *Asteraceae*/Daisy family: endive, chicory, artichokes, sunflowers, lettuces

PLANNING YOUR ROTATION

With the paper slips separated out into vegetable families, you can develop your own crop rotation plan. If any of the groups are particularly large, divide them into two smaller sections to make them more manageable. Your goal should be to have all the groups at approximately the same size. If a family only contains one crop, move it to a smaller group to create a more even balance.

With the equal-sized groupings of paper in front of you, start to arrange them in a logical order. Begin with the legumes (beans and peas), which feed the soil. Follow them with heavy feeders like sweetcorn. Put brassicas before legumes. Potatoes are a suitable crop to follow sweetcorn because they tolerate poor soil. And since potatoes produce so much foliage that they inhibit the growth of weeds, follow them with, say, a crop of onions, which are difficult to weed.

Once you have arranged your slips on this basis, you might find that you have an arrangement similar to the twelve-year plan illustrated on page 79. This is a good start but the question remains: how do the rest of the crops fit into the rotation plan? Highlighted in the box to the right are some key rules for crop rotation.

RULES FOR CROP ROTATION

- Never follow this year's crop with another member of the same family.
- Arrange your plan so that heavy feeders always follow legumes, which enrich the soil.
- Potatoes yield best after sweetcorn.
- Grain crops do best after legumes.
- Root crops often take a lot out of the soil, so put them before legumes.
- Having brassicas follow onions is beneficial.
- Tomatoes are narcissistic and do not like to rotate.
- Squashes and cucumbers are beneficial to most following crops.

Summer squashes do not need high nitrogen levels, and leave plenty of nutrients in the soil for crops raised in the bed in the following year.

THE HEALTH-GIVING GARDEN

A well-balanced diet is essential for good health. The basic principles of good nutrition are very simple but need to be clearly understood to ensure a diet made up of vitamins, minerals, fibre, protein, carbohydrates and fat. Here are a few basic guidelines to improving your diet.

EAT ORGANIC FOOD

Studies have shown that many chemical pesticides and herbicides leave a residue on plants. This residue may be toxic to humans and can remain in the soil to be taken up by plants. Thereafter, it enters into our diet. Conventionally grown food may be genetically modified, and the potential dangers of this are still to be discovered. No study has proved that GMOs are safe. Hormones given to animals are passed on in their milk and flesh to humans.

One final concern is that many conventionally grown crops are fertilized with a man-made nitrogen/phosphate/potash (NPK) fertilizer. Crops grown this way, especially root crops, contain less of the trace elements present in organically grown vegetables. Clearly, chemicals such as these are unwelcome ingredients in our diets. Organically grown food is a much healthier option.

EAT FRESH FOOD

The longer food is stored, the fewer vitamins it retains. Bottling and freezing are forms of dead storage, and the nutritional content of the food decreases rapidly. It is best to eat food while it is still fresh, or to preserve it using live storage methods, such as root cellaring, lactic fermentation, or preserving in oil or vinegar (see pp. 276–9). Nothing beats eating food that is newly harvested from the garden, so try to extend

Peas are the easiest vegetable to freeze and they retain almost all their nutrition. They have a high content of vitamin C and disease-fighting phytochemicals. They also contain vitamins B1, K, folic acid, potassium and fibre.

When planning your meals, allot portions of different types of food according to this diagram. Eat less of the foods at the top of the pyramid and more of the foods at the base. Restrict consumption of red meat and sugars, and eat more grains, fruits, vegetables and legumes. Be sure to drink plenty of water; wine is permissible in moderation.

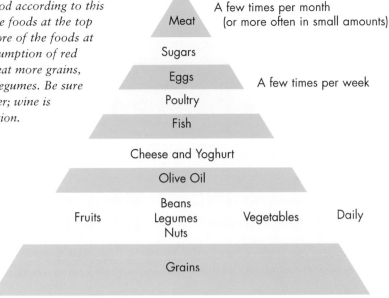

your harvest well into the winter by using cold frames, greenhouses or polytunnels, and by choosing hardy vegetables. When buying meat, it is worth asking whether it was frozen during transport, as freezing may result in nutrient loss.

EAT UNPROCESSED FOOD

In terms of nutrient loss during storage, the issue of food processing should be raised. Take wheat, for example. Wholewheat that has been ground for flour is nutritious, but most of the flour sold in shops has had the germ or outer shell removed and this is where most of the nutrients are concentrated. The remainder of the wheatgrain, the endosperm, is ground for flour. Iron, B vitamins and folic acid are added before the flour is sold, but personally, I feel that wholewheat flours make a much better choice than artificially enriched flours.

Most raw vegetables provide many more vitamins than cooked vegetables, because the heat breaks down vitamins. Uncooked foods also provide more fibre. As for the ready-prepared convenience foods available from supermarkets,

eat them as infrequently as possible, if at all. These foods are usually heavily processed and have lost much of their nutritional value.

EAT A VARIETY IN MODERATION

The only way to achieve a proper balance of nutrients is to eat a wide variety of foods. The saying 'Too much of a good thing' holds true: any food, eaten in excess, can be bad for you. Many people restrict their intake to just a few types of vegetable, even though a wide and diverse range is readily available.

Moderation means that no foods need be blacklisted from your diet, unless for medical reasons; instead, they can be eaten in proper proportions with other foods. The nutritional pyramid above illustrates how to allot portions of different types of food to maintain a well-balanced diet similar to that of Mediterranean regions. Foods at the apex of the pyramid are limited to small amounts that may be eaten occasionally, while those at the base can be eaten daily in larger amounts. Portion control is also necessary for good health.

IMPROVING YOUR EATING HABITS

Change your diet slowly. If you change it rapidly to eliminate unhealthy eating habits, the end result will probably be failure. You are more likely to suffer from cravings for much-loved foods and gradually revert to an unhealthy diet. Slow changes work better and are more likely to last. Begin by reducing the portion size of foods that should have less emphasis in your diet. At the same time, increase the portions of foods that should have more emphasis. Introduce new vegetables to balance your diet, and vary the foods used in your meals to ensure a good balance and to keep your meals interesting.

Aim to reduce and eventually avoid snacks. Snacks tend to be the least nutritious foods you eat. They are convenient when you are hungry and, more often than not, you find yourself eating them out of habit rather than hunger.

Well-planned nutritious meals need not be elaborate or time consuming to make. Studies have shown that several small meals are healthier than three large meals a day. Moreover, eating several small meals a day will reduce your dependence on snacks. One widely recommended meal plan for good health is six small meals which provide a daily allotment of milk, protein, carbohydrate, fruit and vegetables.

GARDENING FOR EXERCISE

Feeding your body well is only one half of good health; the other half is getting proper exercise. A combination of nutritious food and exercise is the key to a healthy body. And what better way to exercise than to work in your organic garden? Double digging beds, raking, weeding, and harvesting can be just as good exercise as walking, swimming and other sports.

Plant Swiss chard (left) in a cold frame in early autumn to extend the harvest well into winter.

Eaten fresh or baked in pies and tarts, cherries (right) are packed with goodness. They are an excellent source of beneficial phytochemicals, vitamin C and fibre.

VITAMINS & MINERALS

Vitamins are derived from plants and animals. They are organic substances that assist the body in processing other nutrients, like proteins, fats and carbohydrates. Minerals, unlike vitamins, are inorganic substances and do not break down. They assist enzyme function in the body.

VITAMINS

In addition to helping the body break down nutrients, vitamins are also used in the formation of blood cells and nervous system chemicals, and in the production of DNA. They are needed by the human body in extremely small quantities. Remember that too much of any nutrient can reach toxic levels – this can pose a very real danger if vitamin supplements are overused.

MINERALS

Iron, copper and other minerals are similar in function to vitamins. They help the body to break down nutrients by assisting enzymes in their activities. Minerals are usually not broken down by cooking or preserving food, but some leach out of foods that are cooked in water. They can be divided into two categories: macrominerals that are needed in large quantities, and trace elements.

VEGETARIANISM

If you choose to eat only a vegetarian or vegan diet, it is important that you take supplements of vitamin B12. This vitamin is only available from animal foods but it is essential to your diet for the formation of red blood cells. Anaemia, pale skin, loss of balance, and general weakness are just some of the symptoms that can be caused by a deficiency of vitamin B12.

TOP 10 VEGETABLES IN VITAMINS AND MINERALS

1. Broccoli
2. Spinach
3. Brussels sprouts
4. Butter beans
5. Peas
6. Asparagus
7. Artichokes
8. Cauliflowers
9. Sweet potatoes
10. Carrots

Carrots are particularly high in minerals and beneficial phytochemicals, including vitamins, and they are easy to store for use throughout the year.

VITAMINS AND MINERALS FOR HEALTH

VITAMIN	BENEFIT	MINERAL	BENEFIT
Vitamin A	Healthy skin and hair, good night vision, bone and tooth development, needed for reproduction.	**Macrominerals** Calcium	Builds bones and teeth, aids in blood clotting, aids absorption of B12, activates some enzymes.
Vitamin B1/ Thiamin	Aids breakdown of fats, proteins and carbohydrates.	Chloride	Activates some enzymes, necessary for stomach acid; regulates body pH.
Vitamin B2/ Riboflavin	Aids breakdown of fats, proteins and carbohydrates.	Magnesium	Needed to build bones and make proteins; aids nervous system functions.
Vitamin B3/ Niacin	Catalyst for energy production in cells.	Phosphorus	Builds bones and teeth; breaks down fats, proteins and carbohydrates.
Vitamin B6	Helps the body use fats and proteins; catalyst in red blood cell formation.	Potassium	Needed to regulate balance of water and dissolved solids inside cells.
Vitamin B12	Necessary for formation of red blood cells; helps nervous system functions.	Sodium	Needed to regulate balance of water and dissolved substances outside cells.
Vitamin C	Helps prevent breakdown of other vitamins; blocks some cancer-causing chemicals; helps in collagen formation.	Sulphur	Needed to build amino acids and many proteins.
Vitamin D	Aids in bone and tooth formation; aids in phosphorus and calcium absorption.	**Trace elements** Chromium Copper	Needed to metabolize sugar. Needed for red blood cell formation and for building many enzymes.
Vitamin E	Aids in cell formation, including muscle and red blood cells; prevents vitamin A breakdown.	Fluoride	Aids in formation of teeth and bones.
Vitamin K	Helps with blood clotting.	Iodine	Needed for reproduction, and for proper function of thyroid.
Folic acid	Combined with B12, aids in the formation of red blood cells.	Iron	Helps red blood cells to carry oxygen.
Pantothenic acid	Aids breakdown of fats, proteins and carbohydrates; helps to regulate nerves.	Manganese	Breaks down carbohydrates, proteins and fats. Necessary for brain function.
		Selenium	Antioxidant interacts with vitamin E, prevents breakdown of vitamin A.
Biotin	Aids breakdown of carbohydrates.	Zinc	Building block of many enzymes.

FUNCTIONAL FOODS

Strictly speaking the term 'phytochemical' applies to all chemicals synthesized by plants, including starches, sugars, oils and vitamins. However, when people refer to phytochemicals they are usually talking about a particular group of chemicals which are physiologically beneficial to humans because of providing protection against cancer and other diseases.

WHAT DO PHYTOCHEMICALS DO?

There are literally hundreds of different phytochemicals present in vegetables and fruits. Scientists are only now beginning to identify many of them, and to understand how they work. It is hoped that by increasing our intake

TOP FRUITS, VEGETABLES AND NUTS FOR GOOD HEALTH

1	Strawberries	12	Onions
2	Tomatoes	13	Garlic
3	Peppers	14	Blueberries
4	Apples	15	Raspberries
5	Cabbages	16	Blackberries
6	Beans	17	Plums
7	Cherries	18	Lettuce
8	Winter squash	19	Walnuts
9	Apricots		
10	Peaches	plus the Top 10 Vegetables
11	Grapes	listed on page 86

High in beneficial phytochemicals, peppers come in a range of striking colours and shapes. Their crisp skins and succulent flesh can be eaten raw or cooked. Hot peppers are especially high in phytochemicals.

of physiologically beneficial phytochemicals, our diet may be used to protect the body against disease. Many of the compounds identified so far are antioxidants that bind with highly reactive substances, called 'free radicals', which damage DNA. It is believed that these free radicals are among the factors responsible for cancer and heart disease. Other phytochemicals have been shown to boost the immune system, or block the action of viruses.

Although scientists have only recently identified physiologically beneficial phytochemicals, humans have long been eating large amounts of them. This is important because these compounds are needed in rather

Grow brassicas in the garden for a year-round supply of nutritious food which is rich in vitamins, minerals and phytochemicals.

large quantities for good health. One of the easiest ways to increase the beneficial phytochemical content in our diet is to eat more raw vegetables and fruits. When food is cooked, many of these delicate phytochemicals are destroyed.

Another good way to increase our consumption is to choose vegetables that are high in phytochemicals. The top ten vegetables (foods that have the highest content of vitamins or minerals, see p. 86) are also high in health-promoting phytochemicals. To complement these vegetables, it is important to include some other vegetables, fruits and nuts for a well-balanced supply of phytochemicals (see box, left). In addition to these, consider adding the following produce for a highly nutritious, well-balanced diet: potatoes, cantaloupes, tangerines, mangoes, pineapples and watermelons.

PLANNING A YEAR'S SUPPLY

Planning the organic garden so that there is something to harvest throughout the year will enable you to have fresh vegetables in winter. Some vegetables are tolerant of cold weather (cold hardy) and may be harvested in the winter; others may be harvested from storage.

EXTENDING THE HARVEST

The primary premise in having vegetables to harvest all winter long is quite simple: extend the growing season as long as possible by using a combination of hardy plants with cold frames

 ### EXTENDING THE HARVEST

There is a significant difference between extending the growing season and extending the harvest season. In order to extend the growing season, you will need a greenhouse, heating equipment, overhead plant lights, and a lot of labour to coax plants; even without all this, more often than not the results are unsatisfactory.

In contrast, extending the harvest season is quite easy and economical. Plants are grown during the summer and autumn and then protected from the cold throughout the winter for a later harvest.

A hardy member of the brassica family, kohlrabi is well suited to live storage in a frost-freee place, such as a shed, and will not lose any of its valuable nutrients.

and unheated greenhouses; and then extend the harvest after the plants are grown. Heating a greenhouse or using other expensive and complicated strategies is not necessary.

Start the plants and get them growing in warm weather. When the cold sets in, they should be ready for harvest. Rather than removing them from the ground, however, protect them from the cold – there in the garden – for a later harvest. Crop protection, in this case, means that the vegetables should be sheltered by cold frames, greenhouses, polytunnels, soil, hay bales or some other method of insulation (see pp. 94–8).

Another benefit of winter harvesting is that it cuts down on the need for preserving food. The labour of bottling, freezing and so on is not necessary when the vegetables are stored just where they grew in the garden.

LABOUR-SAVING PLANNING

Planning for a year-round harvest actually makes your work in the garden easier because it eliminates the effort needed for a major spring planting as well as the frantic rush to harvest and preserve crops in the autumn. By successional planting, the effort is spread out through the entire growing season, with some vegetables planted in spring, others in summer, and still others in autumn. The harvest is not all in the late summer and autumn, but instead is spread out across the entire year. Dismiss the idea of 'putting the garden in' during spring. With a year-round harvest, there is always something to plant and something to harvest. For example, when you carry out your weekly harvest of lettuce, replace the mature plants with seedlings that you have started indoors. Instead of it being time to thin the beets, it is actually time to harvest some beet greens for salad or soup. When the peas are done in early summer, seize the opportunity to replant the area with some radishes or bok choi.

If you miss planting something because you are busy or the weather is poor, there is no need to worry: just skip that planting and continue with the next. This means that if you are too busy when the peas are finished to replant the area with a summer crop, all you have to do is plant the area later, when you have time, with an autumn crop. If your sweetcorn failed to germinate because of the weather, you need not bother trying to plant it again if it is too late – simply refer to your crop rotation plan and plant something else in its place.

The garden is always there and something will always be ready for harvest. There is no need for one small problem to overturn and destroy your plans; you just need to change them a little.

Grow lettuce in a bed that you can cover with a cold frame in winter. Frequent sowings of lettuce and other greens will permit fresh salads throughout the year in most climates.

SUCCESSIONAL SOWING

Successional sowing is the practice of sowing a small amount of the same vegetable in succession throughout the growing season. This should provide a continuous harvest while avoiding gluts. The sowing dates of these vegetables can be brought forward a little if you are sowing under cover.

Beets (beetroot, chard and perpetual spinach) Make monthly sowings beginning in early to mid-spring and continuing until mid-summer.

Spinach Sow every three weeks or so, starting in early spring and continuing until mid-summer.

Lettuce Sow every two weeks, starting in spring

Calabrese Make monthly sowings from mid-spring to early summer.

Peas Sow throughout the spring.

Small radishes Sow every two weeks from early spring to early autumn.

Greenhouses, polytunnels and cold frames provide safe havens for crops that might otherwise succumb to the harsh conditions of winter. The table opposite lists crops normally grown outside, but that will also do well inside during the winter. This list is by no means comprehensive, and experimentation is the key, both with varieties and with sowing dates.

'LIVE' STORAGE

Some vegetables and fruits store extremely well in a shed or other form of live storage (see pp. 276–9). Few of them lose nutrients during storage and some will even increase in nutrition and taste. Harvesting vegetables as needed from live storage is easier than bottling or freezing. The most important requirement of the storage place is for it to be kept cool and moist. The best vegetables to store in this way are root crops, cabbages, kohlrabi and winter squashes. Belgian endive can be stored in a similar way for later forcing. This will produce delicious fresh greens in the middle of winter.

If frost threatens, place cloches over tender plants. In spring, they can be used to start seedlings early, directly in the garden.

PLANNING THE PLANTING

Having considered nutrition, harvesting and your family's preferences, it is time to make a rough estimate of what to grow and in what quantities. Assess how much of each crop your household is likely to eat in a year, and from this determine how many plants of each crop are needed. Only experience will provide the answer. There is enough space even in quite a small garden to grow all of the fruit and vegetables needed to feed a small family throughout the year. To complete a well-balanced diet for your household only meat, fish, dairy products and grain need to be bought in.

INDOOR WINTER CROPS

CROP	WHEN TO SOW
Perpetual spinach	Early autumn.
Endive and chicory	Early autumn.
Lettuce	Early autumn and winter. (Some varieties do better than others over winter, so variety selection is important.)
Chinese greens	Early autumn.
Kohlrabi	Early autumn.
Turnips	Spring and early autumn. Use bolt-resistant varieties for spring sowings.
Peas	Autumn and winter.
Carrots	Mid-autumn and mid- to late winter.
Minor salad vegetables	Early autumn (cold-tolerant varieties only).
Parsley	Early autumn.

SMALLER PROTECTIVE STRUCTURES

Cold frames are very simple structures with glass tops that are used to extend the growing and harvest seasons of crops in the garden. They are most often used to start seedlings earlier than usual in the spring and to extend the harvest of cold-hardy vegetables into the winter.

CLOCHES

These are the simple, portable predecessors of cold frames. They are glass covers which can be placed over individual plants. Cloches are available in a variety of sizes, ranging from models that are small enough to sit on an 8cm/3in pot to 35cm/15in domes which cover larger plants in the garden.

The use of cloches allows seedlings to be started in garden beds earlier in the spring. When frost threatens to damage tender plants, place a cloche over them. Similarly, mature plants can enjoy cloche protection during the autumn to prevent their demise on cold nights. Always remember to remove cloches on warm days because they heat up quickly in the sun. When it is only moderately warm, simply tip up the edge of a cloche on a stone or brick to allow air to enter and prevent overheating.

COLD FRAMES

There are both semi-portable and permanent versions of cold frames. The portable ones are more useful for season extension, especially if they are the same width as your garden beds. If you prefer to buy a cold frame instead of building it yourself, be sure to choose a model that is fitted with an automatic vent opener. This device opens the lid to release the warm air and to let in cool fresh air if the cold frame starts to overheat on a warm day.

You can make a simple cold frame in your garden by using hay bales as supports along your garden paths and covering the beds with old windows. If the frames are painted brown, the windows will blend in with the site and be unobtrusive. On warm days, move the windows slightly to create a 2.5–5cm/1–2in crack between them to allow air to circulate. During cold nights, push the windows together to eliminate the cracks and keep the heat in.

Traditional glass cloches are prized as much for their ornamental value as their practical use in potagers and kitchen gardens.

94

A simple cold frame can be made in your garden from old windows and spare timber. Paint it brown to blend in with the surroundings or white to reflect the light.

If you require a more permanent version of a cold frame, you can construct one from wooden frame walls that are staked into the ground. Again, old windows can be used to cover the frames. Attach them with hinges at one side and consider providing an automatic venting arm to the other side. A good location for this type of cold frame is against the sunniest side of your house. This will provide some additional heat, making it an ideal place to start seedlings in the early spring. Be sure to enrich the soil under these permanent cold frames just as you would for any other bed in the garden.

HOTBEDS

One variation of a permanent cold frame is a heated frame, or hotbed. This contains a source of heat that is either electrical or organic; traditionally, fresh manure was used to generate the heat in the early spring to start seedlings. Hotbeds need to be taller than cold frames if manure is used to generate the heat;

this has the additional benefit of bringing the top to a convenient height for working the bed.

To build a manure-based hotbed, place a 60–75cm/24–30in layer of fresh manure mixed with straw at the bottom of the bed. Wet the manure and cover it with 30cm/12in of garden soil. Close the glass cover of the hotbed and wait for one week. The temperature will rise quickly and then begin to drop. Once the temperature has fallen to 24°C/75°F, the bed is ready to be planted. It will stay warm for several weeks.

A much simpler solution is to use electric heating cable. Dig out the bed to about 30cm/12in deep and place a 10cm/4in layer of coarse gravel at the bottom to ensure good drainage. Do not attempt the electrical installation yourself, but employ a professional electrician to place the cable in equally spaced parallel lines and cover it with a layer of wire mesh to protect it from gardening tools. Add a layer of fine sand followed by another 15cm/6in of garden soil. Check the temperature of the bed regularly.

GREENHOUSES

Greenhouses are simply elaborate cold frames that are large enough to walk into. They can be used to start seedlings and grow crops that are not hardy in your climate, or to extend the harvest season of certain crops into the winter.

GREENHOUSE STYLES

There are two basic kinds of greenhouse: heated and unheated. Unheated greenhouses are just like cold frames. One important use of heated greenhouses is to extend the growing season. Seedlings can be started very early in spring, and many plants can be grown year round. If you garden in a cold climate, a heated greenhouse will also enable you to grow lemons, oranges and other crops that require hot climates.

CHOOSING A GREENHOUSE

It is important to choose a greenhouse that suits your purpose. The most common mistake is to choose a small greenhouse. You will find all too quickly that you have outgrown it. Whatever size you think you will need, you are well advised to buy one that is at least 50 per cent larger. You will never regret the higher initial expenditure.

Greenhouses come in many forms. Freestanding is probably the best choice unless you have a sunny wall, which is ideal for a lean-to style greenhouse. Whether building a greenhouse yourself or buying a kit, automatic ventilation is essential. A greenhouse may overheat rapidly while you are away and literally cook your plants to death.

SITING A GREENHOUSE

If you intend to attach your greenhouse to your house or another building, try to locate it on the sunny side – the south side in the northern hemisphere, and the north side in the southern hemisphere. Eastern or western orientation is acceptable but not as good, because nearly half the day's sun will be lost. There is little point in positioning a greenhouse on the shady side of your house. Whether your greenhouse is freestanding or attached, for the maximum amount of sunlight during winter, orient the ridgeline from east to west.

LIGHTING

Choose the sunniest spot on your property, away from the shadows of trees and buildings. Remember that too much sun is better than too little. During the sunniest months of the year, if shading is necessary, you can install shade cloth or blinds, or wash the glass with shading paint to reduce excessive sunlight. During the least sunny months, and especially during late winter and early spring seed sowing, extra light may be necessary. Full-spectrum 1.2m/4ft fluorescent lamps work well. Keep the lights 2.5–8cm/1–3in away from the plant foliage so as not to encourage the seedlings to become leggy.

TEMPERATURE AND VENTILATION

Ventilation is essential, not only to prevent overheating but also to reduce excessive humidity that causes rot and fungal diseases. Automatic roof vents are the best solution for this problem. These are worked by a non-electric temperature-controlled piston that opens a hatch in the roof to allow hot air out. Even when temperatures are not too high, open the windows (weather permitting) to reduce excessive humidity.

In a large greenhouse, sometimes a small amount of heat will be needed. When you start seedlings in the spring, you might put heat mats under the trays to assist germination. Large greenhouses are often prone to draughts but a small heater is normally sufficient to counteract this problem.

WATERING

If you are starting seedlings or maintaining perennial plants and trees, regular watering is essential. Over- and underwatering both cause significant problems. At cool temperatures, plants need less water, but more is needed as soon as temperatures rise.

An easy solution is to set up a drip irrigation system in the greenhouse. You can run it more often and for longer in hot weather than cold. If you are raising potted plants, you may find that capillary matting fulfils your watering needs.

SUPPLEMENTING PLANTS WITH NUTRIENTS

When growing plants in a greenhouse, two methods are commonly employed. One is to grow plants in pots, and the other is to grow them in a greenhouse bed. The drawback of using beds is that the soil quickly becomes depleted of nutrients. A lack of crop rotation may result in soilborne pests and diseases too. The best solution to this problem is to excavate some soil and replace it with compost each year when cultivating. If plants are grown in pots, you may find that the reduced amount of soil available requires you to supplement the plants with liquid organic feeds. Making your own liquid feed is a simple process (see pp. 49–53) and the feed can easily be applied when you are watering your plants.

Growing a wide variety of plants in your greenhouse will create a balanced environment which will help control pests and diseases.

If your garden suffers from waterlogged ground, build raised beds, which ensure good drainage. The improved growing conditions are worth the labour involved.

CONTROLLING PESTS AND DISEASES

Within the confined space and warm environment of a greenhouse, any pests or diseases, such as mould and mildews, will thrive. Therefore it is especially important that you remove dead and diseased matter from the greenhouse promptly. Cleaning the greenhouse thoroughly on a regular basis is also a good preventative measure. Good gardening practices with an eye towards hygiene are the best defence against potential problems.

One downside of automatic venting is that pests are permitted to enter and, sadly, screens do little to combat the problem. Planting flowers and plants that attract beneficial insects alongside your crops is the best method of pest control. Aphids, whiteflies and red spider mites are the most common greenhouse pests.

POLYTUNNELS

Polytunnels are rather crude structures ideal for gardeners with few DIY skills. The biggest ones come in walk-in sizes similar to greenhouses, and consist of hoops slotted into stakes driven into the ground. Wooden door frames are constructed at both ends, and the whole affair is then covered with plastic normally anchored down in a trench.

The hoops of theses large polytunnels come in a range of set widths, starting with those that stand 3m/10ft wide at ground level. Lengths can vary according to the whim of the gardener; it is just a matter of deciding how many hoops to buy.

Some tunnels come as small, cloche-like structures that conveniently cover individual crops in the main part of the garden. They are easily moved around, and, like the bigger versions, are available in a range of sizes.

RAISED BEDS

When planning the garden it is important to think about good drainage. Raised beds are one method of planting in a wet site. They also offer the gardener the opportunity to create a bed with the specialized growing conditions required by certain plants.

BUILDING A FRAME

The first step in building raised beds is to make a frame. Railway sleepers suit raised beds well; they age to an attractive dark colour and blend in well with the colour of the soil. Be careful to avoid pressure-treated wood, as it can contain arsenic or other toxic chemicals.

Set the frame on the ground on the site you have chosen for your raised bed. The turf must be removed and the soil levelled without digging deeply enough to disturb the compacted earth that will be under the frame. Gravel is often used to level the underlying soil surface. If you are using a wood frame, you may need to drive stakes into the ground on the inside of the bed to attach to the wood.

Loosen the soil in the bottom of the bed with a garden fork, then fill it with soil or compost. If the raised bed is being made to grow a particular crop, use soil or compost that has been enriched with soil amendments specifically suited to that crop (see pp. 54–6).

FRAMELESS BEDS

To build a frameless raised bed, remove the turf from the bed in brick-like pieces. Stack these pieces placing the grass side face-down, along the outline of the bed. Very often these beds last for years before erosion takes its toll and the sides start to slope. You can seed edges that start to slope, but be careful not to tread on these sloping edges.

MAKING A FRAMELESS BED

1 *Mark out the site of the bed using pegs and string. Cut out brick-shaped pieces of turf and stack them grass side down until they are needed.*

2 *Place the 'bricks' along the sides of the bed to form a surrounding wall. Loosen the soil, without disturbing the subsoil, then fill with compost and soil.*

3 *If you are growing a specialized crop, incorporate the necessary soil amendments to ensure ideal growing conditions. Water the bed well.*

EDIBLE LANDSCAPING

The goal of organic gardening is to create a natural balance of planting through diversity. There is a vast array of plants which are not only ornamental but also edible, and edible plants which are also ornamental, which you can use around the garden.

DECORATIVE FRUITS AND FLOWERS
It was quite usual for our grandparents to have apple trees, cherries, raspberries and other fruiting plants interspersed with flowers and vegetables arranged in the garden in a beautiful and decorative way. Many trees have beautiful blossoms and foliage and they also provide wonderful food for the table. With a little imagination and effort, even the vegetable garden can be laid out to enhance the beauty of your home. A large manicured lawn is not the only ideal of beauty.

Edible landscaping is simply utilizing edible plants (namely, fruit trees and bushes, herbs and vegetables) which have decorative value, and decorative plants which are edible (even many flowers).

Many roses produce hips after they flower. These can be used to make syrup or jelly or, if left on the bushes, will attract wildlife in winter.

FILLING THE GARDEN WITH FOOD
When designing your garden, take time to consider where you spend time outdoors. A perfectly natural choice might be to have alpine strawberries along the walk from the front door to your gate. Then, on your way in and out each day, you can pull up a few weeds at the same time as harvesting a handful of strawberries. Either side of the path that runs to the back door is another choice location for planting edibles. On your arrival home, you could harvest some basil and tomatoes to mix in with mozzarella and olive oil to make a wonderful salad for supper. If you spend a lot of time on the patio or terrace during the summer, why not surround it with a narrow vegetable bed, interspersed with flowers and a few bushes that produce fruit? If a patio needs some shade, plant a nut or fruit tree that will also yield fruit in summer and a display of blossom in spring.

Another consideration in landscaping your property is fencing. Instead of building a fence to keep the dog in the garden, why not plant a thick informal hedge of, say, *Rosa rugosa*. It forms an impenetrable barrier, and produces hips that are a good source of vitamin C. Alternatively, grow a thick patch of raspberries to create green 'fencing'. The hedge will also provide a welcome shelter for birds, who will find food in a diversity of plantings. Against the background of your hedge, plant a mix of flowers that will provide colour from early spring through to the autumn, or plant a vine or flowering climber such as a rose or clematis to adorn a wall.

HIGHLIGHTING AND SCREENING

If you want to keep your compost bins from full view but need them to remain close to the kitchen where they will be used, plant a few shrubs or climbing plants around them to act as a screen. Perhaps there is an attractive architectural feature on your property that can be accented? Try flanking the front door with two columnar evergreens that will sway attractively in the wind and frame the entry. If there is a wet area on your plot, consider digging a bed to grow cranberries.

When choosing ornamentals to plant in the garden, search for those that produce edible fruit. Most people think of a dogwood tree as purely ornamental, but the cornelian cherry (*Cornus mas*) produces edible red fruits. A honeysuckle is a beautiful fragrant bush, but you can just as easily choose a variety that produces edible fruit (*Lonicera caerulea* var. *edulis*). The chart below lists bushes and trees that are generally considered ornamentals, but have edible varieties.

YEAR-ROUND TEXTURE

Finally, you also need to think about how the garden will look during the different seasons of the year. In winter, it can still look attractive if the landscape has been planned well. Trees and bushes with striking bark or colourful stems and branches add a welcome splash of interest in winter. European mountain ash trees (*Sorbus aucuparia*) produce orange berries that attract birds, and corkscrew willows (*Salix matsudana* 'Tortuosa') have a more beautiful form in winter than when they are in leaf. Many roses bear huge hips or thorns that remain on the plants into winter; the rosehips are a sure magnet for birds. Evergreen plants can also be put to good use to give structure to the garden in winter. Choose those whose striking foliage will best offset the 'starkness' of leafless trees.

EDIBLE ORNAMENTALS

Please note that only the varieties specified below are edible.

Sugar maple (*Acer saccharum*): used to make maple syrup

'Milky Way' Kousa dogwood (*Cornus kousa* 'Milky Way'): papaya-tasting fruits

Cornelian cherry (*Cornus mas*): the red fruits are edible

Honey locust (*Gleditsia triacanthos*): the dried 'beans' are cooked or ground as flour

Orange daylily (*Hemerocallis fulva*): the unopened flowerbuds are good to eat

Edible honeysuckle (*Lonicera caerulea* var. *edulis*): the blue tear-shaped berries can be eaten

Staghorn sumac (*Rhus typhina*): the berries are made into a drink

Rose (*Rosa* spp.): the petals make a delicately flavoured decoration for salads and puddings, and the hips are used to make syrup or jelly

Nasturtium flowers are a tasty addition to salads and the buds make a peppery substitute for capers.

PLANS & PLANTING IDEAS

The first step in landscaping your garden is to draw a plan. Exact dimensions are not important. Pace off the space and draw a rough plan locating buildings, paths, boundaries, existing trees and shrubs, and any contours in the land. Note which areas receive the most sun.

AVOIDING HAZARDS

If you live in an old property, one important consideration is lead. Lead paint was commonly use for house-painting, and any soil lying close to the walls may be filled with paint chips. If you are concerned that this may be the case, have your soil tested for lead. Look for other areas where you need to avoid growing edibles, for example where the water runs off the driveway, washing away the oil drips from the car. With these things in mind, mark out any areas which will not be suitable for growing food; they can be used for decorative plantings or for lawns.

LOCATING VIEWS

Next, on the plan, mark out the direction of views. Highlight any favourite views, and identify from where they are best appreciated. Note down any unsightly views, and plan to plant trees or shrubs of suitable size to block them.

Use brightly coloured flowers to liven up vegetable plots and add interest. They will also attract beneficial insects to the garden.

SMALL CITY GARDEN

Today the choice of decorative edible plants is greater than ever before. For the boundaries, plant raspberries along the back fence, or mingle them with hazelnuts and thornless blackberries. If you like honeysuckle, there is even a Russian fruiting variety that has blue berries with a wonderful distinctive flavour. Flank a garden path with strawberries or lingonberries, the fruits of which make a tasty sauce that is the perfect accompaniment to roast venison or lamb.

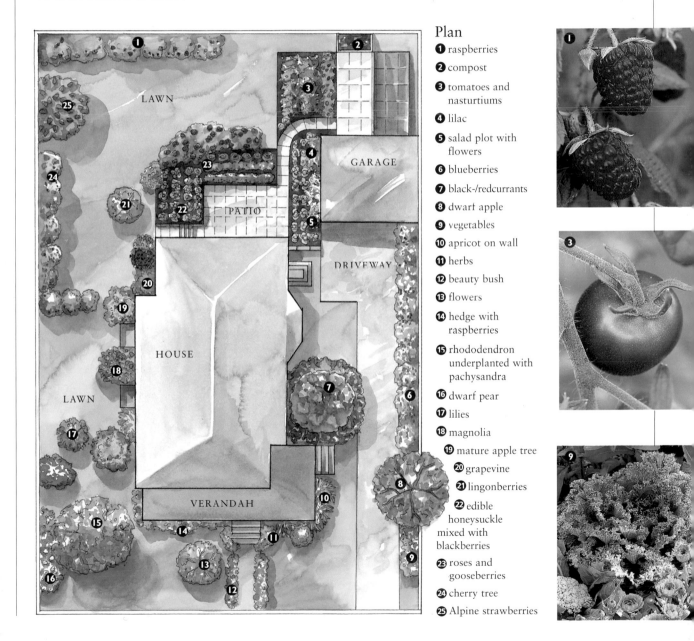

Plan

❶ raspberries
❷ compost
❸ tomatoes and nasturtiums
❹ lilac
❺ salad plot with flowers
❻ blueberries
❼ black-/redcurrants
❽ dwarf apple
❾ vegetables
❿ apricot on wall
⓫ herbs
⓬ beauty bush
⓭ flowers
⓮ hedge with raspberries
⓯ rhododendron underplanted with pachysandra
⓰ dwarf pear
⓱ lilies
⓲ magnolia
⓳ mature apple tree
⓴ grapevine
㉑ lingonberries
㉒ edible honeysuckle mixed with blackberries
㉓ roses and gooseberries
㉔ cherry tree
㉕ Alpine strawberries

LARGE CITY GARDEN

Raspberries are planted outside the fence along the alley, and are a joy to pick when arriving home by car. The terraced back garden leaves lots of room for children to play under the cover of the existing trees. The three raised beds are in the sunniest spot in the garden. The large cherry produces more fruit than a family can eat, and the fruit left on the tree attracts birds. The herbs are grown in partial shade on one side of the house along with rose of Sharon and plants that attract bees and other beneficial insects. The front garden is left more formal with no vegetable production. The pine trees along the south side provide a supply of pine nuts. The row of hemlocks at the rear of the property blocks the prevailing winter wind.

Plan

1 kiwi fruits
2 herbs
3 cherry tree
4 grapes
5 hemlocks
6 raspberries
7 hostas
8 crab apple
9 flowering dogwood
10 apple tree
11 blueberries
12 white pines
13 lilac bush
14 rhododendron
15 evergreen
16 rose bush
17 azaleas
18 columnar arborvitae
19 andromedas
20 rose of Sharon
21 mint
22 astilbe
23 sugar maple
24 herbs
25 climbing roses
26 achillea
27 flowering annuals
28 yew
29 vegetables
30 garlic

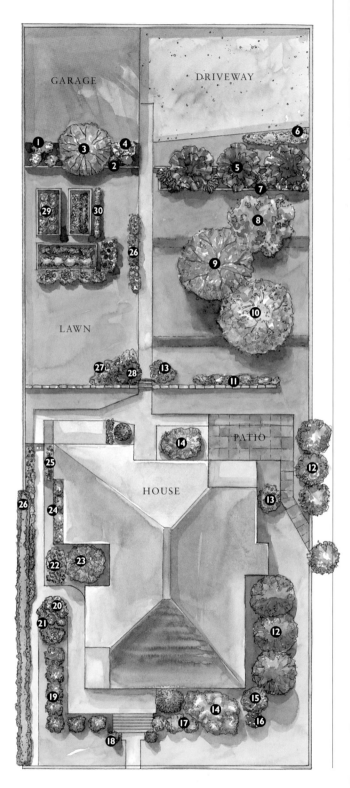

Apples tolerate a range of soils and climates. Choose a variety that is suited to your climate and a rootstock that is compatible with your soil type.

I once lived in a city house where my dining room was so close to that of my neighbour that we could see each other sitting down to dinner. Although we were friends, we both felt the arrangement lacked privacy. The solution was to plant a dwarf apple tree and a honeysuckle to block the view.

In the same house, a dreaded black walnut tree cast shade over virtually the entire back garden. Moreover, its roots produced a chemical that retards the growth of many vegetables, especially tomatoes. This made gardening quite difficult, and also obscured a view from my upstairs rooms of a nearby river. However, after the tree had been removed I discovered that the upstairs bathroom was exposed to the neighbour, so shades had to be installed, depriving the room of sunlight!

PLANNING THE PLANTING

The next step is to choose the location of trees, followed by bushes and perennials. When choosing trees, bushes and perennials, it is very important to consider your climate. Some areas are a great deal more exposed, windy and chilly than others, and some varieties may not grow where you live.

Most good nurseries are able to provide information on the cold tolerance of the plants and trees for sale. In your own garden, tolerance will be influenced by several factors:

● Wind: A windy spot allows trees and bushes to desiccate and results in less cold tolerance.

● Exposure: The sunniest spots in the garden in winter are the warmest. A sunny spot may be an entire zone warmer than a spot that is shaded in winter.

● Elevation: Cold air slides down hills and collects in low spots. A location 90m/300ft away but a drop of 4.5m/15ft in elevation may be −7°C/20°F colder in winter than a high spot.

● Buildings: Garages, houses and other structures may block the wind as well as absorb the warmth of the sun during the day and radiate it back out at night. This process may allow someone with average minimum temperatures around −32°C/−25°F to grow peaches.

SITING TREES

When choosing sites for trees, try to locate them where they will not shade the garden when they mature. Although trees are quite small when you plant them, many of them quickly grow tall and spread wide. In terms of views in your garden, try to site trees so that they block bad views and frame good ones. The most important thing to remember with trees is to start slowly, and not try to plant an orchard in one year. As your plan develops, it will become clear that some existing landscaping needs to be removed. Wait until some of the new plantings are well established before removing existing plantings. Making dramatic changes, such as the removal of several trees and bushes all at once, will not be attractive. It is better to make these kinds of change gradually, replacing the plants removed with your new choices.

Calendulas and anise hyssop not only have edible flowers that can be used in salads but they also attract beneficial insects to the garden.

LARGE SUBURBAN GARDEN

This one acre of land produces nearly all the food needed by a large family for a well-balanced diet. The gardens are in bloom for most of the year. Flowers and bushes attract birds and bees that pollinate vegetables. Hedges and unmowed areas provide habitats for birds and beneficial insects. Bushes have been planted in groups of threes. Note the five peonies in an L-shape – only three are seen at once. No long straight paths are used; a turn in the path creates visual interest and makes the space seem larger.

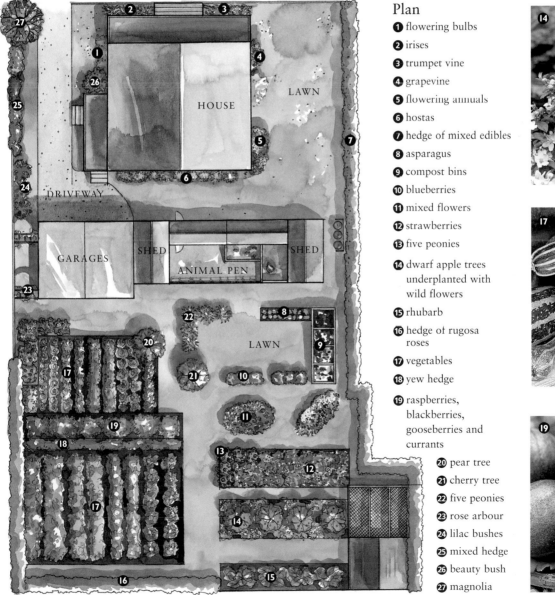

Plan

1. flowering bulbs
2. irises
3. trumpet vine
4. grapevine
5. flowering annuals
6. hostas
7. hedge of mixed edibles
8. asparagus
9. compost bins
10. blueberries
11. mixed flowers
12. strawberries
13. five peonies
14. dwarf apple trees underplanted with wild flowers
15. rhubarb
16. hedge of rugosa roses
17. vegetables
18. yew hedge
19. raspberries, blackberries, gooseberries and currants
20. pear tree
21. cherry tree
22. five peonies
23. rose arbour
24. lilac bushes
25. mixed hedge
26. beauty bush
27. magnolia

THREE-ACRE SUBURBAN GARDEN

This plot is designed to grow enough food to feed a large family. The visual appeal of the garden has been achieved with a mix of edibles and ornamentals. All of the annual flowers and vegetables are grown together. Perennials, which need less care, are planted all around the property, but annuals which need watering and weeding are kept in one location, near a water tap in the area that receives the most sun.

Plan

1. black walnut
2. phlox
3. tree hydrangea
4. rose
5. sugar maple
6. blue spruce
7. hostas
8. crab apple
9. magnolia
10. evergreen hedge
11. rose of Sharon
12. mixed flowers
13. lily of the valley
14. pine tree
15. apple trees
16. ivy
17. peach tree
18. pear tree
19. mature catalpa tree
20. peonies
21. perennial herbs
22. rhubarb
23. currants
24. gooseberries
25. sorrel
26. hedge with mature trees
27. compost bins
28. vegetables and grains
29. vegetables and flowers
30. forsythia
31. elderberry
32. serviceberry
33. edible honeysuckle

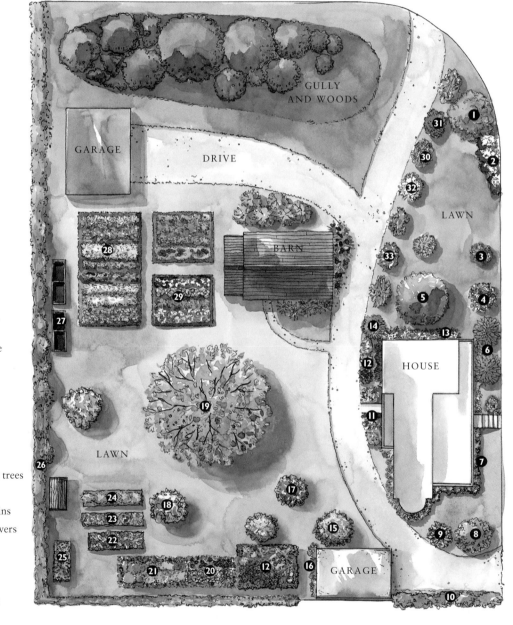

This unusual heirloom potato, known as 'All Blue', stores very well. Potatoes can be stored in a frost-free place throughout the winter.

Another consideration with trees is the climate. In cold areas, consider planting evergreen trees to the windward side of the house. A band of trees will deflect the wind, keeping the house warmer and helping to reduce fuel costs for heating. In summer, the house may be cooled by large deciduous trees planted on the sunny side (see garden plan opposite, item 5). In the winter, the trees will have no leaves and let the sun into the house, but in summer the shade will keep the house cooler.

SITING FRUIT BUSHES

Once the trees are identified on the plan, mark down the site for cane and bush fruits. These are less permanent than trees, but more permanent than vegetable beds. When planning where to put cane and bush fruits, consider whether you will plant flowers and vegetables with them, or keep them separate. A patch of raspberries growing against a fence at the edge of the drive is unlikely to be interplanted with vegetables, but blueberry bushes around the patio will probably be mixed with flowers and more decorative vegetables.

Start with a few bushes, as you can always add more later. Also consult your plan for a year's supply of food, to help you decide on quantities. Many nurseries give significant discounts for ten or more plants, but few

Use scrambling evergreen climbers and shrubs to screen off unsightly objects, such as a compost bin, that might otherwise come into full view during winter.

households could manage to consume the amount of fruit produced by ten bushes of gooseberries, raspberries, blueberries, currants, and so on. For fruiting hedges, plant the bushes very closely. In borders, however, space them wider than recommended to leave room for planting flowers and vegetables.

CREATING WINTER INTEREST

Now is the time to take into account any non-vegetative features of the landscape that become more visible during winter. Will the bare compost bin be an unwelcome sight from the kitchen window in winter? Will the fence be an eyesore when the leaves fall off the forsythia in the autumn? The way garden features look in winter is more important than in summer, when vegetation softens and hides them. A bench

might appear abandoned in winter, so try to give it some visual appeal. This may simply mean siting a hedge or dwarf fruit trees around it or moving it nearer to another feature to form a focal point.

ORNAMENTAL VEGETABLES

Many vegetables are quite attractive and suited to ornamental beds. For example, tomatoes were originally thought to be poisonous and were grown only as ornamentals. They remain a good choice for ornamental beds today. Many flowers attract beneficial insects, and if you mix them with vegetables in ornamental beds, pests can be much less of a problem. Perennial herbs, such as sage and rosemary, are good choices for incorporating into ornamental beds.

SMALL FARM

A small kitchen garden close to the house produces enough fruit and
vegetables for family use. The land is separated into 'outdoor rooms'.
For example, the area of berry bushes is surrounded on all sides by tall
trees, and has two entrances. The large vegetable garden is surrounded
by hedgerows, a wetland, and a pond. These outdoor rooms bring a more
intimate feel to the land because it is broken up into smaller spaces.

Plan

1 kitchen garden
2 black walnut
3 Japanese maple
4 sugar maple
5 kiwi fruits
6 roses
7 apple tree
8 dogwood hedge with trees
9 peach trees against wall
10 gazebo covered with vines
11 vegetables
12 soft fruits
13 white pines
14 hardwood trees
15 vegetables and grains
16 trellised grapevines
17 sugar maple
18 nut trees
19 apple trees
20 evergreen windbreaks

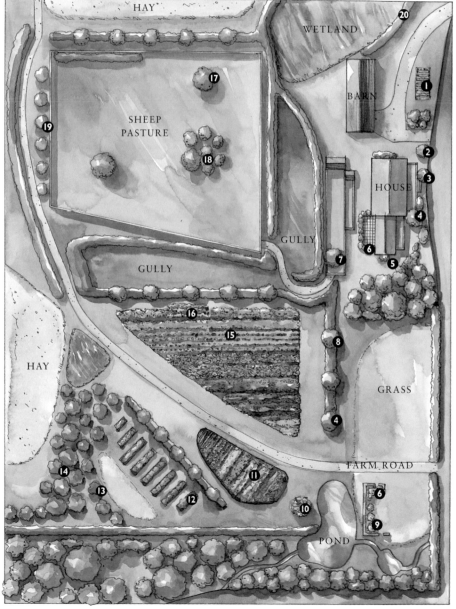

COURTYARD GARDEN

This very small garden appears much larger than it is, and its end cannot be seen from the house. Likewise from the bench at the end of the garden, the house is hardly visible. The curved arrangement of plantings and the height of the trees leaves something hidden, something to be discovered. Here the focus is on ornamentals, but a small vegetable garden has been included. Most of the ornamentals chosen are edible. The herbs and several flowerbeds are all within reach of the kitchen. The dwarf cherry, apple and pear trees provide seasonal food for the table. Together with the Japanese maple and fruit bushes, they give the garden structure, and lead the eye to the roses at the rear.

Plan

1. rose hedge
2. vegetables
3. dwarf cherry tree
4. dwarf apple tree
5. primulas and lupins
6. hydrangeas
7. climbing and bush roses
8. quince bush
9. bay tree
10. clematis
11. potted evergreens
12. strawberry planter
13. chives
14. tomatoes
15. flowers
16. rosemary
17. parsley
18. grapes and kiwi vines
19. flowers and herbs
20. herbs
21. currants and gooseberries
22. Japanese maple
23. thornless blackberries
24. pear espalier
25. figs

PLANTS FOR SCREENING AND STRUCTURE

When considering how to screen a verandah from the summer sun, or cover an unattractive compost bin, it is important to consider the options available. When an architectural feature such as an entrance deserves accent, the right choice of tree or bush can make all the difference. Plants that provide structure and screening should not be an afterthought, but integral to the landscaping design. The individual choices you make depend on your situation, but it is worth visiting other gardens in your area to see what plants and devices have been used.

To screen a verandah from the sun, so that it can be enjoyed throughout the summer, consider planting trumpet vines, or grapevines that will provide not only shade but fruit. Nothing beats the wonderful scent of wisteria. For a shady spot or to create some privacy, use Dutchman's pipe.

Choose tall trees to flank an entrance and low bushes to line the walk to an entry. Using a pair of bushes or trees this way is an exception to a general rule of locating plants in the landscape.

THE RULE OF THREES

Trees and bushes look best grouped in threes. You would need to have a large even number of bushes for it to look as attractive as an odd number. It is hard to determine why this is the case, but almost everyone who looks at a landscape agrees with this rule. When planning to plant bushes that have a separation between them, you will find that an odd number always look better. Where bushes are planted closely and touch one another, as in a close planting of gooseberries, this is not a concern. An even number look fine because it becomes one line of vegetation, not several individuals.

The annual sweet pea (Lathyrus odoratus) can be trained on canes or trellis to create a woven screen of colour and a sweet summer scent.

HERB PLANS & PLANTING

Herbs can be mixed into the vegetable garden or ornamental beds. However, many gardeners choose to create interesting beds exclusively of herbs. These can be incorporated into formal or informal plans and are guaranteed to attract many beneficial insects into the garden.

COOK'S DELIGHT

Locate the herb garden near your kitchen and pick from it frequently as you cook. Herbs that are perennials should not be worked into annual vegetable gardens. The decision as to formal or informal arrangements should match the character of the house and the garden as a whole. If formal hedges of privet surround the garden, consider a classic knot garden or chessboard pattern for herbs. If raspberries, gooseberries and evergreens are mixed with tall trees to form the boundaries of the garden, consider a less formal

design. A cartwheel pattern can fit in with both formal and informal gardens and homes.

Many herbs prefer to grow in sun, but there are some that prefer shade. For this reason, you will probably need to have herbs in two different areas of the garden. In general, annual herbs tend to require direct sunlight and do best in the vegetable garden or worked into a sunny perennial plan. Any herb that is used in great quantities, such as basil or parsley, should be grown in the vegetable garden so that there is enough room to produce the amount needed.

Some herbs are useful the whole year round. Use this to your advantage by growing these herbs in containers or pots that can be brought indoors during the winter. Some of them can be quite ornamental: for example, a pyramidal rosemary can be trained and pruned into a perfect shape, making a welcome decoration in the house during winter.

LAYING OUT A CARTWHEEL BED

1 *Use a central peg and lengths of string with a scoring implement to mark out the rim. Mark out the spokes. Remove the topsoil from these areas.*

2 *Position the pavers on a bed of sand. Gaps can later be filled with gravel to deter weeds. Work plenty of well-rotted compost into the soil.*

3 *Plant the herbs in the bed, keeping in mind the size that they will reach at maturity. For best effect, plant a different herb in each section of the wheel.*

CREATING A HERB BED

Formal herb gardens are often bordered by manicured low hedges of box (*Buxus sempervirens*) or walls made of warm red brick or stone. Most large formal herb gardens feature a central statue or fountain, while smaller plans may feature a particularly eye-catching plant, such as a bay tree in a planter. Most of the work involved in creating these gardens is planning the borders and paths. Stone, brick, or gravel paths together with hedges or walls form the infrastructure of the garden. It is worthwhile spending time and effort initially to build these features well so they will need little maintenance in later years.

The first step is to design the bed. Decide on the type of border and preferred material, then lay out the route of the paths. Choose a central feature, such as an ornament or striking plant that will draw the eye to your design. The next step is to lay out the masonry features in the garden. Brick and stone paths and walls should be built on undisturbed soil. Excavate the turf and set the pavers on a bed of sand. Walls measuring more than 30cm/12in in height will need special footings for support. Consult a reference book or a professional for advice on masonry construction.

When the structure is complete, plant hedge borders or other edging plants that are needed. The final step is to dig the beds between the paths and the edge of the garden. Give perennial herbs a good start by single or double digging the beds; then you are ready for planting out. There are many herbs to choose from, but try to place tall ones at the centre or back of the spaces, and low-growing herbs at the edges. Think creatively about the juxtaposition of colours and shapes.

Purple-leaved basil is one of the many tasty basils available. A group of plants will provide a strong contrast to lighter-coloured foliage in the bed.

FORMAL HERB GARDENS

Formal herb gardens are generally symmetrical in shape, based on a repeating geometric pattern. They are usually edged with paving stones or loose materials such as gravel to separate the paths from the beds. The plantings are often symmetrical, too (see the plan at the bottom of this page, and the cartwheel opposite, below). Also illustrated is a classic knot garden; its intricate pattern is accentuated by a simple planting of just three types of plant.

Knot garden plan
1 thyme
2 rosemary
3 box
4 stone pavers

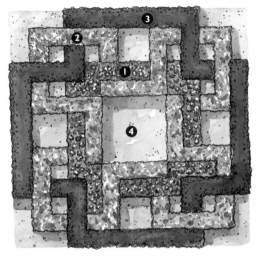

Symmetrical plan
5 box
6 spring onions
7 pyramidal rosemary
8 marjoram
9 hyssop
10 bergamot
11 parsley
12 flowering urn
13 garlic
14 angelica
15 lemon verbena
16 thyme
17 coriander
18 chives
19 sage
20 lovage
21 feverfew
22 epazote
23 Egyptian onions
24 stevia
25 dill
26 sweet Cicely
27 mint
28 ornamental fountain

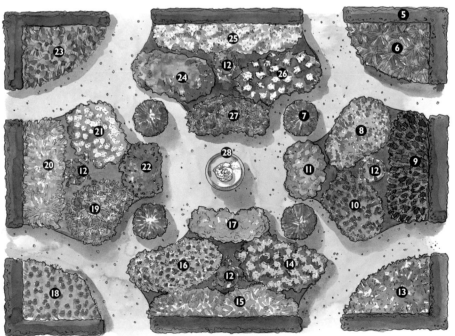

INFORMAL HERB GARDENS

Creating an attractive informal herb garden is much easier than a formal garden. All that is really necessary is to:

● Place tall items at the rear of beds that are up against a building or wall, or in the centre of beds that are viewed from all sides.

● Ensure that the colours of the herbs and their flowers complement each other. The beds can be of any shape, and are easily created by preparing the soil as you would for a vegetable bed – then let your imagination run wild. Look at the drift plan below for inspiration.

Natural drift plan

❶ dill
❷ bay
❸ fennel
❹ lovage
❺ juniper
❻ borage
❼ chives
❽ sorrel
❾ rosemary
❿ spearmint
⓫ tarragon
⓬ sage
⓭ basil
⓮ parsley
⓯ coriander
⓰ thyme
⓱ creeping thyme

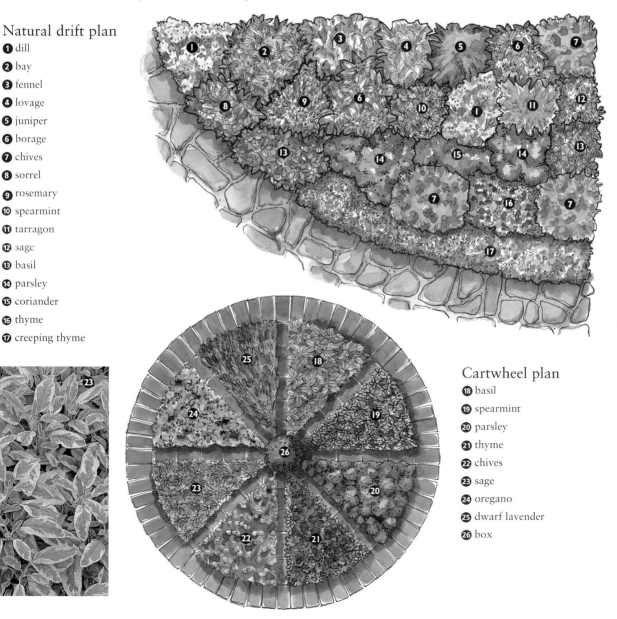

Cartwheel plan

⓲ basil
⓳ spearmint
⓴ parsley
㉑ thyme
㉒ chives
㉓ sage
㉔ oregano
㉕ dwarf lavender
㉖ box

COMPANION PLANTING

Companion planting is the practice of locating particular plants near one another because they enhance plant growth, discourage pests and diseases, or have some other beneficial effect. It also includes ensuring that 'bad companions' are kept apart.

WHEN TO USE

Companion planting is much less effective in discouraging soilborne pests and diseases in the vegetable garden than crop rotation, and wherever possible, you should practise crop rotation (see pp. 78–81). The real benefit of companion planting is in perennial beds where crops cannot rotate.

In fact, very little research has gone into the benefits of companion planting and most of the information that is available about it is anecdotal. However, the tradition of planting certain crops together extends back thousands of years. With this kind of history, companion planting is certainly worth investigating for your organic garden. Though some of the folklore surrounding the practice might make you dismiss this concept as nothing more than an 'old wives' tale', more often than not these companion plantings are based on experience.

The powerful scent produced by a row of marigolds growing next to a patch of cabbages will help to keep many pests away from the crop.

Apples and potatoes Growing potatoes near apple trees can result in blight in the potatoes. Locate potatoes out of the drip line of apple trees.

Black walnuts and many vegetables, especially tomatoes Black walnut trees (*Juglans nigra*) produce a chemical in their leaves called juglone. When it rains, this chemical is washed off the leaves and on to the soil below. Juglone inhibits the growth of many plants, including tomatoes, apples,

potatoes and blackberries. The roots of black walnut trees also produce toxins.

Brassicas and tomatoes When tomatoes are planted close to brassicas, their growth is poor and they do not produce well.

Grass around apples and pears The root tips are the quickest-growing parts of young apple trees and are present near the surface of the soil. Chemicals excreted from the roots of grass can retard the growth of these root tips,

therefore the area close around young apple trees should be kept free of grass.

Maples and wheat The roots of maple trees produce a toxin that deters the growth of wheat, but their leaves have a preserving effect on apples and potatoes.

Spruce trees The effects of spruce trees maintain a presence in the soil long after the tree is gone. While they retard the growth of other trees, they encourage the growth of strawberries.

SUGGESTED PAIRINGS

The best idea is to experiment with companion planting in your garden, and to keep using those pairings that have beneficial effects.

French marigolds (*Tagetes* spp.) These have many benefits in the garden. Dutch scientists discovered that the roots of marigolds excrete a substance that kills soil nematodes. In Holland, chemical sprays were being used (with some success) to combat a problem of nematode infestation in rose beds. The Dutch Plant Protection Service tried interplanting French marigolds with the roses in some beds and found that the nematodes were controlled in those beds. The beds that were not interplanted still suffered from an infestation of nematodes.

This is one of the many uses of marigolds in the garden. They are also grown in greenhouses used for tomatoes, to discourage whitefly. The scent of marigolds is offensive to many insects and other pests. One year I surrounded an entire garden bed with marigolds, and while there was no conclusive evidence that there were fewer pests, the decorative effect was so striking that the following year I planted French marigolds

around all the vegetable beds. It might have been coincidence, but I found that squirrels raided less from the garden that year.

Parsley and carrots Mixing parsley and carrots deters carrot flies because of the masking aroma of the parsley.

Tomatoes and asparagus Tomatoes repel asparagus beetles. Tomatoes planted in the asparagus bed after the spring harvest will protect the asparagus plants during their summer growth season, and the fern-like foliage of the asparagus will provide an attractive backdrop for the tomatoes.

Borage and strawberries Planting borage around strawberry beds makes potassium, calcium and other minerals available to the strawberries.

Pyrethrum (*Tanacetum cinerariifolium*) This is a common organic insect repellant; a powder is made from its flowers and has been used for thousands of years. Growing this wild plant in your garden can discourage many pests.

Stinging nettle (*Urtica dioica*) As its name suggests, the stinging nettle is somewhat painful to touch, but consider growing it nonetheless – it is an excellent deterrent of pests.

BENEFICIAL WILDLIFE

Inviting wildlife into your garden will bring many benefits. Some insects and animals are predators which will eat the numerous pests that invade the garden. All that is necessary is to attract these predators with flowers and herbs, and provide them with a habitat in which to live.

PLANTING FOR BENEFICIAL INSECTS

Traditional English and American gardens shared similar planting styles, which mix flowers, vegetables, herbs and fruit trees and bushes. It was common to find garlic growing with roses, and tomatoes being grown for their decorative value interspersed with marigolds, zinnias and herbs.

It rarely occurs to most gardeners today that the beneficial insects which were attracted by this mix of flowers, herbs and vegetables in traditional gardens are the reason why pests were rarely a problem. Today most gardeners avoid planting carrots alongside the tomatoes, or siting the fritillaries in the same bed as cabbages. The current preference for large mown lawns provides very little habitat for beneficial insects. In the past, the number of pests in the garden was kept under control by planting a varied garden which attracted natural predators.

FRIENDS OR FOES?

The most effective means of controlling pests is to welcome beneficial insects and birds into the garden by providing them with a habitat. Birds, bees and ladybirds are just some of the many predators that will keep pests out of the garden.

Plant an area with flowers that are known to attract beneficial insects. An area of lawn can be left unmown and sprinkled with flower seeds.

Since spiders enjoy a carnivorous diet of flies, caterpillars and other garden pests, they are welcome visitors to the organic garden.

Planting flowers that attract these predators is a simple step in the right direction to controlling pests. Another option is to plant flowers and bulbs that ward off pests, such as onions and sage which repel carrot fly and some other pests. For more information on specific beneficial insects, please refer to the section on pests and diseases on page 173.

ATTRACTING BIRDS

One of the best ways to encourage birds is to create a habitat for them – to build nests and to provide them with food when it is scarce.

The deliciously scented flowers of lavender attract bees and butterflies to the garden. Leave the seedheads for the birds to enjoy in the late summer and autumn.

Plant trees and shrubs that produce berries that can be eaten by birds throughout the winter, encouraging them to live near your garden. European mountain ash trees are a good example. They produce wonderful orange-red berries that birds enjoy feeding on. Rosehips, especially from Rosa spp. and R. rugosa, also provide nutritious food. Snowberries and the black berries that form on ivy are also a good source of food for many birds.

During the growing season, many plants provide seeds for birds. The flowerheads of golden rod, lavender and globe thistles all provide food. Find a spare corner of your plot for growing sunflowers and millet, so that the seeds can be saved as winter feed for the birds.

Dense hedges make an excellent nesting site for birds. The leaves and debris that collect under dense hedges is a wonderful habitat for hedgehogs. They may even overwinter under the hedges if it is not too wet. When planting hedges, leave about 90cm/36in of width to provide ample room for the bushes to grow. The composition of hedges depends on the type of hedge you prefer. For formal hedges, choose slow-growing bushes such as yew (*Taxus baccata*) or holly (*Ilex aquifolium*). This will reduce the necessary labour in clipping and maintaining them. Let the seeds or berries remain on the bushes in winter to provide food for the birds.

Informal hedges can be composed of a variety of bushes. Forsythia (*Forsythia* spp.) is a favourite nesting place for birds, and hawthorn (*Crataegus monogyna*), raspberries, gooseberries, currants and blackberries are all good choices too. Use just one species to make up three-quarters of the hedge, then mix in the others to complete the planting. For example, starting at one end of a hedge, plant 75 per cent *Rosa rugosa* mixed with raspberries for the first

9m/30ft; then plant 75 per cent gooseberries mixed with holly, blackberries, and an apple tree in the next 9m/30ft. After every 3m/10ft, include an evergreen to provide winter protection for nesting birds. Repeat this process until the entire length of the hedge has been done.

Providing birdboxes for nesting and birdbaths for drinking and bathing will further encourage birds to live in your garden. Squirrel-proof birdfeeders filled with sunflower seeds in addition to a thistle feeder will provide necessary winter nutrition and will help encourage migrating birds to return in the spring.

ATTRACTING BEES

Bees are wonderful to have in the garden. They pollinate squash and other vegetables, and feed upon small insects. Different flowers attract different types of bees. This is supposedly because different varieties of bees have different tongue lengths. Growing a wide range of different flowers will attract many varieties of bee.

It is important to do this because more than one-third of the food we eat is bee pollinated, and we need all kinds of bees in the garden. Most of the above-listed methods of attracting birds and beneficial insects to the garden will also attract bees.

An upturned lid of an old dustbin, filled with water and placed on the ground, provides a drinking pool for birds and small creatures.

 BENEFICIAL PREDATORS

There are several different classes of predator, and attracting them requires different methods.

Animals	Insects
Bats	Ladybirds
Birds	Beetles
Frogs	Hoverflies
Toads	Centipedes
Hedgehogs	Lacewings
Shrews	Earwigs

ATTRACTING BATS

Bats feed on a wide range of flying insects, including flies and mosquitoes that attack humans. Bats are mammals and look very much like winged mice. They hibernate during the winter; if you find a family roosting in your house – they usually settle in the eaves of a roof – do not disturb or try to remove them from your property, as they are a protected species.

They can easily be attracted to nest in your garden by providing a simple bat house, which can be made or bought. Contact your local bat conservation society for more information.

The bright yellow flowers of dandelions attract insects. Harvest the young foliage for early spring salads, but leave a few seedheads for birds to enjoy.

ATTRACTING FROGS AND TOADS

Frogs and toads eat slugs and small insects; they even eat some snails. A small pond is a great way to encourage them; however, it is not essential. Water is only necessary for them to breed. They will live and hibernate happily in sheltered dark damp places where they are safe from predators.

ATTRACTING HEDGEHOGS

Native to Europe, hedgehogs feed on caterpillars, slugs and millipedes. As noted above, hedges are wonderful habitat for hedgehogs. They do not like wet places, and are found in cities and the country. You may not know you have hedgehogs in your garden because they hide during the day and hunt at night. If you do not have hedges, leave a shady section of unmowed lawn where they can hide during the day. A small heap of twigs will also provide them with a good home. Encourage hedgehogs to hibernate in your garden in winter by leaving wet cat food or dog food for them near the hedges.

FLOWERS TO ATTRACT BENEFICIAL WILDLIFE

When considering which flowers to plant in order to attract beneficial insects and animals into your garden, start by planting the wildflowers that are native to your local area. Try creating different styles of habitat. For example, a woodland edge is by far the most attractive area to beneficial insects. Beneath some tall trees, plant an understorey of bushes and flowers. Choose shade-tolerant varieties that will provide pollen in early spring, when food is scarce. Other popular habitats are lawns and grass. Leave a section of the lawn unmowed and allow weeds and meadow flowers to flourish. Here are some plants that are recommended.

Bulbs for naturalizing in lawns

Anemone (*Anemone nemorosa*)
Glory of the snow (*Chionodoxa* spp.)
Snow crocus (*Crocus chrysanthus*)
Species crocus (*Crocus* spp.)
Winter aconite (*Eranthis* spp.)
Snowdrop (*Galanthus nivalis*)
Star flower (*Ipheion* spp.)
Snowflake (*Leucojum* spp.)
Grape hyacinth (*Muscari*)
Daffodil (*Narcissus* spp.)
Scilla (*Scilla siberica*)

Wild flowers

Try to use only wild flowers that are native to your area.
Yarrow (*Achillea millefolium*)
Queen Anne's lace (*Anthriscus sylvestris*)

Snapdragon (*Antirrhinum majus*)
Columbine (*Aquilegia* spp.)
Cornflower (*Centaurea cyanus*)
Daisy (*Leucanthemum* spp.)
Coreopsis (*Coreopsis tinctoria*)
Foxglove (*Digitalis purpurea*)
Purple coneflower (*Echinacea purpurea*)
Baby's breath (*Gypsophila elegans*)
St John's wort (*Hypericum perforatum*)
Flax (*Linum usitatissimum*)
Birdsfoot trefoil (*Lotus corniculatus*)
Baby blue eyes (*Nemophila menziesii*)
Poppy (*Papaver somniferum*)
Phlox (*Phlox drummondii*)
Black-eyed Susan (*Rudbeckia hirta*)

Annuals and biennials

Hollyhock (*Alcea ficifolia*)
Calendula (*Calendula officinalis*)
Aster (*Callistephus chinensis/Aster novae-angliae*)
Celosia (*Celosia* spp.)
Cosmos (*Cosmos* spp.)
Foxglove (*Digitalis purpurea*)
Sunflower (*Helianthus annuus*)
Heliotrope (*Heliotrope arborescens*)
Morning glory (*Ipomoea tricolor* var. 'Heavenly Blue')
Alyssum (*Lobularia maritima*)
Marigold (*Tagetes* spp.)
Feverfew (*Tanacetum parthenium*)
Mexican sunflower (*Tithonia rotundifolia*)
Flowering tobacco (*Nicotiana* spp.)
Zinnia (*Zinnia* spp.)

Orchards

Buckwheat (*Fagopyrum esculentum*)
Clover (*Trifolium* spp.)

CHAPTER 4

WORKING THE

ORGANIC GARDEN

CREATING NEW BEDS

Preparing new beds is an important step in gardening. The effort and time you invest digging and enriching the soil will result in bountiful harvests. Make sure that the size, position and shape of the plots suit your overall design, and that the beds are easily accessible.

THINKING AHEAD

When breaking ground for new beds the first thing to consider is their size and shape. I usually make mine about 1.2m/4ft wide so that they can be worked from the edges without stepping on them. The soil quickly becomes compacted if it is trodden on and will need double digging again to restore the soil structure. Short gardeners may find a width of about 90cm/36in more manageable. If you plan to put a cold frame over the bed, make the width the same as that of your cold frame. If you build simple cold frames using hay bales and old windows, allow enough space between the beds for the bales as well as room to walk (see p. 94).

In small gardens, irregularly shaped beds work best as they can incorporate awkward corners and combine several small areas of land. Curved beds can bend around the corner of a house or patio, or follow the course of a path or contour of the land. Provided that they are not too wide, curved shapes are just as suitable for the organic vegetable garden as regular ones. If the site requires a wide bed, build a small stepping-stone path to the centre to avoid walking on the soil.

MARKING EDGES

Once you have decided on the size and shape of a bed, mark out the edges with string. To achieve straight edges, drive stakes into the ground along

A series of shaped flowerbeds or vegetable plots works well within a symmetrical garden design, or can be placed to accentuate the contours of a site.

the perimeter and tie string tightly between them.

Mark out curved beds by laying string or a garden hose directly on the ground. Stand back to view the overall shape, then adjust the outline until the desired shape is achieved. Following the outline, slice through the turf with a garden spade or half-moon edger.

A common mistake is to mix turf into the bed. If the area where you are creating a new bed is covered with turf, remove the turf and add it to the compost heap, leaving behind as much soil as possible in the bed. Once you have removed all the turf from the new plot, the surface is likely to be lower than the level of the path around the bed. Do not worry about this now; the process of double digging and incorporating compost will make up for this difference in levels. When establishing new beds, it is especially important to test the soil for deficiencies and to establish its pH level (see p. 34). This is the most appropriate time to carry out these tests.

DOUBLE DIGGING

Although it may appear to be a laborious technique, double digging repays the time and effort spent as it ensures a thorough cultivation of the soil. As well as being used in the preparation of new beds, double digging is a good solution for beds with poor drainage or where a hard layer of subsoil has formed. Once it has been double dug, a bed is unlikely to need this treatment again. The process involves turning the soil in two separate layers, and mixing in compost and additives. Its effects are:

- To loosen compacted soil, which allows plant roots to grow with ease.
- To improve drainage, which reduces waterlogged soil and enables the bed to warm up earlier in the spring.
- To allow air to penetrate the soil, which is necessary for plant roots to grow.

 ## RULES FOR DIGGING

There are several rules for digging the soil that apply to both single and double digging.

- Do not dig the soil when it is wet as you are likely to damage the structure and cause compaction. If the soil sticks to your shovel, fork or boots, it is too wet to cultivate. Wait until it dries out or dig the beds in the autumn instead of the spring.
- Do not dig the soil when it is too dry. Heavy soil will be very difficult to dig and the wind will carry away a light topsoil. You may need to water the area before digging. Allow several days of watering before trying to dig in very dry clay soil.
- Use a spade that is suited to your height (see pp. 270–72). Let the weight of your entire body provide the force to drive the blade into the ground, not muscular force from your foot. When lifting a spade of dirt, do not toss it but let it slide off your spade where desired. Both of these techniques take less effort and allow you to dig for longer.
- When digging, you may need to step on the bed. To avoid compacting the soil, always stand on a large board that is long enough to reach across the width of the bed. This will spread your weight across the surface.
- Always remove weed roots from the bed.

DOUBLE DIGGING A BED

1 Mark out the edges of the bed with stakes and string. Once you have obtained the desired shape and size, cut the turf around the edge of the bed using a spade. Lift and remove the turf, leaving behind as much soil as possible.

You may find it useful to divide the bed into 30cm/12in strips across the width of the bed, using wooden stakes to mark the width of each trench.

2 Excavate a trench of soil from the bed. The trench should measure about 60cm/24in wide by 25cm/10in deep. Put the soil to one side, either in buckets or a wheelbarrow. It will be used at the other end of the bed to fill the trench left there after digging.

3 Using a garden fork, loosen the subsoil in the bottom of the trench. Work along the length of the trench, plunging the tines deep into the heavy subsoil to break it up. The subsoil should be loosened to a depth of 25cm/10in. The total depth of the loosened soil will be about 50cm/20in below the surface. Return some of the turf, grass side down, to the bottom of the trench.

4 Using a spade, begin digging the second trench about 30cm/ 12in wide and 25cm/10in deep, adjacent to the first. Toss the soil on top of the turf in the first trench. Add a 2.5cm/1in layer of compost on top of the soil. Dig the other half of the second trench, again about 30cm/12in wide and again to a depth of 25cm/10in, and toss it on top of the compost in the first trench.

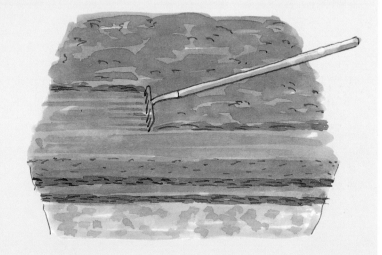

5 The first trench now contains layers of turf, topsoil, compost and more topsoil, all sitting on loosened subsoil. The second trench is empty. Repeat steps 3–4 until you reach the other edge of the bed. Loosen the subsoil in the last trench and cover it with a layer of turf. Add half the soil from the wheelbarrow, cover with a 2.5cm/1in layer of compost, then add the balance of the soil.

6 In spring, rake the bed smooth with a garden rake. Now is the time to add and gently work in any soil amendments that are necessary. A soil test will indicate which, if any, soil amendments should be added. Only if the bed is showing severe signs of compaction, or if drainage is poor, will it be necessary to double dig the bed again. This most often happens in heavy clay soils.

RENOVATING EXISTING BEDS

Double digging rarely has to be repeated once a bed has been established. Provided that the soil does not become compacted or waterlogged, light cultivation of the top layer of the bed, without disturbing the soil structure, is all that is needed to maintain and improve a bed.

ANNUAL TOPSOIL IMPROVEMENT

When a crop is harvested, nutrients are removed from the soil. These nutrients need to be replaced before the bed is replanted. The technique shown on the opposite page allows the gardener to aerate and loosen the soil without repeating the labour-intensive work of double digging. The first essential step is to remove weeds and debris from the previous crop. Make sure that the weeds are removed in their entirety, roots and all; add them to the compost pile. However, if the previous crop was a legume, leave its roots in the bed because they contain nodules of nitrogen. Using a garden rake, smooth the bed and remove any rocks or other debris from the bed.

Well-nourished soil will support abundant quantities of closely planted vegetables to provide food throughout the year.

ADDING SOIL AMENDMENTS

Now is the time to test the soil, if you think that there may be any deficiencies of nutrients (see pp. 32–4). Then spread an even layer of well-rotted compost over the entire bed. On top of this, spread any required soil amendments, such as lime (to increase the pH) or rock dust (a good source of calcium, magnesium and iron). If you apply fresh manure or other soil amendments that may burn, allow the bed to rest for several weeks before planting.

The next step is to work the compost into the bed. The best tool to use for this is a garden fork. This process also helps to loosen the soil and eliminate any compaction that may have occurred during the previous season. Always start from the edge and work your way towards the centre of the bed, so that soil is pushed towards the centre rather than on to the paths. The majority of the compost should remain close to the surface of the soil, where it is needed most.

The third step is to smooth the bed and break up any clods of hardened earth that remain near

BED WIDTH

For practicality, the maximum width for your beds should be no more than 1.2m/4ft. This ensures that all parts of the bed can be reached from the edges, allowing you to incorporate compost and organic fertilizers without having to step off the garden path and tread on to the soil. You will also be able to carry out planting, routine duties such as weeding and watering, as well as harvesting, without causing compaction.

the surface. Mix the compost into the top 5–8cm/2–3in of soil with a slight twisting action using a rake or a garden fork. The final height of the bed will be about 8–10cm/3–4in above path level. The bed is now ready for planting. If it is the end of your growing season and you do not wish to plant crops in the bed at this time, you do not have to leave the bed empty. Consider instead planting a hardy cover crop or green manure, to prevent erosion and to further nourish the soil (see pp. 57–61).

MAINTAINING A BED

1 After clearing the bed of weeds and residue from the previous crop, spread well-rotted compost in an even layer about 5cm/2in deep over the surface of the bed.

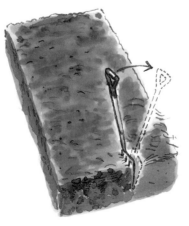

2 Plunge the fork tines to their full depth. Gently rock the fork to loosen the soil so that the compost sifts down. Work across the bed in rows 8cm/3in apart.

3 Break up any clods of earth and mix the compost into the top layer of soil with a slight twisting action. Using the back of a rake, even out the surface.

SOWING & PLANTING OUT

Now that the beds have been prepared it is time to plant them. Whether transplanting seedlings or sowing directly in the garden, you must consider the spacing of the plants in the bed. The best choice is equal spacing of plants to completely cover the bed.

NATURAL SEED DISPERSAL

In nature, seeds are sown in many ways. Birds scatter them in their droppings; the wind carries seeds over long distances; and animals carry seeds with burs. When sowing, remind yourself that nature does not sow seeds in tidy little rows with walking paths between, so try to follow suit. In nature, soil is rarely left bare. Growing in rows leaves large areas of bare earth, which only encourages weeds to grow and rain to wash away the soil. Instead, grow the seeds or seedlings at equal distances from each other in the bed and

close enough so that the leaves of mature plants will touch and leave no bare earth visible. This will not only crowd out weeds but also allow the roots of the plants to stabilize all the soil in the bed to prevent erosion and nutrient loss. The canopy of leaves over the bed will prevent sunlight from reaching the soil and causing evaporation and germination of weed seeds; the bed will require less watering and weeding.

ASSESSING PLANTING DISTANCES

The optimal way of positioning plants in a bed is with hexagonal spacing (see below), where the plant are equidistant from one another. Much closer spacing can be achieved this way, which results in a greater harvest from less space as well as less labour digging, weeding and watering. The exact distance between the centre of each plant is determined by what is being grown. Spinach may be spaced just 18cm/7in apart while

Space plants hexagonally so that when they mature, their foliage will create a canopy that prevents light from reaching the soil. This reduces moisture loss.

pepper plants might require a spacing of 45cm/
18in. Any planting scheme that covers the bed
with vegetation and avoids exposure of bare soil
is a valid plan to consider.

SOWING SEED OUTDOORS

Direct seeding is the process of starting seeds
directly in the garden beds. Many vegetables
will not survive transplanting and must be sown
directly in their permanent locations. Other
vegetables are so easy to get established that
they do not need transplanting. As a general rule,
when seeds are sown in the garden, they should
be planted to a depth equal to their length. For
example, a bean seed that is 2cm/¾in long should
be planted 2–2.5cm/¾–1in below the surface of
the soil. Some seeds need light to germinate, so
it is best to consult planting directions specific
to the vegetable being grown.

HEXAGONAL SOWING PLAN

When seeding directly in the garden, follow the
hexagonal planting illustrated on the opposite
page. Sow one seed at each corner of the
hexagons and one in the centre of each. You may
find it easier to mark a line across or along the
length of the bed using string attached to stakes.
Using the recommended spacing for the vegetable
seed being sown, make holes in the bed with a
dibber or narrow-bladed trowel, and place a seed
in each. Sometimes it is easier to make a furrow
along the entire row, rather than a series of
planting holes. Do not cover the seeds with soil
yet, or it will be difficult to assess how to plant
the next row to achieve a hexagonal pattern.
Move the string the appropriate distance over
and plant the next row, offset from the first so
that all the seeds are equidistant. Continue this
process until the whole bed, or allotted area of
the bed, has been planted. Now, using a rake or
handtool, cover the seeds with a thin layer of
soil. It is a good idea to water the bed if the

*Where recommended planting distances are minimal,
you may find it easier to make a furrow rather than
a series of planting holes.*

soil is dry, but take care not to deluge the soil so
that the water uncovers the seeds or washes them
away. Always label the area sown to identify the
vegetable and variety planted.

Sowing in a cold frame should be treated just
like sowing outside in a bed. If you sow hardy
vegetables in a cold frame, you can start them
much earlier in the spring (see pp. 94–5).

BROADCASTING SEEDS

Green manure crops are usually broadcast by
hand. This can be difficult to do evenly without
practice. Even seeding, however, is not essential
with cover crops. Simply grab a handful of seed,

When one crop of vegetables is harvested, replace it with another crop, using seedlings that were started indoors.

and while gently waving your arm back and forth, let the seed slip between your thumb and index finger and land on the bed. Rake the bed lightly to cover the seeds.

USING A BROADCAST SEEDER
If you are seeding a large area, a broadcast seeder is essential. Also known as a broadcaster, this seeder is made of a canvas, metal, or plastic hopper that drops seed on to a spinning plate to sow the seed evenly. The speed with which you turn the handle determines the width of the path sown; your pace determines how densely the area is covered. The opening can be adjusted to suit the size of the seed.

USING A PLATE SEEDER
Another common tool for direct seeding is the plate seeder. It is only appropriate in the largest of gardens. This seeder has a hopper that picks one seed at a time and drops it down a chute into a furrow created in the soil. The seeder has a flange or chain to cover the seed with soil. There are two drawbacks with this tool: you must walk on the bed to use it, and the spacing and depth can be very difficult to control.

HARDENING OFF SEEDLINGS
Seedlings that have been started indoors need to move out to garden beds when the weather and conditions are appropriate. Many plants can suffer root damage and must be transplanted with care. After growing indoors, seedlings are not accustomed to the harsh conditions outdoors and have to be acclimatized in a process called

A broadcast seeder is useful for seeding large areas. The seeder disperses seed evenly via a spinning plate that is operated by hand.

Seeds are sown individually in furrows created by the plate seeder as it is pushed along the ground; a flange or chain then covers the seed with soil.

STARTING SEEDS

Homemade seed mix

Try making your own seed mix for soil blocks (see pp. 140–42), using compost and coir. Remember to keep the ingredients fine. A good way of doing this is to put the finished mix through a 0.5cm/¼in sieve; this type of sieve is generally available in hardware shops.

The composition of a good mix for soil blocking consists of:

- 3 parts well-rotted compost
- 1 part garden soil
- 4 parts coir

Use compost that is about two years old and quite fine (see p. 48). The garden soil should be fine textured and fertile; harvest it in the autumn, before the ground freezes. The coir has good moisture-absorbing abilities and will help to hold the block together. If your garden soil is heavy, you may find it helpful to mix in a little sand.

Mix the ingredients thoroughly in a bucket and then add enough water to moisten the mix well. You will learn to judge the right amount of water with experience.

Sterilizing equipment

It is important to sterilize seed-starting trays, pots and equipment before they are used. Wash them well and dip them in a dilute bleach solution. Allow the items to dry and then rinse them well under running water.

Sowing extra seeds

When sowing seeds directly in the garden, it is important to remember that germination does not have a 100 per cent success rate. This may cause gaps to appear in the bed, allowing bare soil to be visible, and creating an opening in the canopy of foliage. For this reason, sow seeds more closely together or sow more seeds than necessary. The extras can be thinned out later and, depending on the vegetable, they can be used young in the kitchen or composted.

Germination

Some seeds need special treatment to assist germination. Some need to be scarified – nicked with a sharp knife – to allow moisture to penetrate; others need to be soaked in water overnight. Some plants need light to germinate and others require total darkness. Some

seeds even need to be wrapped in moist paper towels and refrigerated until they sprout. Specific advice on the germination of seeds is given under individual entries in Chapter 5 (pp. 178–269). Most seeds will germinate better indoors if their trays are covered with a clear plastic dome, which should be removed immediately after germination; otherwise damping off (see p. 143) may occur.

Booster feeds

As seedlings grow in trays indoors, there may come a time when they use up the nutrients in the soil block and need an additional boost to keep growing well. A good choice for a booster is an organic liquid feed of fish emulsion. Be sure to dilute it exactly according to the manufacturer's instructions and bottom-water the seedlings with the feed.

'hardening off'. Starting a couple of weeks before transplanting, set the young plants outdoors for an hour or two each day. They will gradually adjust to the stronger light and wind. As the time for transplanting draws near, let the seedlings stay outdoors for longer periods; the differences in temperature will prepare the plants for life in the garden. Once the seedlings have hardened off, they are ready for transplanting.

TRANSPLANTING SEEDLINGS

In the same way as you would mark out the bed for sowing seeds directly outdoors (see pp. 134–5), use string and pegs to mark out the planting rows in a hexagonal pattern. With a hand trowel or dibber, make a hole in the soil that is wide and deep enough to receive the seedling. Some seedlings, such as tomatoes, prefer to be planted very deep, but many vegetables will not survive if they are planted too deeply in the ground. Most seedlings need to be set at the same soil level as when they were growing in a soil block.

SOWING IN HOTBEDS

When starting seedlings in hotbeds, make sure the soil in the hotbed is about 24°C/75°F before sowing. Sow the seeds very closely in the hotbed, equidistant in a hexagonal pattern. The seedlings must be transplanted into the garden when they are small, before the roots grow together. To extract the seedlings, hold them by one leaf and dislodge the roots by lifting with a wooden plant marker. If seedlings are spaced far enough apart, they can be dug out with a trowel.

Remove the soil block from the tray with a spatula or bricklayer's trowel and place it in the hole. Push the earth around the soil block and firm it gently. Water the seedlings thoroughly after planting, taking care not to wet their foliage. After the initial watering, let the soil dry out somewhat to encourage the roots to develop. This 'mini-drought' will prompt the roots to branch out and head downwards through the soil in search of water.

If protected by a cold frame, tender vegetables can be started when it is still chilly in early spring.

SOWING INDOORS

There are many reasons why you might need to sow seeds indoors. Some plants need special cultural conditions to be able to germinate. Some need to be started indoors in winter, or they will not be able to mature and produce fruit before autumn. Others are started indoors to provide an early harvest.

USING SOIL BLOCKS

The best method of sowing indoors is to use soil blocks, which have many advantages over seed trays and pots:

- Plant roots are not disturbed when transplanting (see p. 139) because they are contained within the soil block.
- The plant is unlikely to become pot-bound because each block is surrounded by air.
- Soil blocks are inexpensive to make and easy to handle.
- The use of soil blocks is good for the environment because it decreases the use of disposable plastic trays and peat pots.

The concept of using soil blocks has been around almost as long as agriculture itself. When pots and containers for planting were scarce, soil was packed into pots and then turned out on to a flat surface, in the same way as a child builds a sandcastle at the beach using a bucket and sand. By this method, many more seedlings can be started with only a few pots.

There have been improvements on this method that have resulted in a special tool called a soil blocker. This tool is available in cubes of several different sizes, from 2cm/¾in to 10cm/4in; the most useful size for the home

To make soil blocks that will not fall apart when you work with them, ensure that the mix is thoroughly moist, but not waterlogged.

gardener is the 5cm/2in version. Smaller cubes may save some space but they tend to be more difficult to handle. Equally, larger cubes can be very difficult to handle and often fall apart. Plants that will need a lot of soil should be started in 5cm/2in blocks and transplanted into 10cm/4in blocks when the seedlings require more root space.

MAKING SOIL BLOCKS

Using a soil blocker is easy if the seed mix you are trying to form into blocks has the right proportions of soil, compost and coir. If you buy a commercial organic mix, try to choose one that does not contain peat, the harvesting of which causes damage to wildlife habitats and the environment. Alternatively, make your own seed mix (see p. 138), which is just as effective.

Practice makes perfect: don't worry if your first few efforts are unsuccessful, just toss the soil back into the bucket and start again. The first step is to put 10–13cm/4–5in of the properly moistened seed mix in the bottom of a shallow flat-bottomed tray. It is also essential that the mix is not too dry or moist. When squeezed it should not feel like a drenched sponge, but should release a little water. Hold the soil blocker by the metal flange, not the handle, and drive it forcefully into the mix. With the blocker pressed against the bottom of the tray, twist it back and forth – clockwise and counter-clockwise – several times. This loosens the soil from the bottom of the tray and allows the blocker to be removed easily. Lift the blocker and ensure the holes are full of mix before gently pressing the blocks out on to a seed tray.

SOWING IN SEED BLOCKS

Start seedlings in soil blocks arranged on a rigid seed tray. Choose one that will last a long time and that can withstand rough handling. The tray should also be completely watertight. I prefer a heavy rigid tray that is about 2.5cm/1in deep, with sloped sides. Place the filled soil blocker on the tray, and gently push down on the handle as you lift the tool, keeping the mix in contact with

SOWING SEED IN SOIL BLOCKS

1 *Place the filled soil blocker flat on a rigid watertight tray. Lift the blocker carefully while pushing slowly down on the handle to release the blocks.*

2 *Gently drop one or two seeds into the dimple on the top of each soil black. Push a little of the seed mix over the top of the seeds so that they are lightly covered.*

3 *Place the seed tray in your sunniest window or under an artificial light. Consider covering it with a plastic dome. Make sure that each tray is clearly labelled.*

the bottom of the tray. Place the blocker directly on the tray and lift it slowly as you push the blocks out so that they do not break apart.

If possible, sow an entire tray at once. Seeds can be started off under shelter, in a greenhouse, polytunnel or cold frame or in the house. Heat-loving plants started early in the year may need a little extra warmth till the weather turns. Seedlings started in the house may not get enough sunlight for good growth. Fortunately, specially made lights for indoor growing are available from nurseries and specialist suppliers.

In the dimple in the top of each soil block, place one or two seeds. Use a small wooden plant marker to cover the seed with a little of the mix. Just push some soil from the top of the block over the dimple that contains the seed. Some seeds require light to germinate and should not be covered. Always be sure to label the seedlings clearly. Some plants, like onions, do extremely well when several seeds are planted in the same

block. This saves space indoors and does not harm the growth of the plants. For example, if four onion seeds are sown in one soil block, when transplanted outdoors the bulbs will grow and push away from each other. The result will be four onions ready to harvest at once. The proximity will not cause deformed bulbs, but, when planting out, the blocks should be placed farther apart in the hexagonal pattern than if each block contained only one seedling.

SOWING SEED IN POTS AND TRAYS

There are other methods of starting seeds: in pots or module trays. The best kinds of trays are made of heavy plastic and will last many years. Choose a type fitted with a tray to keep them together; this also makes them easier to water from the bottom.

Many gardeners like to use the styrofoam trays that are set up with a water reservoir and capillary matting. This makes watering easier,

Seed trays come in a variety of shapes and materials. Choose trays that are strong, rigid, reusable and easy to water.

142

but has several drawbacks: the roots of the plants tend to grow into the matting; the roots often become damaged when you remove the plants for potting up or transplanting outdoors; the capillary matting has to be replaced every year; and the production of styrofoam damages the environment. Both plastic pots and styrofoam trays allow seedlings to become root-bound, while soil blocks do not.

SOWING PROBLEMS

The two most common problems that occur when starting seeds indoors are damping off and leggy seedlings. Damping off is a fungal disease that is promoted by excessive watering, over-fertilizing, or lack of sun or air circulation (see p. 176). The best way to prevent this is to water the seedlings from the bottom. This also encourages deep roots to develop more quickly.

Leggy seedlings are usually the result of inadequate light. If you are using an artificial light source, it may be that the seedlings have been placed too far away from the lamp. Position the light bulbs no farther than 5cm/2in from the seedling foliage. If the seedlings are on a windowsill, they are receiving enough direct light. Place them in the sunniest window, or use extra artificial light. Turn the trays often to get even lighting. Brush the seedlings with your hand or blow on them to imitate the wind. This helps to harden off and prevent leggy seedlings.

WATERING SEEDS

Seeds sown in soil blocks can be easily watered from the bottom. Gently pour water into the tray and the blocks will absorb and wick it up quickly. Be sure to put enough in so that the blocks in the middle of the tray get moisture too. If you are growing seedlings in pots, take the entire pot and sit it in a saucer of water, about 1.5cm/½in deep. The water will be wicked up into the soil very quickly. Stand watered pots in a

Courgettes grow well in a confined space. Sow seeds directly in the container once all threat of frost has passed.

tray that has a ridged base to allow excessive moisture to drain out of the holes at the bottom of the pots. If placed on a flat tray, the soil in the pots may become waterlogged.

POTTING ON

If seedlings become too large for the 5cm/2in soil blocks, move them into 10cm/4in pots; square pots provide much more soil and growing space than round ones. Line the bottom with a 5cm/2in layer of moistened mix. Using a kitchen spatula, lift up the entire soil block and place it gently in the pot. Fill around the block with mix. Make sure that the seedling is no deeper than the top of the soil block, unless the seedling is a plant that needs deeper planting.

WORKING WITH VEGETABLES

Once a bed is planted, it needs only minimal care. Watering, weeding and mulching are most commonly needed. Occasionally a crop will need a liquid organic feed to give it a boost. When harvesting, replant the area soon to another crop to prevent erosion and nutrient loss.

WATERING

The goal of any gardener should be to minimize the use of water. Reducing or eliminating watering saves time and labour; it is also good for the environment. Salt water covers most of the Earth, while fresh water accounts for just

All plants can wilt a little in the hot summer sun, especially at midday. Water them if they fail to recover when the day cools down.

2 per cent of available water. The rain and water in ponds and streams is known as surface water, while water from deep wells is called ground water. When we draw ground water, we deplete the underground storage supply of fresh water – usually converting it to waste water.

For this reason, we should try to limit our consumption of this precious supply of fresh water to surface sources. I am fortunate enough to live in a house supplied with surface water from a spring. In all but the worst of droughts, the water supply is more than sufficient. If your water supply is from a deep well, as is the case in most cities, it is especially important for you to conserve water. To this end, consider installing a rainwater collection system in your garden. These devices attach to the gutters and down pipes from your house, diverting rainwater into a storage tank where it can be kept until needed for garden watering.

Plants use water continuously. The best way to reduce the need for constant watering is to prevent moisture loss in the soil by mulching – mulch all of your vegetable and perennial beds with a thick layer of organic matter to conserve moisture – close plant spacing, and working in plenty of compost to improve water retention in the soil. Heavy soils are less prone to drying out than light soils.

DRIP IRRIGATION

When you do need to water the garden, be as economical as possible by watering only where it is needed. In this respect, the use of an overhead sprinkler is not advisable because it is unable to direct water to specific plants. The best way to conserve water is to use a drip irrigation system. Many gardeners never consider using this equipment, but simple models are very

RULES FOR WATERING

- Water less frequently, but water deeply enough to soak the soil.
- Water plants only when the soil is dry, but before the plants begin to suffer drought.
- Watering fruits that are nearly ready for harvest can cause fungus problems.
- Water newly transplanted plants, unless you are lucky enough to have timed the planting to be followed by rain.
- If a hard crust forms on top of the soil, cultivate it before watering, so that the water can penetrate and reach the roots.
- Do not water during the sunniest part of the day – much of the water will evaporate. Do not water in the evening – cool nights can encourage mould and fungus. Water plants in the early to mid-morning.

- Water plants slowly, allowing water to soak into the soil and reach the roots rather than run off.
- Watering fruits immediately before harvest dilutes the flavour – dry conditions at harvest time make fruits sweeter.

- Watering frequently in small amounts results in a shallow root system that can be very sensitive to minor droughts.
- If overhead watering is used, set out a bucket to measure how much water has been applied.

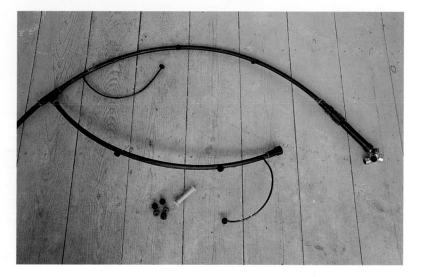

inexpensive and invariably pay for themselves many times over in the savings that you make on your water bill.

When considering a drip irrigation system, look for the simplest model. It needs to have a filter and a pressure-reducing valve from which a purpose-made hose is run around the garden. It is best to run it in a line close to the house and around the perimeter, avoiding the central areas of lawn where it may easily be damaged. Make sure that the hose is not left exposed where it may be severed by the lawn mower accidentally, or trip someone up. Pierce small holes in the hose so that water emitters may be inserted. Use standard emitters for flat gardens and pressure-compensating emitters for hilly or steeply terraced sites.

If you need to put an emitter at a distance from the main hose, use a smaller-size tube to branch off. Some emitters act like tiny sprinklers and can be useful for watering delicate plants. Very often a timer is used to turn the water on and off once or twice a week. This allows you to control how much water the plants receive. Soaker hoses are sometimes used in combination with drip irrigation systems, but they are prone to clogging up with sediment from the water. Look for a special hose with pre-made holes spaced about 2.5cm/1in apart; this is useful for garden beds and can be used like a soaker hose, but will not clog.

You should only use your irrigation system when watering is necessary; the exception to this is when starting fruit trees (see p. 158).

RULES FOR WEEDING

- Remove weeds when they are quite small – this will make your workload much easier.
- Remove perennial weeds, roots and all.
- Always remove weeds before they go to seed.
- If you weed on a hot sunny day, most hoed weeds can be left in the bed as mulch. The sun will dry them out and kill the roots.
- Perennial weeds can be killed by frequent cultivation of the soil, which keeps these weeds from ever sending out shoots to the surface where they can thrive in the sunlight.

WEEDING

Hoeing is the most common method of weeding in organic gardening. You will have very little to do if you have prepared your beds well and mulched them well. Two types of hoe are necessary in the garden: the draw hoe and the three-tine cultivator (see p. 273). Both have long handles that allow you to work from a standing position. Use the draw hoe to cut off small weeds just below the surface, and tackle larger weeds with a three-tine cultivator.

If you are weeding around seedlings, or small delicate plants such as strawberries, kneel down and pull the weeds out by hand or use an onion fork to avoid damaging plants.

In certain circumstances, weeding is more easily accomplished with a flame weeder or a strimmer. Grass and weeds that grow up between flagstones in a patio or paving bricks can be easily removed with a flame weeder. Flame weeders are particularly useful on hard gravel paths. When using a flame weeder, direct the flame on to the weed just long enough for the foliage to change colour; do not let it burn completely. The singed foliage will die and decompose.

Strimmers can be turned at an angle and used to eradicate weeds from hard surfaces.

MULCHING

There are four purposes to mulching:
- To prevent evaporation of moisture.
- To discourage weed growth.
- To stop erosion.
- To add organic matter to the soil.

Mulching is the practice of covering garden beds with a thick layer of organic material. Many types of organic matter may be used as mulch (see pp. 40–43 and below). In nature, the leaves of plants drop to the ground during the autumn and become a mulch; try to imitate this process in the garden. Mulching has been practised for thousands of years. For example, there is a long tradition of using straw to mulch

Use the draw hoe to cut off small weeds below the surface. Hold the hoe with both hands; keep your back straight and the hoe blade parallel to the ground.

146

strawberries, which have very shallow roots that are easily damaged by weeding and cultivation. The straw mulch forms a protective layer that keeps weeds at bay and saves you from having to weed frequently.

Organic mulches retain a lot of moisture and provide an excellent barrier to soil evaporation. A thick mulch keeps the soil cool in the heat and bright sun of summer. If the sun cannot reach the soil, water will evaporate at a much slower rate. Another benefit is that weed seeds are discouraged from germinating. When annual weed seeds are buried beneath a layer of organic matter, they most often die before the foliage reaches the surface. Occasionally, well-established perennial weeds do manage to send out shoots that are strong enough to penetrate the surface. If you notice emerging weed shoots, pull them out by hand immediately.

Apply mulch to the garden beds in the spring,

Mulch strawberries with a thick layer of straw to keep weeds at bay and to protect the fruits from being soiled.

after the soil has warmed. Most gardeners plant the bed and wait for the seedlings to emerge before adding the mulch, but some seeds can grow through the mulch. However, if you are transplanting seedlings, it is best to allow them to become established for a week or so before applying a mulch. If any weeds have germinated, remove them before mulching. Add them to the compost heap.

During the gardening year, a mulch will begin to decompose and provide nutrients to the soil. At the end of the growing season, any surplus mulch can be added to the compost heap. Or you can just rake it to one side for the time being and use it elsewhere in the garden in the course of the following year.

MULCHING MATERIALS

All unrotted organic material, including pine needles, grass clippings, straw, hay, and woodbark, shavings and sawdust should be allowed to mature well before being used as mulches, or they may rob the soil of nitrogen.

Pine needles A 10–15cm/4–6in layer provides a good mulch around acid-loving plants.

Grass clippings Use as mulch around young seedlings. Follow with a thicker mulch of leaf mould or straw.

Leaf mould A 10cm/4in layer provides a good barrier against weeds. When leaf mould is incorporated in the autumn, add lots of organic matter to build good soil structure. Leaf mould provides an excellent habitat for worms and insects that aerate and loosen the soil (see Making leaf mould, p. 49).

Compost A 8–13cm/3–5in layer makes an excellent mulch. However, if compost is too fine, it may be washed away by rain.

Straw Excellent, when well matured, for use around strawberries as it contains few weed seeds. Use a 15–20cm/6–8in layer to prevent light reaching the soil.

Hay A 10–20cm/4–8in layer of well-matured hay makes a good mulch. You may be able to get hold of spoiled hay that is unfit for animals – it is often available free. The only disadvantage of hay is that it does tend to contain weed seeds.

Shredded bark A common decorative mulch for perennial beds. A 5–10cm/2–4in layer will give good results. As bark decomposes, it robs the soil of nitrogen; however, a dressing of 25g/1oz per 1m²/1yd² of a high-nitrogen organic fertilizer will counteract this loss. Do not turn the bark under in the autumn. If you buy shredded bark, make sure it was not treated with any chemicals.

Sawdust and wood shavings Again, you need to be sure that sawdust and shavings come from untreated wood. Let them mature well before use to prevent nitrogen depletion. Do not turn them under in the autumn. Use a 2.5–5cm/1–2in layer.

Black plastic Avoid using black plastic because it may leach chemicals, especially DEHA, into the soil. Plastic also prevents rain from soaking into

Mulch vegetables in the garden with a thick layer of organic matter. A 10cm/4in layer of hay makes a good mulch around potatoes.

A thick layer of organic matter will suppress weeds and help to retain moisture, encouraging strong growth in a plant.

the garden beds and does absolutely nothing to enrich the soil. It may even harm plant roots because it prevents oxygen from entering the soil.

Newspapers Avoid using these unless you are certain that the ink and dyes are not synthetic.

SUPPLEMENTARY FEEDING

When watering the garden, you may notice that some plants need a nutrient boost. Many vegetables are annuals that require lots of nutrients to produce an abundant harvest. For instructions on how to make and use liquid feeds, see pages 50–53. Be sure to dilute these feeds carefully or the plants may be burned. Any commercial liquid organic feed should be diluted

exactly according to the manufacturer's directions. For other additives, see pages 54–6.

Bulbs Potassium supplements are often needed to ensure good flowering in bulbs. Apply soil amendments and mulch the plants after the foliage dies back, during the growing season, but not in spring before they bloom.

Bush and tree fruits/Vegetables Many plants, bushes, and trees will benefit from a side-dressing of solid feeds. Add compost, well-rotted manure and soil amendments as a mulch, then gently mix them into the top 5cm/2in of garden soil.

Container plants Potted plants need more feed than those grown in the ground. Liquid organic feeds are the best source of nutrients for container plants, and should be applied every two to four weeks in the growing season. Top-dress perennials in containers with compost once a year. Slow-release organic fertilizers can be mixed into the soil when planting in a container.

Perennials Beds of perennials will benefit greatly from a mulch of seaweed every three to five years to add trace elements and organic matter. Apply fresh mulch every year and add soil amendments at the same time if necessary. Testing the soil will indicate which amendments are needed. Any high-phosphorus or high-nitrogen feeds needed should be sprinkled on the bed before mulching in the spring.

CONTROLLING EROSION

When rain falls on bare soil, each drop hits with great force. Soil particles are dislodged and washed away with the water that runs off the bed. The force of the rain hitting the ground compacts the soil, preventing moisture absorption and causing the water to wash away more of the soil on the surface. A thick, loose mulch absorbs the force of the rain and lets the water trickle down to reach the soil.

CHOOSING FRUIT

Fresh organic fruit from the garden is a wonderful treat. Nothing can compare in flavour and freshness with the first apple of the season or a succulent strawberry still warm from the afternoon sun. The fruit available in shops has usually been transported long distances and rarely retains its fresh-picked taste and texture.

HEIRLOOM VARIETIES

Fruit trees make excellent specimen trees and provide beautiful flowers in spring. Along with cane fruits and bushes, trees provide structure in the garden. Their placement can frame a beautiful view or obstruct an unsightly one.

One of the biggest concerns about growing fruit organically is the prevalence of pests and diseases. As with vegetables, choosing resistant varieties provides a good defence. Old heirloom fruits are often quite resistant to diseases but it can be difficult to find suppliers that stock them (see p. 280). Even if you choose resistant varieties, you may experience problems with pests and diseases, but there are several effective organic methods of control available (see pp. 168–72).

OBTAINING BENCHGRAFTS

Some nurseries are dedicated to preserving heirloom varieties of fruit trees and bushes. They raise a wide selection of heirloom plants and may be prepared to graft a variety of your choice on to your preferred rootstock. These types of plant are called 'benchgrafts' (see pp. 154–5). Since the upper part of the plant, or scionwood, has just been grafted on to a rootstock, it will need special care until the graft heals.

Benchgrafts and delicate or weak plants should first be planted in pots in a rich compost, where they will receive tender loving care and daily attention. They can be planted out in their permanent locations in the autumn. Fruit trees, bushes and canes that are large, hardy and vigorous should be planted directly in the ground in their permanent locations. When buying fruits, avoid being tempted to over-order, otherwise you may find yourself with more bushes than you are able to plant – they will not survive for long out of the ground. Planting trees and bushes is hard work; fortunately this task needs to be done only once, but the benefits will last for decades.

Although they are not hardy, olives can be grown under glass in cool climates. When grown outdoors, olive trees can eventually reach 9m/30ft in height.

Consider nutrition when planning your planting. Blueberries are a good source of beneficial phytochemicals and many vitamins and minerals.

Most of the common problems encountered in establishing new fruit trees, bushes and canes arise from working with poor-quality stock. So you should be sure to order your fruitstock from a reputable nursery. Arrange for delivery in late winter or early in the spring, when the weather is still cool. (Alternatively, in warmer climates, have plants delivered in early winter and plant straightaway.) Shipping in hot weather often results in plant damage caused by excessive heat.

One important point to remember when growing fruit trees is that many bear fruits biennially, not every year, and most trees will not produce in the first few years after planting.

Choosing the right site

When planning the fruit garden, you need to consider climate (see box, left) as well as the topography of the land. The site may be sloped and provide frost pockets in low areas. Make use of features such as a brick wall or the side of a house to provide shelter for tender plants. You can create a microclimate on the sunny side of the house by protecting fruits from the wind. This will allow you to grow some tender fruits in climates that are usually too cold for them to succeed.

Making your selection

When choosing plants, it is important to consider the nutrient content they offer, as some fruits have higher nutritional value than others (see pp. 86–9). Select young trees wherever possible as older trees often suffer shock from

---

PREFERRED CLIMATES

Consider your climate carefully when deciding which fruits to grow. You need to take into account their cold hardiness and heat tolerance as well as disease resistance and flavour. Some fruits can only be grown in cool climates and others only in warm climates; a few plants perform well in both.

Cool climates Apples, cherries, plums, pears, blueberries, raspberries, blackberries.

Warm climates Oranges, lemons, limes, olives.

Cool/warm climates Grapes, currants, quinces.

transplanting and take longer to bear fruit. A one- to two-year-old tree is a better choice than a large three- to four-year-old tree – a small tree involves less work when planting too.

Buy healthy, disease-free plants from a reputable nursery. The plants should be dormant when shipped so that they suffer less shock when transplanted. Plants that are shipped from the nursery are most often bare-rooted. This simply means that they were dug up when dormant and the soil was removed from their roots. If they heat up or dry out during shipment they may die. When they arrive at your home, it is imperative that you tend to them immediately.

Unless you happen to have a particularly good local nursery, it is generally best to place an order with a specialist mail-order nursery. The selection and quality from mail-order nurseries tends to be much better. Local nurseries often sell fruit trees and bushes after they break dormancy which, in fact, is the worst time to transplant them. It is usually much more cost-effective to buy bare-root plants in winter and arrange for delivery at the proper planting time in spring.

Remember to check the expected full-grown height of the plant. For example, an apple variety can be grafted on to many different rootstocks, which determine its mature size. One rootstock may permit the tree to reach full size (about 10.5m/35ft) while another may dwarf the tree so that it only reaches 2.5m/8ft.

ROOTSTOCKS FOR FRUIT TREES

Another consideration is the compatibility of the rootstocks with your soil type. There are rootstocks better suited to sandy soils, while others perform well on clay. For example, the apple rootstock M9 makes a good dwarf tree

Hang a bottle part-filled with sugar water near your apples to lure sweet-toothed pests away from your crop and into the bottle trap.

on fertile clay but struggles on dry free-draining sandy soil. The most trouble-free apple rootstock is probably MM106, which makes a very strong root system but is not so dwarfing.

In some commercial orchards experiments have been carried out in grafting M9 on to MM111, and then adding the cultivar. The M9 becomes an interstem, conferring a dwarfer habit while benefiting from the strong roots of the MM111. Normally, however, interstems are only used where there is incompatibility between the cultivar and the preferred rootstock. In Chapter 5, rootstocks are recommended for each tree fruit if appropriate (see pp. 250–56).

SELECTING FOR POLLINATION

There are many different varieties of almost every type of fruit. Some varieties store well, others are best eaten fresh; some are sweet and others tart. Some bear fruits early, others bear late. In order to have an extended harvest, it is a good idea to choose several different varieties: you will have fruit to pick throughout the season, and the different varieties will cross-pollinate each other.

Pollination is essential for most plants to set fruit. It is primarily accomplished by insects in fruit trees, and by the wind in nut trees. Many fruits are self-sterile and need the pollen of other varieties in order to produce fruit. This can be a challenge in small gardens, if there is not enough room for two varieties of the same fruit. The easy solution is for one rootstock to have two or more varieties grafted on to it, so that different branches bear differing varieties of the same fruit. Many nurseries sell trees grafted in this way with popular varieties, or you can graft your own combinations at home – scionwood or budwood can be bought for this purpose (see pp. 162–3).

Equally, you may not need to have more than one variety of a fruit in your garden if other varieties exist in a nearby garden. Visiting insects will cross-pollinate your tree.

PLANTING FRUIT

When your fruitstock arrive, they are in a state of shock from being dug up and transported. They need to receive immediate care if they are to survive their ordeal. Submerge their roots in water straightaway and heel them in. Pot them up, or plant them as soon as possible.

BARE-ROOT CARE

When fruitstock are dug up at the nursery, they are bound to lose some roots. During delivery, the wet packing material in which they are shipped begins to dry out, leaving them subject to drought. For this reason, it is important to soak the roots in water before planting. It is also a good idea to wrap them in wet hessian before carrying them to the planting site. Keep the plants in a shady spot until they can go in the ground; if you are unable to plant them in their permanent spot within a day or two of delivery, pot them up or heel them in.

To heel plants into the garden, dig a trench and lay each plant down at an angle of 45° with its roots in the hole. Cover the roots with a mound of garden soil and keep them very moist with regular watering. Remember to provide shade for the exposed parts of the plant. And, of course, they should be moved to their permanent position as soon as possible.

If the ground is frozen, pot up bare-root plants in compost. Keep them moist and place the containers in an outbuilding to protect them from extreme temperatures. During the daytime, open the door to provide the plants with necessary sunlight.

PLANTING BENCHGRAFTS

Benchgrafts are trees that have been grafted specifically at the gardener's request (see p. 150).

A benchgrafted tree is created from the top growth of one plant and the rootstock of another. Note the V-shaped graft on the apple tree above.

They may still be quite delicate when they are delivered to you and need extra care to give them a good start. Pot them in pure potting compost until they are well established. Keep a close eye on their progress and supplement the compost with liquid organic feed as necessary. They may be planted out in their permanent locations during the autumn after the growing season.

The grafts are generally covered with wax or a rubber band, and you will need to unpack your plants carefully to avoid damaging them. Prune off any obviously dead roots and soak the plant in water for about twelve hours. Place the tree or bush in a pot of appropriate size – it is acceptable to bend the roots to make them fit. If any specific soil amendments are required, mix them with the compost, then add the mixture to the pot and press down firmly with your fists. It is essential to have good contact between the compost and the roots. Add more of the mixture and press down again, more gently this time. Water the plant thoroughly and label it.

As benchgrafts grow, buds may form on the rootstock or interstem. These must be removed or energy will be diverted away from the grafted variety that you wish to grow. Remove any suckers that emerge. They do not overwinter well in pots, so they should be planted in their permanent location in the autumn.

PRUNING

Unless it has already been done by the nursery, it is essential that you prune back the top of the fruit tree once it is in the ground. This will concentrate the energy of growth into developing a healthy root system. The aim is to compensate for the roots that the plant lost when it was dug up at the nursery. Pruning back the tops after planting creates a balance between the top of the plant and its roots. A good rule of thumb is to remove half of every side branch of a tree or half the height of a multi-stemmed plant. For more information on pruning, refer to pages 164–7.

Fresh fruits – to be eaten raw, served in pies, or preserved as jellies or jams – make a welcome summer harvest.

PLANTING OUT

Soak bare-root plants in water for twelve hours before planting; plants in containers should be watered and moist, but not waterlogged. If you are not planting the tree in a cultivated bed it is important to dig a large hole and loosen the soil deeply. Without good drainage, the plant's roots will become waterlogged. Choose a fertile site and collect any soil amendments that will be necessary to provide for the specific requirements of the plant.

Prepare the site by digging a hole twice the size needed for the rootball of the plant. This is important to provide the best conditions for growth. Add rock phosphate to the bottom of the hole to encourage root development. Coir or lime can be used to change the pH depending on the plant's requirements. Avoid incorporating high-nitrogen amendments because they will encourage too much tender growth in the autumn. Mix any required soil amendments with the compost and some of the excavated earth in a wheelbarrow.

Remove the bare-root plant from the water and prune off any dead roots. Wrap the roots in wet hessian and carry the plant to the prepared site. If the plant was in a container it can be transplanted when not dormant. Remove the plant from the container carefully, keeping as much of the soil with the roots as possible. If the plant is balled and wrapped in hessian, remove any ties before planting the tree. Cut the hessian tied around the trunk and tuck it back under the rootball. Check to see whether the plant has become root-bound, and use pruners or a knife to slice into the spiralling roots. This will encourage new growth and help the plant to become established.

Place the plant in the hole and adjust the mound of soil beneath its roots until the plant is at the same depth as it was before being dug up by the nursery. Use a stake across the planting hole to assess the correct soil level. Dig the hole deeper if necessary or add some of the soil mix beneath the roots to raise its height. Make sure that the trunk is perpendicular to the ground.

PLANTING A BARE-ROOT FRUIT TREE

1 *Dig a hole twice the size of the root system. Loosen the soil deeply to ensure good drainage. Mix the excavated soil with compost and any soil amendments.*

2 *Prune off any dead roots and gently loosen the rootball. Place the tree in the hole and backfill with soil so that it is vertical and at the same planting depth as before.*

3 *Firm the soil down to ensure good contact with the roots and eliminate any air pockets. Add more soil and firm again more gently. Water the tree thoroughly.*

Stake tall trees after planting, to give them additional support during strong winds. Smaller trees and bushes rarely need staking.

Fill the soil mix around the roots and press firmly by treading down the soil with the heel of your boot to ensure good contact between the roots and the soil. This eliminates any air pockets. Add more soil on top and firm again gently. The turf may be used to form a mound, or berm, around the base of the tree to retain water. If you use turf instead of soil to make the berm, place it upside down to discourage competition for nutrients from the grass.

Water the plant thoroughly, being careful not to cause erosion of the berm or of the soil around the roots. Put a permanent label on the plant; plastic ones often fade after one season, so use a metal label that can be written on by making an impression with a ballpoint pen.

STAKING AND PROTECTION

If you have planted a tall tree, make sure that it is well staked to protect it from damage in strong winds and gales. Bushes and small trees rarely need staking.

Pound three wooden stakes into the ground outside of the berm, spacing them evenly around the tree. Using twine, tie the tree to each stake. Be sure to wrap the trunk with a soft cloth so that the twine does not injure the bark. Do not tie the tree too tightly or it may be damaged. As an alternative to twine, use a purpose-made rubber tree tie that can be adjusted as the tree grows.

In areas where damage from mice, voles or rabbits is likely, you will need to protect the base of the tree. Girdling by animals (see p. 159) is a common reason for failure of a newly planted fruit tree or bush.

One way of doing this is to wrap a length of wire mesh or chicken wire around the base of the tree and secure it with twine. Remember that the wind can rock the tree and cause it to rub against the wire and so damage the bark. Be on the alert for this and take steps to prevent it if necessary. Sink the wire into the soil to prevent rodents from burrowing underneath.

WORKING WITH FRUIT

Once fruit trees, bushes and cane fruit are planted, they require regular care. Watering, weeding, mulching and feeding are essential, and the fruits themselves must be protected from birds and other pests. It is important to protect the bark of newly planted trees and bushes from rodents.

WATERING

Correct watering is essential to produce good fruit. Some plants produce fruit best in dry conditions, while others need copious amounts of water to produce fruit. Consult Chapter 5 to ascertain the watering needs of specific fruits (see pp. 248–67). When they are establishing themselves, plants often need significantly more supplementary water than they will need when mature. Most fruit trees will bear fruits a year or two sooner if they receive consistent thorough watering during their first two to four years of life. The best way to accomplish this is with a drip irrigation system (see pp. 144–5). Start with a small emitter and gradually add additional emitters on a side tube as the tree grows.

Young trees are often planted with a mound of earth around the base to retain water (see p. 156). Older and established trees benefit from having a large mulched area around their base to prevent competition from grass. Bushes should also be planted with mounds of earth around them to retain water. As with watering vegetables, it is important always to water deeply to soak the soil (see Rules for Watering, p. 145).

The lack of water stresses trees and many bushes long before the signs of wilt are evident. A good way to test whether watering is needed is to dig down 12–25cm/5–10in below the surface. If the soil there is dry, it is time to water. Always apply water slowly so that it can penetrate the surface and be absorbed, rather than run off. Keep watering until it has soaked deeply into the soil. Avoid watering your fruitstock immediately before harvesting, except in a drought. Excessive watering makes the fruits swell with juice that dilutes the flavour. Some of the best-tasting fruit is grown in semi-~ drought conditions.

MULCHING

Fruit plants should be mulched to conserve moisture. As the mulch decomposes, it adds organic matter and nutrients to the soil. Using

Apply a thick mulch around the base of newly planted trees and bushes to help retain moisture in the soil and prevent the growth of grass.

Throw soft netting over your fruit crops as they near maturity to ensure that you rather than greedy birds get to enjoy the fruits of your labour.

mulch also prevents the growth of grass around the base of a fruit tree. Young fruit trees have many shallow, quick-growing roots that enable the tree to become established. The growth of these shallow roots can be retarded by a substance released from grass roots. When mulch is used, be sure to pull it away from the trunk of the plant in winter or it will encourage mice and voles to chew on the bark and girdle the plant.

UNWELCOME VISITORS
Fruit trees and bushes can be damaged by rodents and rabbits chewing on their bark. When a plant has had its bark stripped off all the way around the trunk, it is called girdling. Even mature trees that are 9m/30ft tall can be killed by voles after just a few days of chewing. Girdling most often occurs in winter when there is little food for animals to eat. As a start, each autumn

you should clear away any grass or other vegetative growth from around the base of each plant to discourage rodents from choosing it as their winter home. You will probably also need either to surround the plant with a barrier of wire mesh or chicken wire held in place with twine or canes, or to place a proprietary tree guard around the trunk. These are widely available from nurseries and garden centres and range from guards made of wire mesh through heavy-duty plastic ones to flexible plastic wraps, and even degradable plastic net.

In cool weather climates, consider the height of the snow in winter. Whatever type of guard you use, it needs to extend well above that level or rabbits may chew on the tree while standing on the snow. Push the base of the guard well into the soil in order to prevent rodents from getting under the barrier.

PROTECTING FROM BIRDS

All soft fruits and some tree fruits are susceptible to damage and theft by birds when the fruits near maturity. There are two techniques for saving fruits. One is to plant a tree to lure birds away from the crops. For example, a fruiting mulberry will attract birds away from your soft fruits. A second is to use nets. Soft netting can be thrown over bushes and trees as the fruits near maturity. Plants that cannot withstand the weight of the netting will need to be supported by stakes, but it is rarely necessary to build elaborate cages to exclude birds. Do not cover plants with nets during the growing season because this prevents birds from eating the pests. Plants only need to be covered as the fruits become ready for harvest.

FEEDING

One of the most effective ways of feeding fruit plants is to side-dress the plants with well-rotted manure. The manure can even be used as a mulch. If soil tests indicate deficiencies, sprinkle soil amendments on the soil before adding a mulch. Remember that the root system of a plant is as extensive as its top growth. Therefore, when feeding trees do not simply concentrate on the immediate area around their trunks; you need to cover an area that extends as far as the drip line of the tree.

If the soil is deficient in trace elements, apply a seaweed meal every three to four years. Add compost or manure every three years to maintain fertility. If you choose to surround your fruits with turf, use a dibber or rod to make holes and fill them with soil amendments. In this way, the fruit trees and bushes rather than the grass will receive the amendments.

Another option for feeding fruits is to plant a green manure crop. This will discourage the growth of weeds and turf, and when turned under it will provide organic matter to the fruit trees and bushes (see pp. 57–61).

Almond trees produce delicate pink or white blossom in spring, followed by a harvest of tasty nuts (right) in the autumn.

You may need to support drooping fruit-laden branches (left) to prevent damage to the tree. After harvest, the supports should be removed.

GRAFTING

Grafting is immensely satisfying. Every gardener should try it. The technique has been commonplace for more than 2,000 years, is an inexpensive way to propagate existing trees and bushes and provides you with the opportunity to add new fruit varieties to your garden.

GRAFTING

Most cultivated fruits and nuts do not come true from seed. They are usually propagated by grafting a bud or piece of wood on to a compatible rootstock. This may mean grafting a different variety of apple on to one branch of an apple tree in your garden or it may mean grafting a variety directly on to a rootstock.

Often an orchard or a neighbour will let you take a small cutting from one of their trees to use as scionwood. Finding a compatible rootstock is very easy. If you have a fruit-bearing plant in your garden, the rootstock is likely to have sent out a sucker. This sucker can be dug up and grown in a pot (or elsewhere in the garden) and used for grafting. Otherwise, rootstocks can be bought from nurseries, generally at a fraction of the price of a cultivated variety.

The technique of grafting is most commonly used for propagating fruit trees, nuts and a few flowering bushes such as roses. There are two basic methods: bud grafting and whip grafting.

BUD GRAFTING

Budding, or bud grafting, is best done during late summer. Though this method is most often used for roses, it is appropriate wherever the size of the scionwood differs from that of the rootstock.

First, using a sharp knife, make a T-shaped cut in the bark of the rootstock. Be careful when doing this not to damage the greenish cambium layer under the bark.

BUD GRAFTING

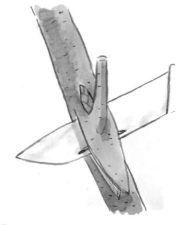

1 *Using a sharp knife, make small cuts into the bark of the rootstock to form a T-shape. Gently ease back the flaps of the bark on either side of the cut.*

2 *Select a healthy bud on the scionwood. Cut from the base towards the tip, taking a slice of the bark and the green cambium layer beneath.*

3 *Place the bud inside the T-cut so the two cambium layers are in contact. If necessary, cut off the top of the bud wood to make it fit. Wrap with tape.*

Using pruners, remove a ripened shoot from the current season's growth of the tree you wish to propagate. Strip off the foliage, leaving about 2.5cm/1in of each leaf shoot intact. At the base of each leaf shoot is a bud that will produce growth in the next growing season. Select a healthy bud and, again using your sharp knife, cut it off, taking a slice of the bark and the green cambium layer beneath. Do not worry if you accidentally take a little of the wood, but be very careful not to damage the bud.

Place the bud inside the T-cut that you made on the rootstock, making sure that the cambium layer of the bud stays in contact with the cambium layer under the bark of the rootstock.

Gently fold back the flaps to cover the bark attached to the bud, being careful to leave the bud (and leaf stem, if there is one) exposed. Using a rubber band or grafting tape, secure the flaps. Remove the rubber band or grafting tape after about a month. Prune off the top growth of the rootstock in late spring after the bud has developed and grown a little.

WHIP GRAFTING

Whip grafting is used when the scionwood and the rootstock are of approximately equal size. The rootstock in this case might, for instance, be a branch on which the scionwood is to be grafted. This form of grafting should take place in early spring, when the plants are still dormant.

Using pruners, cut a healthy shoot approximately 23cm/9in long from the scion tree, cutting obliquely just above a bud. Cut the rootstock horizontally 13–25cm/5–10in above the ground, then make a slanting cut, exposing the cambium layer to receive the scion. Using a sharp knife, make a V-shaped slit in the exposed cambium layer. Cut a matching point at the bottom of the scionwood, being careful not to damage the bottom bud.

Slot the two pieces together. If they are not

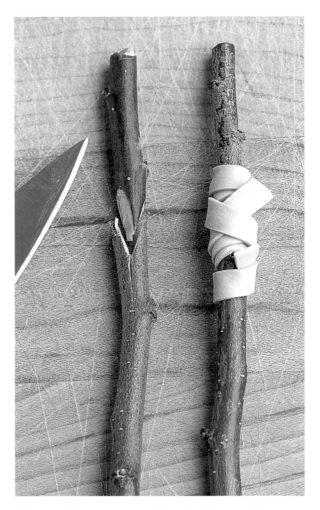

Wrap grafting tape or a rubber band around the graft union to hold it together until plant growth heals over the wound.

exactly the same diameter, ensure that the bark of the rootstock fits flush with the bark of the scionwood on one side, even if it does not line up on the other side. Wrap tape or a wide rubber band around the graft, starting below the union and working your way upwards to cover the whole union. Tuck the end of the band under and pull it tight.

The rubber band will hold the graft together until plant growth heals over the wound and binds into one piece. Remove the band after about six weeks.

PRUNING

Pruning is an art. When you prune fruit trees and bushes, you selectively remove parts of the plant to eliminate dead or diseased wood, promote the production of fruit and flowers, and improve the shape of the plant. Pruning keeps a plant healthy and vigorous.

MAINTAINING THE BALANCE

Pruning is necessary to balance the top of the plant with its roots when transplanting has taken place. When plants are dug up at nurseries for resale, their roots are inevitably damaged. Some roots are lost and so the tops need to be pruned to compensate for the smaller root system.

Many plants will not set much fruit if their branches are crowding one another. By thinning out the plant, more high-quality fruit will be produced. When pruning, it is possible to shape the plants into different forms for various locations. In a small garden, a fruit tree may be pruned into a flat fan shape against a fence or wall to save space. In a larger garden, a fruit tree may be allowed to mature into a fine pyramidal specimen tree. Or a fruit tree can be pruned and trained into a stepover, with just two branches held horizontally 30cm/12in above the ground, to border a vegetable garden. The possibilities are endless (see Training trees into shapes, p. 167).

RULES FOR PRUNING

- Do not injure the bark when making a cut. All trees, bushes, vines and cane fruits rely on this thin layer of tissue to supply the water and nutrients. It provides the pathway from the leaves to the roots.
- Remove dead, diseased and damaged portions of the plant as soon as they are discovered. Waiting may permit the disease to spread.
- Where branches rub against one another, remove one to prevent bark damage on both.
- Prune lightly every year instead of heavily every few years. This is easier work and promotes plant health and fruit production.

Correct cut – *clean, angled cut made about 0.5cm/¼in above a healthy bud.*

Too short – *the tip of the bud is extending beyond the cut and will be vulnerable to damage.*

Too high – *cut is too far above the bud, which will lead to stem dieback from the cut downwards.*

Poor angle – *cut slopes towards the bud and will allow rainfall to run directly on to the bud.*

- When a limb is removed or a branch is headed back, a callus forms over the exposed wood to protect it from decay. Do not hinder callus formation with paint or tar.
- With a few exceptions, most trees are best pruned during the late winter or early spring when the plant is dormant. Do not prune when the weather is extremely cold. Pruning in autumn often promotes tender new growth that is likely to be damaged during the winter.
- Remove unwanted suckers as soon as they appear. If left to be pruned later, they will unnecessarily utilize the plant's nutrients and resources.
- A branch that is headed back will grow in the direction of the last bud, so prune at a bud facing away from the centre of the plant to discourage crowding.
- Before pruning, have a structure in mind and understand the reasons for pruning the plant in that particular way.

TYPES OF PRUNING CUT

When pruning a tree there are two basic cuts that can be made, each with a different purpose:

- Heading back is the process of pruning off parts of branches in order to improve the shape of the tree, to increase fruit production or to remove dead or diseased wood. When heading back a branch, leave one strong bud at the end to ensure the branch survives. The new growth will follow the direction of the bud.
- Thinning out is the process of removing branches to improve the structure of the tree and prevent overcrowding. The goal is to ensure good air circulation and that light reaches the centre of the tree.

REMOVING LARGE BRANCHES

When removing a branch it is important to avoid leaving a stub which will cause decay and leave the tree vulnerable to insect damage. Cut back large branches in three stages to prevent damage

Cut out dead, diseased or damaged portions of branches. This eliminates crossing branches and often increases fruit production.

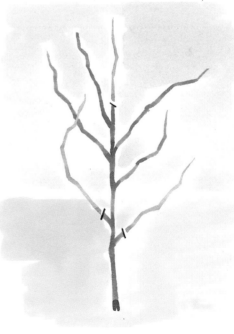

Remove entire branches to improve the structure of the tree. This ensures good air circulation and prevents overcrowding.

The crown of the tree has been trained to create an open centre that allows sunlight to reach the lower branches.

to the bark and to ensure a smooth finished cut. First make a cut from the bottom of the branch upwards, about 2.5–5cm/1–2in away from the trunk of the tree. Make the second cut from the top of the branch downwards, slightly farther away from the trunk than the first cut. This will detach the branch from the tree. Make the final cut close to the trunk, but not so close that the saw damages the bark on the trunk.

TRAINING FOR BETTER FRUIT TREES

Several standard methods of pruning fruit trees ensure that sunlight reaches the centre of the tree and that crowding does not occur:

- When a central leader is created, the tree has a clear vertical line running from the trunk through the crown of branches. Trees shaped in this way are strong and able to resist damage from wind and ice.
- If the main leader is headed back, the side branches will become nearly as large as the new leader. This type of structure is known as a modified leader.
- An open-centre structure allows for air circulation and plenty of light to reach the centre of the tree. This is used for stone fruits.

Early pruning of a tree will determine its shape at maturity. After the initial thinning out, the main branches should not need altering. Removing secondary branches and heading back is the only pruning that should be done. If heavy pruning is performed on an older tree, its yields will be temporarily reduced. However, pruning can also generate new growth in mature trees.

A fruiting spur often forms on one- or two-year-old wood on most types of fruit trees. Every time fruit is set, a new shoot forms on the other side of the spur. Fruiting spurs are therefore often zigzags of growth. As a tree gets older, its production of fruiting shoots and spurs decreases. Removing some of the older wood, stimulates new vigorous growth, resulting in improved yields of fruit.

TRAINING TREES INTO SHAPES

Espalier Espaliering is an ancient art in which each year two horizontal branches of a fruit tree are allowed to grow and all others are removed. The tree is usually planted against a wall or fence. The espalier becomes taller with the addition of two more branches until it reaches three to six laterals. It is then kept at this level with regular pruning of any unwanted stems. Espaliered trees take up little space and produce a good harvest.

Fan Fan training is the process of growing a fruit tree or bush against a wall. The lateral shoots are pruned to be generally symmetrical. Once the fan is formed, prune regularly to maintain its shape.

Festooned A festooned tree is most often grown as a specimen tree. Instead of heading back the branches, they are bent down and tied to the trunk; this restricts the sap flow and encourages the production of fruits. Be careful not to break the branches when bending them down, or to damage the bark when tying down the branches. Prune back any fruiting spurs to 8cm/3in. Remove the ties after a few years, when the branches are permanently bent.

Step-over A step-over is an espaliered tree that has only one lateral at 30cm/12in above the soil level. Often used as a border around

Fan training is ideal for stone fruits such as plums and peaches. The trees are trained against a wall or fence with the main branches spread out from the trunk.

Espaliering is most commonly used for apple and pear varieties. Paired branches are trained out horizontally from the main stem.

PESTS & DISEASES

The best way of dealing with pests and diseases is to grow healthy plants in a healthy environment. Thriving plants are less likely to get diseases. A healthy environment filled with a diversity of plants encourages beneficial insects that keep pests under control.

PREVENTION AND CONTROL

Conventional thinking on pests and diseases is to find chemicals that kill or control them. Many organic gardeners have taken this same approach and sought out organic pesticides and fungicides that do the same job. This is flawed thinking because healthy plants, in the right conditions, grow vigorously and almost never require chemical protection against pests and diseases.

Studies show that deficiencies or excesses of nutrients cause imbalances in plants, which make them more susceptible to pests and diseases. Other studies show that plants grown in well-prepared beds, with good soil structure, have superior root systems and are more resistant to pests. Soil testing (see pp. 33–4) is useful in the organic garden to ensure that the soil has a balanced supply of nutrients. Good soil structure can be encouraged by double digging beds (see pp. 128–31).

Pests and diseases attack weak plants. Healthy vigorous plants may be attacked but the negative effects are most often minimal. Only when growing conditions are deficient in some way, and plants are stressed, are opportunities created for pests and diseases to flourish.

Sometimes weather or climate conditions can foster disease – for example, excessive rainfall can provide favourable conditions for fungal diseases. There is little you can do to counteract this kind of stress.

Since the best method of pest and disease control is prevention, choose resistant varieties that are suited to the local climate (often the ones that are traditonally grown locally), and practise crop rotation. Even in a small garden, rotating crops will discourage pests and diseases (see Crop rotation, pp. 78–81). If you plant a diversity of crops in the garden and avoid planting large areas to a single crop, pests are unlikely to get out of hand. Pests that affect a particular crop will not reproduce ceaselessly without an endless supply of food. A variety of plantings, which include habitats for beneficials, will encourage insects, birds, and other animals to live in the

Slugs and caterpillars can damage lush green foliage. As they do so, they leave behind these tell-tale, crinkle-edged holes.

garden and eat pests (see Beneficial wildlife, pp. 121–5).

Good garden hygiene will help to prevent the spread of disease (see p. 270). In addition, there are many biological controls that can be used. For example, if you introduce parasitic wasps (*Encarsia formosa*) into your greenhouse (see p. 172), these insects will feed avidly on whiteflies.

Beneficial insects and natural predators are a better means of pest control than pesticides. If you can create an environment that is friendly to them, there will be a natural balance in the garden. There will always be some pests, and there will always be some predators, but neither will have large populations that get out of control.

BARRIERS AND TRAPS

Sometimes pests cannot be controlled by the above methods, and you will need to take further action. One strategy is to create a barrier. Floating row covers can be placed over plants and secured at the edges or the covering can be fitted over a frame just as if you were building a small tunnel.

Another strategy is to set traps. Sticky cards can be placed in the garden or greenhouse to catch pests. Some beneficial insects may be caught in these traps, and they should certainly never be used where biological controls are in operation. However, traps can be very helpful in identifying an unknown, unseen pest, so that a specific control can be chosen.

A further strategy of pest control is simply to remove the pests from the plants. Pick them off and squash them, or wash them away with a hose – whatever works!

USING ORGANIC PESTICIDES

The use of simple organic pesticides and fungicides can be an acceptable form of organic gardening, but try to regard them as a last resort.

Blackfly typically cluster together around stems or on the undersides of leaves, where they suck the sap from healthy plants.

Pesticides and fungicides do not cure the underlying problem. When using them, try to search out the cause of the problem and take the necessary steps to prevent it from occurring again in the future. (Note too that some organic certifying organizations restrict the use of certain organic pesticides and fungicides.)

I try never to use any organic pesticides or fungicides unless it is absolutely necessary. When Colorado potato beetles attacked my potatoes one year, I did try spraying with a soap solution (see p. 171) but this barely deterred them. So instead I harvested the crop as new potatoes rather than full-sized ones. I was interested to note that one variety of potato was unaffected by the beetles and planted more of that variety in the following year.

A single snail can cause immense damage to a plant, leaving large holes in the leaves. Encourage predators to tackle the problem.

PESTICIDES AND FUNGICIDES

A poison is a poison is a poison. Every time we use pesticides and fungicides we attack the garden with a form of warfare. Organic pesticides and fungicides can be just as poisonous as their synthetic, agribusiness-produced counterparts. Therefore, great care must be taken in their handling and use. Nature can make chemicals that are as dangerous as those made by a chemist in the laboratory; the primary difference is that most of nature's chemicals are biodegradable. Listed below are some organic pesticides and fungicides which I have used, but be sure to check the legal situation in your country. For example, in the UK, under the Control of Pesticides Regulations 1986, it is illegal to use any pesticide other than those officially approved and listed in the current UK Pesticide Guide. You should also check with your local organic certifying agency before using any pesticide.

Pyrethrins Extracted from *Tanacetum cinerariifolium*, pyrethrins kill aphids and most other insects – including beneficial insects. They should be used only with caution.

Sulfur Used against powdery mildew and scab. May not be permitted by some organic certifiers. Some plants are burned by sulfur.

Diatomaceous earth The fossilized shell remains of diatoms have microscopic sharp edges that cut soft-bodied insects. The pests die from dehydration. I have used diatomaceous earth to control caterpillars, slugs, aphids and other soft-bodied insects.

Garlic I sometimes make a spray by finely chopping a head of garlic and steeping it in mineral or olive oil overnight. I then strain the oil and mix it with a little soap and an equal amount of water. Sprayed on plants this seems to deter pests, at least temporarily.

Chilli pepper I have also made a spray by finely chopping a chilli pepper and mixing it with water. I find that if this is sprayed on plants it will deter squirrels and other large pests. A dusting of cayenne pepper on foliage is sometimes enough to deter a mammal.

Soap I have occasionally used a solution made by mixing half a teaspoon of soft soap (not washing-up liquid) with one tablespoon of olive oil in 2l/½gal water. Sprayed on plant foliage this kills a wide range of pests. Insecticidal soap, which contains a potassium salt to increase effectiveness, controls aphids, whitefly and others, but also kills some beneficial insects.

I sometimes use a spray made of thinly sliced chilli peppers, mixed with a little water, to deter pests that attack the crops in my garden.

Stinging nettle I sometimes make a spray by chopping nettle foliage and steeping it in water. I spray the solution on plants to deter pests.

BIOLOGICAL CONTROL

Biological control is the importation of specific natural predators to control pests. Some biological controls, such as *Bacillus thuringiensis* (*Bt*), can be used outdoors, but they are most often used in greenhouses.

Obtainable from specialist suppliers, these agents are now virtually the only effective treatment against many common pests that have developed resistance to conventional pesticides.

Have recourse to biological controls at the first signs of infestation. This is important, since the effect of such controls may take some weeks.

Aphidius matricariae A parasitic wasp that is used to control aphids in greenhouses.

Bacillus thuringiensis (Bt) This is a bacterium that prevents caterpillars from eating – which effectively kills them – yet is relatively harmless to animals, humans, and most insects. Sadly, *Bt* is quickly becoming ineffective because of its widespread use in genetically modified corn (see p. 70). Resistant varieties of pests have developed rapidly in the US in recent years, but it is still a useful biological control in the UK.

Encarsia formosa A parasitic wasp that is used to control whitefly in greenhouses. They can be bought in the form of pupae. The wasps lay their eggs in the scales of the whitefly.

Heterorhabditis megidis A nematode that controls vine weevils, in greenhouses or, in warm areas, outdoors.

Phasmarhabditis hermaphrodita A nematode that can can be used to control slugs in warm areas. However, a more effective method is to set a slug trap (see p. 175).

Phytoseiulus persimilis A predatory mite used to control red spider mites in greenhouses or outdoors.

Organic pesticides will usually kill beneficial insects, like this monarch butterfly caterpillar, along with the pests. Any pesticide or fungicide, even if organic, may have the negative side-effect of killing micro-organisms in the soil.

PEST OR BENEFICIAL?

It is important to be able to visually identify the insects and animals that visit your garden so that you know what actions, if any, to take. Some of them will be unwanted pests while others are welcome beneficials that can be encouraged to stay in the garden (see pp. 121–5).

BENEFICIALS

Bats These reduce the number of insects in and around the garden.

Bees Bees are responsible for the pollination of more than one-third of the fruits and vegetables that we eat.

Centipedes Centipedes eat a wide range of soil-dwelling pests.

Domestic fowl Chickens and ducks eat insects and slugs.

Frogs and toads Frogs and toads feed on insects, snails and worms. They are also a good form of slug control.

Ground beetles These prefer to live in areas with ground-cover plants. They eat cutworms, caterpillars, slugs and snails and the eggs of cabbage rootfly and other pests.

Hedgehogs Eat a wide range of pests, including slugs and snails, caterpillars and millipedes.

Hoverflies The adults, like parasitic wasps, lay their eggs near pest colonies. Their larvae help to control aphids.

Lacewings These will reduce the number of aphids, whiteflies, larvae, mites and thrips.

Ladybirds Also known as ladybugs and ladybeetles. The adults and nymphs eat aphids and other soft-bodied insects (but mostly aphids).

Spiders Spiders build delicate but deceptively strong webs that catch many pests.

Wasps Parasitic wasps lay their eggs in pests. When the eggs hatch, the pest is destroyed.

A pond-lover in spring, the common toad roams on land for most of the year feeding on many pests in the garden.

PESTS/BENEFICIALS

Ants Ants aerate the soil and clean up weed seeds and other debris. They also eat the sticky substance that is created by aphids, and in the process transport pests to other plants. If the aphids are controlled, ants will not cause problems.

Birds Birds can be the gardener's best friend. They control many pests. However, sometimes they attack a crop before harvest. Place nets or floating row covers over brassicas and young fruits. Another tactic is to plant a tree such as a mulberry that will serve to attract birds away from crops for the table.

Earwigs Earwigs prey on many pests and their eggs. Unfortunately, they also eat young leaves and the tips of buds just before they flower. Set an earwig trap by stuffing hay or dried grass into a pot and support it upside down on a stick near affected plants. The earwigs are nocturnal and will occupy the trap during the day. Empty the trap daily.

Nematodes Nematodes, also known as eelworms, are microscopic. Some are pests and others are beneficial. Those that feed on insects are often useful in controlling pests. Root knot nematodes, stem and bulb nematodes and potato cyst nematodes are only a few examples of the many types that are pests in the garden. Crop rotation is an effective control of some of these pests (but not cyst nematodes). Destroy any affected plants.

PESTS

Aphids Aphids are also known as greenfly and blackfly and in fact come in many colours. They affect virtually all plants, bushes and trees, making the leaves sticky or blistered and spreading viral diseases. Control them with ladybirds and other beneficial insects, or remove aphids from plants by spraying them with a blast of water.

Beetles and weevils Weevils are a type of beetle. Predatory wasps and birds are the primary natural predators of all beetles and weevils.

Flea beetles are notable because they jump when the plant is touched. If flea beetles are a problem, clear plant debris out of the garden in the autumn to discourage recurrence. Protect plants with floating row covers or apply parasitic nematodes to the soil.

Asparagus beetles only affect asparagus. Pick them off by hand.

Pollen beetles attack many plants, especially brassicas. There is no effective method of control except for applying floating row covers before a problem occurs.

Vine weevils are hard to pick off, as they only feed at night, hiding by day. Clear away plant debris to reduce their hiding places.

Caterpillars Caterpillars are the larvae of moths and butterflies. Most eat plant foliage and fruit; however, some attack the roots. Pick caterpillars off and destroy them. Look for eggs left behind

Ladybirds are welcome visitors to the garden as they feed on the gardener's enemies, such as aphids, scale insects and mealybugs.

on foliage and remove them. *Bt* may be used as a biological control.

Flies and maggots Whiteflies lay eggs on the undersides of leaves. When the eggs hatch, the maggots eat the foliage. They are very common in greenhouses; control with parasitic wasps (*Encarsia formosa*). The eggs of carrot root flies hatch into maggots that eat into root crops.

Cabbage root maggots (larvae of the cabbage fly) eat and tunnel into roots. Good hygiene is the best defence, so destroy the roots of the previous year's brassicas every spring. Parasitic nematodes may be applied to the soil around the roots of each plant. Apple maggots and the larvae of fruit flies eat into fruits. Good hygiene is essential, so clean up dropped fruit to discourage them.

Celery flies and other leaf miners are controlled by removing damaged plants or branches and destroying them.

Leafhoppers There are many types of leafhoppers and most spread diseases, especially viral diseases. The tops of affected leaves get pale spots. Control them by encouraging beneficials into the garden.

Mammals Deer and rabbits are only excluded from the garden by effective fences. Electric fences work particularly well. Rabbits girdle trees in winter, so protect the trunks either with wire netting or with proprietary tree guards (see p. 159).

Mealybugs These small pests are covered by a white waxy powder and filaments. Control them with mealybug destroyers – these are a type of ladybird. In greenhouses, clean them off with insecticidal soap.

Millipedes Distinguishable from centipedes by their two pairs of legs per body segment instead of one. Millipedes damage potatoes and eat seedlings and soft growth on fruits. They flourish in soils that are high in organic matter. Control with crop rotation, regular cultivation, and good hygiene. Leave infested areas of the garden unplanted for a year or two.

Scale insects A collection of species that suck on plant leaves and stems. They look like tiny bumps. Remove infested plants (or portions of plants) and destroy.

Slugs and snails Slugs and snails eat leaves and seedlings. You may notice a slime trail. Cultivate the soil to kill eggs, and encourage predators like birds and frogs. If you have a lot of slug damage it is worth setting a slug trap, in the form of a steep-sided dish filled with beer. The slugs will be attracted to the beer and drown. Empty the dish and refill it with beer every day until the slugs are eliminated. (Unfortunately, ground beetles, which hunt slugs, can be attracted to the trap and drown too.)

Spider mites Mites produce tiny webs in plants. They rarely kill trees and bushes but can affect annuals. In the greenhouse, use the predatory mite *Phytoseiulus persimilis* to control them. Keeping the greenhouse atmosphere moist may also help.

Thrips Thrips are sap-sucking insects that produce a whitening of the leaves. They feed on the upper leaf surface rather than the underside. They may also affect petals of flowers and prevent them from opening. Predatory mites are an effective control in greenhouses. Since they thrive in dry conditions, water affected plants regularly. They may be treated with pyrethrins.

Wood pigeons If you notice in the winter that your brassicas are being devoured, or that some young plants have been uprooted, the culprits are likely to be wood pigeons. Earlier in the year, they are particularly partial to blackcurrants and the seeds of peas and beans.

Scarecrows, foil strips or other devices may scare them away in the short term, but the only really effective long-term protection is netting.

The trunk of this tree was damaged by rabbits during the winter. If a little more bark had been stripped away, the tree might have died.

COMMON AILMENTS

Name	Symptoms	Name	Symptoms
Bacteria			leaves. The upper side develops yellow blotches. To control the problem, avoid overhead watering and ensure good air circulation.
Wilt	There are many types of bacterial wilt. Each is specific to a single plant or a group of plants in the same family. Often the plants get a grey, fuzzy growth that looks like botrytis.	Botrytis	Also known as grey mould. It may attack seedlings in damp weather. Plants with soft leaves are at risk. Dead, discoloured patches develop on stems, causing the plant to die. The best cure is prevention – remove dead plant debris from the garden regularly. Ensure good air circulation and avoid overhead watering.
Canker	Bacterial and other cankers affect many fruit trees, causing sunken spots on the stems which release thick, coloured liquid. Remove affected branches and destroy. Clean tools well after pruning.		
Blackleg	Affects plant cuttings and potatoes. The stems collapse at soil level and the plant dies. It is caused by poor garden hygiene. Destroy affected plants. Only buy certified seed potatoes.	Fusarium wilt	Affects most plants, causing black patches on the stems and leaves. Crop rotation is the most effective method of control. Remove diseased plants and soil from around their roots and destroy.
Moulds/mildews		Verticillium wilt	Affects plants in the garden and greenhouse, creating long brown stripes on the stems. Remove diseased plants and soil from around their roots and destroy.
Damping off	Affects seedlings. The stem collapses at soil level, killing the plant. The only solution is good air circulation and bottom-watering.		
Rust	Small bright orange or brown spots on leaves, caused by mould spores.	Crown rot	A soilborne fungal disease that is prevented by good drainage. Keep mulch away from the stem.
Fungal leaf spot	Round blotches of fungus on leaves or fruits.	Foot/Root rot	Affects a wide range of plants. This fungus causes the stem to discolour, wilt and die. Crop rotation and good drainage are the best prevention.
Blackspot	A fungal disease that attacks roses.		
Powdery mildew	Affects most plants. A white powder-like mould appears on the upper side of leaves. Avoid dry conditions to discourage the problem.	Tomato/Potato blight	Starts as soft brown patches on leaves. Spread is very rapid and the whole plant quickly succumbs. Spores are washed into the soil and potato tubers underground become smelly
Downy mildew	Affects most plants. White fluffy fungal growth develops on the under side of		

COMMON AILMENTS

NAME	SYMPTOMS	NAME	SYMPTOMS
	and almost liquid. Tubers in store can also be affected. At the first signs cut off all haulms, wait two or three weeks, and then lift the tubers.		potassium levels inhibit the plant's uptake of magnesium.
		Nitrogen deficiency	Causes pale green leaves with a yellow tint.
Onion white rot	A fungal disease that affects alliums by causing a white fungus on the bulbs. Crop rotation is the only effective method of prevention. If you develop a problem with onion white rot, do not grow any alliums in that location for a decade.	Potassium deficiency	Causes leaves with a bright yellow or reddish edge.
		Phosphate deficiency	Slows plant growth and the leaves may appear to be yellow.
		Boron deficiency	Can cause cankers, discoloration, and bad taste and texture. Fruit can be small and disfigured.
Scab	Affects many fruit trees, causing dark brown patches on the leaves and fruit. Plant resistant cultivars. Remove any affected branches immediately and destroy. Consider an open-centre tree shape to encourage air circulation and allow sunlight to reach the centre of the tree.	Calcium deficiency	Affects fruits and causes blossom end rot in peppers and tomatoes. Causes bitter flesh and pitted skin.
		Other problems	
		Speckle leaf	Dark spots on the leaves of many plants – said to be caused by high ozone levels. Choose a resistant variety.
Clubroot	Stunts brassica plants by causing swollen and disfigured roots. Remove and destroy infected plants. Do not plant brassicas on the land for at least twenty years.	Drought	Causes the foliage to wilt, dry, discolour, and fall off. Plants may be stunted or even die.
Viruses			
Mosaic virus/ Cucumber mosaic virus	Viruses cause disfigured flowers and foliage. Can affect all plants. Most viruses are brought into your garden by insects. Good hygiene is essential. Clean tools well after pruning infected plants. Buy plants that are certified virus-free. Destroy infected plants.	Excessive watering	Turns leaves yellow and the plants may wilt.
		Irregular watering	Causes distorted leaves and flowers.
		Transplant shock	Causes leaves to wilt, turn yellow and drop. Harden off seedlings before transplanting.
Deficiencies			
Magnesium deficiency	Very common in potted plants. Leaves show yellow or red discoloration. Acid soils and heavy watering decrease magnesium levels. High	Frost or low temperatures	Cause many plants to defoliate and die back or die.

CHAPTER 5

DIRECTORY OF FRUIT & HERBS

VEGETABLES,

GUIDE TO DIRECTORY

When grouping vegetables for crop rotation, it is important to consider their botanical family. Members of the same plant family are often susceptible to the same diseases and should not be grown in a bed where another member of that family was grown the previous year.

HOW TO USE THE DIRECTORY

In this directory, the plants have been separated into botanical families (see panel opposite). Each entry provides advice on how to choose the most appropriate site for the crop and indicates any specific soil preferences or needs. It discusses the

With so many varieties to choose from, the hardest part of planning a garden can often be deciding which ones to leave out of your planting scheme.

NUTRITION RATINGS

Excellent source *40–100+% of RDA per serving.*
Good source *25–39% of RDA per serving.*
Significant source *10–24% of RDA per serving.*
Source *Less than 10% or lack of quantitative data.*
Phytochemicals *Limited available data means that only vegetables that are very high in phytochemicals are listed as an excellent source; all other vegetables are sources of phytochemicals.*

best sowing or planting techniques for that plant as well as routine care and maintenance needed during the growing stage. Key pests and diseases that may pose a threat to your crop are identified too. A selection of recommended varieties highlight some of the most popular varieties grown as well as some with unusual features.

VEGETABLES, FRUIT & HERBS

The vegetables, fruits and herbs described in this directory are grouped according to their family to help you when drawing up a crop-rotation plan.

Vegetables

Goosefoot Family
Chenopodiaceae
Beets 182
Spinach 183

Daisy Family
Asteraceae
Endive 184
Chicory 185
Globe Artichokes 186
Sunflowers 187
Jerusalem Artichokes 188
Lettuce 189–91

Morning Glory Family
Convolvulaceae
Sweet Potato 192

Mustard Family
Brassicaceae
Kales 193
Cauliflowers 194–5
Cabbages 196–7
Brussels Sprouts 198
Kohlrabi 199
Calabrese and Broccoli 200
Swedes 201
Turnips 202
Radishes 203

Gourd Family
Cucurbitaceae
Watermelons 204
Melons 205–7
Cucumbers 208
Summer Squash 209–10
Winter Squash 211–13

Grass Family
Poaceae
Wheat 214–15
Sweetcorn 216–17

Pea and Bean Family
Papilionaceae
Beans 218–23
Peas 224–5

Onion Family
Alliaceae
Onions 226–8
Leeks 229
Garlic 230

Asparagus Family
Asparagaceae
Asparagus 231

Buckwheat Family
Polygonaceae
Buckwheat 232
Rhubarb 233

Nightshade Family
Solanaceae
Peppers 234–5
Tomatoes 236–8
Aubergines 239
Potatoes 240–41

Carrot Family
Apiaceae
Celery 242–3
Carrots 244
Parsnips 245

Minor Salad Vegetables 246–7

Tree fruits

Mulberry Family
Moraceae
Figs 248

Rose Family
Rosaceae
Quinces 249
Apples 250–51
Apricots 252
Cherries 253
Plums 254
Peaches 255
Pears 256

Nuts

Walnut Family
Juglandaceae
Walnuts 257

Hazel Family
Corylaceae
Hazelnuts 258

Beech Family
Fagaceae
Chestnuts 258

Soft fruits

Heath Family
Ericaceae
Blueberries 259
Cranberries 260

Rose Family
Rosaceae
Strawberries 261
Raspberries 262
Blackberries 263

Saxifrage Family
Saxifragaceae
Gooseberries 264
Currants 265

Kiwi Fruit Family
Actinidiaceae
Kiwi Fruits 266

Grape Family
Vitaceae
Grapes 267

Herb Selection 268–9

Beets *Beta vulgaris*

Plant type Biennial

Nutrition Significant source of vitamin C and folic acid. Source of potassium.

Uses Beets are grown both for their roots and for their greens. Some are used for animal fodder, others to make sugar, and most to eat fresh, cooked or pickled.

SITE AND SOIL

Choose a deeply cultivated site enriched with compost. Light soils are preferred to clay soils. Make sure the soil is not deficient in boron. A pH of above 6.0 and cool temperatures produce the best colour. Good drainage is essential.

SOWING

To speed up germination, soak seeds in warm water for fifteen minutes. Start seeds indoors in early spring or sow direct outdoors when the soil has warmed up. For the earliest crops use bolt-resistant varieties. Sow 1cm/½in deep, 5cm/2in apart, at monthly intervals until mid-summer.

CARE AND MAINTENANCE

Weed regularly, taking care not to damage roots. Thin to 8cm/3in. Do not over-water, but keep the soil moist. Add high-nitrogen compost in summer.

Pests and diseases Boron deficiency. Damping off in seedlings. Leaf spots may develop.

HARVEST

Using a garden fork, lift beets from the soil. Small beets can be pulled by the tops. Use the greens; they are ideal in salads. Store the last harvest at cool temperatures (0°C/32°F) at high humidity through the winter. Before storing, twist off the leaves well above the root: cutting tends to make the stems ooze juice. Storing the roots in the

In areas with mild climates, beets, such as 'Boltardy' (above), can be left in the ground throughout the winter to produce the first spring greens of the season.

garden over winter is possible in warm climates, but cold tends to make them rather woody.

VARIETIES

Boltardy A dependable red-rooted variety that is resistant to bolting.

Bull's Blood Grown for its dark red leaves.

Chioggia Popular candy-striped root.

Golden Rich orange-coloured sweet roots.

Libero Bolt-resistant. For early and main sowings.

LEAF BEETS

Leaf beets (*Beta vulgaris* var. *cicla*) are grown for their leaves and stems, which are braised, or used lightly cooked in salads. Leaf beets are quite cold hardy and crop over a long period.

Bright Lights Stems in a range of different colours.

Perpetual Spinach Narrow green leaf stems.

Rhubarb Chard Has delicious ruby-red stems.

Swiss Chard Leaf blades attached to white stems.

Spinach *Spinacia oleracea*

Plant type Annual

Nutrition Excellent source of phytochemicals and vitamin A. Good source of vitamin C and folic acid. Significant source of iron and magnesium. Source of potassium, B2, B6, calcium and protein.

Uses Smooth or textured spinach leaves are used fresh in salads or cooked as vegetables.

SITE AND SOIL

Spinach is fast growing and tolerates a wide range of soils. It is quite cold hardy, but at high temperatures tends to bolt. It also tolerates partial shade, which it prefers during the heat of summer. Spinach grows best in a soil pH of 6.5 to 7.5.

SOWING

Sow seeds directly in the garden, starting as soon as the soil can be worked in early spring. For a continuous harvest, continue sowing at three-week intervals from spring to autumn. Germination tends to be erratic where soil temperatures exceed 29°C/85°F. Space the seeds at intervals of 2.5–5cm/1–2in, sowing them 1cm/½in deep. Sow them in rows 30cm/12in apart.

CARE AND MAINTENANCE

Water and weed as necessary. If the plants start to bolt, harvest them immediately.

Pests and diseases Caterpillars may eat the leaves. Downy mildew is the main problem. Remove affected leaves and thin plants out.

HARVEST

An entire plant or just several leaves at a time may be harvested. Thin out as necessary, by harvesting young plants and serving them fresh in salads. Try to use them as soon as possible after picking. Perfect unblemished leaves may be frozen.

PEST CONTROL

Spinach leaves may be eaten by caterpillars. Regularly check the leaves for damage. Remove pests by hand and destroy.

VARIETIES

Avanti Resistant to powdery mildew.

Giant Winter Very hardy large-leaved variety.

Strawberry Spinach (*Chenopodium capitatum*) Mild-flavoured, with strawberry-like fruits.

The small strawberry-like fruits borne on the stems of the strawberry spinach can be eaten or left to provide ornamental interest in the vegetable garden.

Endive *Cichorium endivia*

Plant type Annual or biennial

Nutrition Significant source of vitamin A and folic acid. Source of calcium, iron and fibre.

Uses This leafy vegetable is sometimes cooked but best served fresh as a salad vegetable. Blanching increases sweetness.

SITE AND SOIL

Endive is a cool-season crop that likes a moisture-retentive rich soil.

SOWING

Sow early varieties in late spring for a summer crop; sow in summer for an autumn crop and again in early autumn. Sow directly outdoors at 5cm/2in intervals and thin to 20cm/8in; close spacing helps self-blanching.

CARE AND MAINTENANCE

Endive is fast growing. Water as necessary. For five days prior to harvest, place a 10–15cm/4–6in cardboard disc on top of the plant or a bucket or clay pot over the entire plant. Blanch nearly mature plants one at a time. Eat straight away because blanched plants tend to spoil quickly.

Pests and diseases Slugs and aphids cause the most problems.

HARVEST

Between seven and thirteen weeks after sowing, harvest blanched plants by cutting across the crown. The plant may re-sprout and produce another crop. Leaves may be individually harvested as needed. Endive does not store well.

VARIETIES

Fijne Krul Groen (Moss Curled) Very hardy.

Indivia Riccia Romanesca da Taglio A tall variety.

Jeti Hardy, smooth leaves, self-blanching.

Monaco Frizzy leaves. Slow to bolt and resists tipburn.

Nummer Vijf 2 (Batavian Broad-leaved) Crumpled leaves that are tasty in salads.

Endive can have curly, serrated leaves (like those of 'Monaco', left) or long, broad leaves. It has a slightly bitter taste and is best mixed with other greens in salads.

Chicory *Cichorium intybus*

Plant type Biennial

Nutrition Source of vitamin A, folic acid, calcium, iron and fibre.

Uses Sometimes cooked, these slightly bitter greens are best in salads. The roots of some varieties are forced in winter.

SITE AND SOIL

Chicory requires a long growing season to harvest the roots for forcing. It is cold-tolerant, and does not require nitrogen-rich soil.

SOWING

Sow seed in spring. For an extended harvest, make another sowing in early autumn. Thin to 20cm/8in apart.

CARE AND MAINTENANCE

Weed regularly and keep watered during drought.

Pests and diseases Slugs and aphids.

HARVEST

Some chicories are eaten fresh while others are forced for winter greens. For forcing, dig the roots in the late autumn and cut off the leaves; save only thick roots. These may be stored in sand, like carrots, for later forcing. Belgian chicories may be forced in the garden in areas with mild winters. Cut off the greens and cover the crowns with soil about 15cm/6in high. New tops will grow in eight to twelve weeks, depending on temperature. To force plants indoors, trim the root tips and any side-shoots, leaving a carrot-like root about 20cm/8in long. Plant the roots in moist potting compost in a deep pot. Leave space between the roots and the edge of the pot, and leave the crowns exposed. Cover with another pot (opaque) and keep at 10–18°C/50–65°F for three to five weeks. Harvest the resulting regrowth by cutting just above the crowns. Compost the root. Radicchio may be harvested directly from the garden or forced.

VARIETIES

Witloof chicory produces a cos lettuce-like head; radicchio or red chicory produces a reddish green head with a tight heart. Leaf chicory can be harvested just twenty-eight days after planting. Belgian chicory produces yellow-tinged heads when forced in the winter.

Palla di Fuoco Rossa Popular red chicory variety.

Red Rib Red dandelion-type.

Variegata di Castelfranco Red chicory variety.

Zoom Belgian chicory variety.

Radicchios, such as 'Palla di Fuoco Rossa' (above), are particularly suitable for forcing indoors and provide a welcome note of colour in winter salads.

Globe Artichokes *Cynara cardunculus* Scolymus Group

Plant type Perennial (annual in cool climates)
Nutrition Excellent source of phytochemicals. Significant source of vitamin C, folic acid and magnesium. Source of potassium and fibre.
Uses Serve sepals with mayonnaise or melted butter. Mature globes are used as cut flowers. The hearts may be pickled or used in salads.

SITE AND SOIL

Artichokes need a sunny, sheltered site with a soil pH of 6.5. They tolerate light frost. Remember that they may grow to 1.5m/5ft tall with a 90cm/36in spread. Enrich the soil with compost or well-rotted manure.

SOWING

Sow indoors in late winter, in moist compost in 5cm/2in soil blocks. Germinate at 21–27°C/70–80°F. Once seedlings emerge, grow at 16–21°C/60–70°F. Transplant to the garden in late spring. Space 90cm/36in apart. In areas where temperatures do not fall below –8°C/18°F, seeds may be sown in autumn for a spring harvest: the plants will mature about twenty days earlier than those grown from transplanted seedlings.

CARE AND MAINTENANCE

Protect plants from heavy frosts. Weed regularly and mulch heavily to prevent the roots from drying out. Ensure the plants have plenty of water.
Propagation Shoots can be taken from plants in the garden, or you can propagate plants by division. To do this, use a sharp knife, or a spade, and divide an established plant so that each half has two or more shoots and a good root system. Do this in the spring and replant both halves about 90cm/36in apart. Plants last only about three years.

Pests and diseases Slugs may cause problems, especially when the plants are young.

HARVEST

In early summer to early autumn, cut mature buds before they begin to open. A second harvest may be possible later in the season.

VARIETIES

Green Globe Needs a long growing season and mild winters.
Purple Globe Romanesco Has an attractive colour and good flavour.

The globes of artichokes (such as 'Purple Globe Romanesco', shown here) are actually flowerbuds, prized for their fleshy base.

Sunflowers *Helianthus annuus*

Plant type Annual
Nutrition Excellent source of vitamin B1.
Source of vitamins B2 and B3, calcium, iron,
potassium and fibre.
Uses Good source of organic vegetable oil for
cooking in the kitchen. Seeds can be eaten whole,
baked in bread or used as bird food. Large
flowerheads bring height, colour and ornamental
interest to the garden.

SITE AND SOIL
Sunflowers tolerate a wide range of soils. Choose
a site where the height of these plants will not
shade other vegetables.

SOWING
Sow directly in the garden after all chance of frost
has passed. Sow them 1cm/½in deep and
15–30cm/6–12in apart depending on variety.
Germination takes two to ten days at 21°C/70°F.

CARE AND MAINTENANCE
A mulch may be helpful in retaining moisture.
Weed as necessary until plants become tall. Keep
soil evenly moist for a large harvest.
Pests and diseases Birds often attack the crop
before harvest.

HARVEST
When the heads of the sunflowers begin to droop,
it is time to begin harvesting. Using pruners, cut
the stem 2.5cm/1in below the flowerhead and
hang to dry in a warm place. The heads may
become mouldy but this will not affect the seeds.
For birdseed, the heads may be hung outdoors as
they are. Typically seeds are removed by rubbing
the heads against a coarse screen, or against
another flowerhead. Store the seeds in a cool dry
place. To eat, soak for twelve hours in warm
water, then spread the seeds on a baking sheet and
dry roast them in a warm oven until they are crisp.
Oil is produced by cracking the seeds with
a mill and pressing. Filter the resulting oil
through cheesecloth.

VARIETIES
Helianthus cucumerifolius Multi-stemmed, long-
flowering.
Italian White Unusual cream-coloured flowers,
excellent for cut flowers and seed production.
Russian Giant Just as it sounds, with very large
seedheads.

*Bright yellow sunflowers are easy to grow and are
useful as well as attractive. Their seeds are a nutritious
food for humans as well as for birds.*

Jerusalem Artichokes *Helianthus tuberosus*

Plant type Perennial

Nutrition Significant source of vitamin B1 and iron. Source of vitamins B2 and B3, calcium, potassium and fibre.

Uses Roots have a sweet flavour and are very nutritious. Their tall stems with yellow flowers are useful for adding height in the garden.

SITE AND SOIL

Jerusalem artichokes tolerate a wide range of soils. They can easily take over the entire garden, so grow them by themselves, surrounded by grass. Mow around them regularly; if they overwhelm the site, simply return the bed to lawn.

PLANTING

Cut large tubers into smaller pieces before planting. Plant 12cm/5in deep, 30cm/12in apart as soon as the ground can be worked in early spring. Cover and gently firm the soil.

CARE AND MAINTENANCE

If the plants do not appear extremely vigorous, soil may be mounded up around the bases. Water during dry periods in the first year. Depending on the variety, the tops may range in height from 1.5–6m/5–20ft. They may be trimmed back to 1.5m/5ft in mid- to late summer if desired.

Pests and diseases Few pests or diseases bother Jerusalem artichokes.

HARVEST

Lift as needed for the table with a garden fork. They store well in the ground, but may be harvested and stored in a very moist and cool location for winter use in colder climates. Be sure to leave some in the ground to grow in future years.

VARIETIES

Fuseau Bears long, smooth tubers.
Red Excellent flavour.

Jerusalem artichokes (also known as sunchokes) are very easy to grow, but can take over the entire garden if not controlled.

Lettuce *Lactuca sativa*

Plant types Annual
Nutrition Excellent source of phytochemicals.
Source of vitamins A, B and C, calcium, fibre
and potassium. Romaine is a significant source of
folic acid and a good source of vitamins A and C.
Uses Ideal for salads. Look effective when grown
in ornamental beds.

SITE AND SOIL

Lettuces can be divided roughly into the hearting
types, which include the tall cos varieties and the
rounded crispheads and butterheads, and the non-
hearting or loose-leaf lettuces.

The key to growing good lettuces is quick
growth under good conditions. In temperate
climates, given the help of a cold frame,
polytunnel or greenhouse, it is possible to harvest
lettuces for most of the year. Lettuces need very
fertile soil with lots of nitrogen. Ensure soil is not
deficient in boron. Working rich compost into the
soil will help retain moisture. Rotate their location
from year to year to deter pests and diseases.

SOWING

While it is perfectly acceptable to sow seeds
directly in the garden, starting them indoors three
to five weeks before transplanting will provide
optimum conditions for germination. Transplant
outside as soon as the soil can be worked in the
spring. Every two weeks or so, start more
seedlings indoors. Each time a lettuce plant is
harvested from the garden, replace it with a
seedling started inside. As the seasons change,
choose varieties suited to the changing light and
temperature regimes. For example, a garden plot
planted with cos and loose-leaf lettuce in the
spring might have iceberg and a heat-tolerant leaf
lettuce in the summer, and a butterhead and cos in

the autumn. For an extended harvest, try an early
autumn and a winter sowing of a hardy variety
such as 'Kelly.', 'All the Year Round' or 'Flandria'.
Set transplants in the garden spaced appropriately
for the variety. Start seedlings indoors in 5cm/2in
soil blocks and germinate at between
10–20°C/50–68°F. A basement may be suitably
cool for germination. After seeds germinate, move
to a sunny location. When transplanting be sure to
match the soil level; planting too deeply can be a
problem. Water thoroughly after transplanting.

CARE AND MAINTENANCE

Keep weed-free and add a little compost when
replacing a harvested plant. During a drought,

*Crisphead lettuce, also known as iceberg lettuce,
has crispy leaves that form a large solid heart which
is cabbage-like in appearance.*

PEST PREVENTION

A ring of sharp objects such as crushed eggshells placed around each plant will protect young lettuce leaves from being eaten by slugs.

water regularly. In adverse conditions, plants may bolt. Watch for the heads becoming soft on icebergs, or cos and loose-leaf lettuce suddenly growing tall. Taste a leaf for bitterness. Pinching back the top of a cos or leaf lettuce may help prevent bolting, but it is best to harvest the plant early and transplant a new seedling to replace it. In warmer weather, choose varieties resistant to bolting and tolerant of heat. Cos gets bitter quickly if the soil dries out.

As winter approaches, the most cold-tolerant varieties should be planted in the garden. Before frost damages the crop, cloches or cold frames should be put over the plants. The plants will not grow much after frost, but they will remain fresh well into winter in the cold frames. A simple preservation method is to surround a bed with hay bales, and then place old windows over the tops of the bales, creating a large cold frame at little or no cost. If very cold weather threatens, bales of hay may be placed over the glass to provide more insulation.

Pests and diseases Greenfly, root aphids, slugs and snails are common pests (see Pest prevention box, above). Cutworms, downy mildew, and mosaic virus may also affect plants. Botrytis, also known as grey mould, may attack seedlings in damp weather. Remove any afflicted plants and dispose of them carefully. Floating row covers can be used to shade the plants. This will discourage bolting.

HARVEST

Lettuce is best harvested in the morning, when it is most crisp. Its flavour and nutritional value are at their peak just after picking. Hearting lettuces should be harvested when the heart is firm. Remove the entire plant and compost the roots and outer leaves. Some lettuces, especially loose-leaf lettuces, can be harvested by picking the outer leaves, leaving the inner leaves to mature. Lettuce loses most of its vitamins in storage. It may be refrigerated for up to a week in a sealed container (to retain moisture), but is best eaten fresh.

CRISPHEAD VARIETIES

This type of lettuce is also known as iceberg, when its outer leaves are removed. It has a cabbage-like appearance, with crispy leaves that form a large

The slender, crisp leaves of cos or romaine lettuce are noted for their good flavour. The striking white stems look and taste rather like fresh celery.

solid heart. Although crispheads are the least nutritious of the lettuces, they are the most common type found on sale in shops because they travel well and tolerate warm weather.

Floreal Iceberg/butterhead cross. Good flavour with pest and disease resistance.

Iceberg Long-lasting variety grown for its crunchy leaves.

Kellys An older variety that often does well during winter in a greenhouse or polytunnel.

Butterhead varieties

Butterheads form small rounded heads of smooth soft leaves. The outer leaves are green, and the inner leaves are yellow to white. Butterhead lettuces are particularly high in vitamins.

All the Year Round A hardy variety with a slightly looser head. It can be grown under low light conditions in a greenhouse.

Flandria Good for greenhouse growing from mid-winter. Green, resists downy mildew and bolting.

Libusa Green, slow to bolt; resistant to downy mildew and less troubled by mosaic virus, root aphid and tipburn.

Cos varieties

Also known as romaine, cos lettuces have long broad leaves with thick juicy stems. They hold their leaves upright in a tight bunch. They usually take longer to mature than other types of lettuce.

Corsair A well-flavoured variety.

Erthel Tender and bolt-resistant.

Little Gem Dwarf, quick maturing, and resistant to root aphid.

Little Leprechaun Red semi-cos. Slow to bolt and tolerant of hot weather.

Pinokkio Good flavour, with disease resistance.

Vaux Self-folding Old variety with good flavour.

Loose-leaf varieties

Loose-leaf lettuces tolerate much warmer conditions than most hearting lettuces. They hold

Loose-leaf lettuces, especially the frilly and red-splashed varieties, such as 'Lollo Rossa' (above), add a decorative element to the vegetable garden.

their leaves up and out in a very loose and open fashion.

Black-seeded Simpson An early variety with tasty curly leaves.

Blushed Butter Oak Oak-leaf type with pink-veined leaves.

Lollo Rossa Variety with red frilled leaves.

Malibu Resistant to mildew.

Frisby Quick maturing, green. Some resistance to tipburn, downy mildew and bolting.

Red Fire Dark leaves, very frilly; slow to bolt.

Red Salad Bowl Leaves rarely turn bitter. This variety will last well if its leaves are harvested at regular intervals.

Valdai Red oakleaf type; resistant to bolting and downy mildew.

Sweet Potato *Ipomoea batatas*

Plant type Perennial

Nutrition Excellent source of phytochemicals and vitamins A and C. Significant source of vitamins B2, B6 and copper. Source of calcium, magnesium, iron, potassium, fibre and protein.

Uses Grown as annuals for their delicious roots, attractive flowers and colourful leaves. The young leaves can be picked and used like spinach.

SITE AND SOIL

Sweet potatoes grow best inside a polytunnel or greenhouse, in soils with good drainage and a high level of nitrogen. A well-drained fertile soil is best, with a pH level between 5.5 and 6.5. To create the best conditions, grow them in containers or in raised mounds of compost above soil level.

PLANTING

Sweet potatoes can initially be grown from roots bought from a shop. Place a few of the roots in moist soil in a propagator and keep them at 24°C/75°F. When the shoots reach 20–25cm/ 8–10in long, cut them off and plant into 15cm/6in pots. Transplant to their permanent site in the tunnel or greenhouse in early summer. For next year's crop, cut the tips of the vines off in the autumn. Grow them on in pots located on a warm,

sunny window sill, until they can be transplanted in the following year.

CARE AND MAINTENANCE

Keep sweet potatoes well watered and weed regularly. Make sure that container-grown crops are not allowed to dry out. A thick mulch will help retain moisture. An application of organic liquid fertilizer may help to produce larger tubers, though too much may promote lots of leafy growth. If the vines are allowed to root, a very large quantity of small tubers will be produced instead of fewer decent-sized tubers, so it is worth deterring vines from rooting by gently lifting them.

Pests and diseases Aphids and caterpillars may cause problems.

HARVEST

Probably the best time to harvest sweet potato roots is in the autumn. Using a garden fork, lift the roots gently, trying not to damage their fragile skins. To store the roots, cure them at 27°C/80°F and 80–90 per cent humidity for one week, then store them in a cool (10°C/50°F) place with high humidity.

VARIETIES

Generally, there is not a lot of choice when it comes to choosing varieties. On the whole, it is just a matter of finding something you like in the shops and propagating it from year to year. If you are fortunate enough to be able to choose, it is worth looking for one of the following varieties.

Centennial A good short-season variety.

Jewel High-yielding. Deep orange flesh.

Sweet potatoes thrive in hot, humid climates. In cooler climates, they need the protection of a polytunnel or greenhouse.

Kales *Brassica oleracea* Acephala Group

Plant type Annual or biennial

Nutrition Excellent source of phytochemicals and vitamins A and C. Significant source of calcium and copper. Source of potassium and fibre.

Uses Young leaves of broad-leaved types are used raw in salads; the older leaves are cooked like spinach or added to soups.

SITE AND SOIL

Kales prefer a fertile, well-drained soil that has been deeply cultivated. They prefer medium rather than high levels of nitrogen, so work in well-rotted compost only.

SOWING

Sow directly in the garden in late spring. Sow at intervals of 8cm/3in; thin seedlings to 23cm/9in spacing. Kales can also be started indoors for an earlier crop. Four weeks after sowing, transplant seedlings to the garden at 23cm/9in spacing. Seeds germinate best at 24°C/75°F.

CARE AND MAINTENANCE

Water frequently and keep free of weeds. Mulching will help to retain moisture.

Pests and diseases Birds, flea beetles, slugs and snails, caterpillars, cabbage root fly, whitefly and aphids can all cause problems. Diseases include mildew and clubroot. Seedlings can suffer from damping off.

HARVEST

Starting in the autumn and continuing into winter, harvest individual leaves by cutting with pruners. After overwintering, pick new leaves at 10cm/4in long in the spring. Kales freeze well. In severe winter climates, hardy dwarf varieties can be grown under cloches for a continuous harvest.

VARIETIES

Kales survive –15°C/5°F and, surprisingly, some varieties also survive heat. Many kales are grown as ornamentals or as garnishes. Some American kales are known as collards. These generally have broad, flat, rounded leaves.

Cottager's Pre-1900 variety, green tinged with red.

Dwarf Green Curled An old, very hardy variety.

Pentland Brig Crops from late autumn to late spring. Excellent flavour.

Redbor Crinkly purple-red leaves. Very hardy and attractive enough for a flower border.

Red Winter Purple stems but green leaves. Use immature for stir-fries.

Russian Red Purple-veined grey-green leaves that are very tender. Great for salads and stir-frying.

Kales are the hardiest of all the brassicas, and their flavour increases noticeably after a frost. 'Redbor' (above) has attractively coloured leaves.

Cauliflowers *Brassica oleracea* Botrytis Group

Plant type Biennial

Nutrition Excellent source of vitamin C and other beneficial phytochemicals. Significant source of vitamin B6, folic acid and pantothenic acid. Source of fibre and potassium.

Uses Most cauliflowers have a white head that tastes best after a frost. Young leaves surrounding the head are cooked or eaten fresh in salads.

SITE AND SOIL

As with all brassicas, crop rotation is very important to discourage soilborne diseases. Plant cauliflowers in a fertile, humus-rich soil that retains moisture. Do not plant them in high-nitrogen soils or they will become soft. Cauliflowers have a spread of up to 90cm/36in and a height of up to 60cm/24in, so allow enough space between the plants for each one to develop fully. Cauliflowers that are going to be overwintered need a protected site.

SOWING

Success depends on planting the correct variety at the appropriate time and in the right location. Dunking the seeds briefly in hot water before sowing indoors may help to prevent disease. Start seeds indoors five weeks before transplanting outside. Germinate at 21°C/70°F and then reduce the temperature to 16°C/60°F. Plant outside when the seedlings are ready.

CARE AND MAINTENANCE

Water regularly during the growing season. Do not let the soil dry out. Apply a high-nitrogen liquid feed to overwintered cauliflowers in the spring to encourage them to set seed, which can be saved for future planting. Heirloom varieties and those maturing in the summer may need to be blanched to prevent discoloration of their white curds. Wrap the leaves around the head and bind them with soft twine or pin them together with a toothpick. Weed regularly after planting until the leaves are large enough to shade out the weeds.

Pests and diseases As for kales (see p. 193).

HARVEST

Refer to the table below to establish the correct time to harvest your crop. Using pruners or a knife, cut just below the head when it is still firm and tight. Summer/autumn varieties mature in about fifteen weeks; winter varieties in about forty weeks. After harvest, remove the entire plant to deter soilborne diseases, and add to the compost.

CAULIFLOWER TYPES			
TYPE	WHEN TO SOW	WHEN TO HARVEST	COMMENTS
Late winter/Spring	Late spring	Spring to early summer the following year	Grow these types only in areas with mild winters.
Summer	Mid-autumn or early spring	Early summer or mid- to late summer	Autumn sowings should be overwintered in cold frames or tunnels, and transplanted in early spring.
Autumn	Mid- to late spring	Late summer to late autumn	There are interesting coloured varieties.

WINTER VARIETIES

The Walcheren Winter varieties 'Armado April', 'Pilgim' and 'Markanta' do well over winter.

Maystar Ready for harvest in late spring.

Purple Cape Hardy purple variety.

Snowbred Early to mature, heavy yield.

Vilna Relatively late variety.

SUMMER VARIETIES

All the Year Round An older variety, good for autumn and spring sowing.

Nautilus Good-quality variety that can be sown in both the spring and the autumn.

Snowball Good for autumn and spring sowing.

AUTUMN VARIETIES

Alverde Medium- to dark green curd. More vitamin content than most cauliflowers.

PEST PREVENTION

Plant brassica seedlings inside a small collar of heavy paper or cardboard to protect the plant from damage by cutworms.

Idol White-curded. At 15cm/6in spacing will produce mini-heads.

Limelight A dependable green-curded type.

Marmalade Light orange in colour.

Minaret Green 'Romanesco' type with pointed, pyramidal curds.

White Rock White-curded.

Most cauliflowers produce a white curd-like flowerhead. There are also attractive purple and green varieties.

MUSTARD
BRASSICACEAE

Cabbages *Brassica oleracea* Capitata Group

Plant types Biennial

Nutrition Excellent source of phytochemicals and vitamin C. Significant source of vitamin B6. Source of calcium, fibre and potassium.

Uses Can be eaten fresh or cooked. One of the easiest vegetables to store.

SITE AND SOIL

Cabbage needs fertile, humus-rich soil that holds moisture. The soil should be rich in nitrogen and have a pH level above 6.0. Discourage disease by planting in a location where brassicas have not been grown for three years.

SOWING AND PLANTING

Sow seeds indoors. Germinate at 24°C/75°F, then, once seedlings have germinated, reduce the temperature to 16°C/60°F. Transplant outside at 25–30cm/10–12in spacing.

CARE AND MAINTENANCE

Mound up soil around winter cabbages for stability as they grow. Keep the soil moist. Use row covers if necessary to protect from pests. Feed with high-nitrogen compost once during the growing season. Splitting is a problem with spring varieties, caused by rapid new growth after heavy rain or irrigation after a dry period. Deep cultivation near the roots may prevent splitting.

Pests and diseases As for kales (see p. 193).

HARVEST

Remove entire plant from garden when the head has matured and feels firm. Cut off the root and compost it to help eliminate soilborne diseases. In areas with cold climates, harvest winter cabbages and store them at 0°C/32°F in a dark place with high humidity.

The hardy variety 'January King Hardy Late Stock 3' needs fertile soil and a high level of nitrogen to produce healthy heads of large, red-tinged leaves.

VARIETIES

Cabbages are often grouped by their time of maturity. Summer and autumn varieties are sown from early spring and harvested from early summer to autumn. They typically have large round heads. Winter varieties are sown in the late spring and harvested in early winter. Spring varieties are sown in summer for a spring harvest, and often have small heads or loose leaves.

SUMMER VARIETIES

Greyhound Dwarf, pointed, good flavour.

Minicole Round, slow to bolt, particularly good for small gardens.

AUTUMN VARIETIES

Cuor di Bue Pointed Winnigstadt type.

Red Drumhead Rich red; good for pickling.

WINTER VARIETIES

January King Hardy Late Stock 3 Attractive red-tinged cabbage with good flavour.

Vertus (Savoy) Very hardy.

SPRING OVERWINTERED VARIETIES

Duncan Hearts up quickly.

Pyramid Excellent dark green variety for spring greens or full-sized cabbage.

ORIENTAL BRASSICA VARIETIES

These Asian specialities have a mustardy flavour. They may be stir-fried or used as salad greens.

Bok Choi (Pak Choi) *B. rapa* var. *chinensis.*

Chinese Cabbage *B. rapa* var. *pekinensis.*

Mibuna *B. rapa* var. *japonica.*

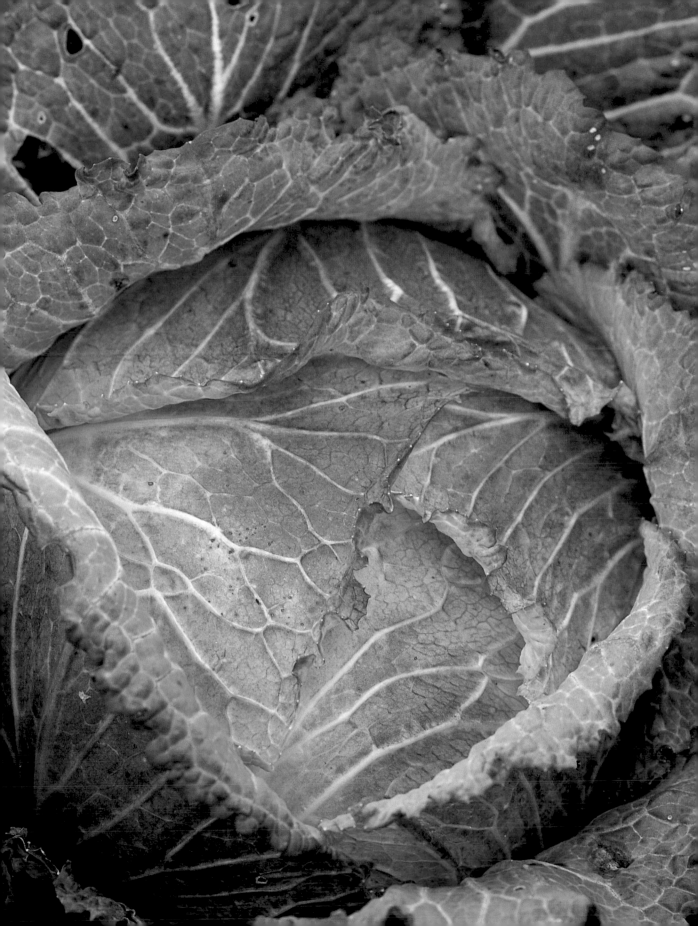

Brussels Sprouts *Brassica oleracea* Gemmifera Group

Plant type Biennial
Nutrition Excellent source of phytochemicals and vitamin C. Significant source of vitamins A and B6, and folic acid. Source of fibre and potassium.
Uses Brussels sprouts taste best when quickly blanched. They are eaten cooked.

SITE AND SOIL
Brussels sprouts prefer a moisture-retentive soil. A pH between 6.5 and 7.0 produces the best crop. For tight, firm sprouts, do not grow in beds that have recently had rich compost or manure added.

SOWING
While seeds can be sown in the garden, for best results start seeds indoors in late winter or spring. For an extended harvest, choose early types as well as late-season ones. Transplant 45cm/18in apart, and plant deeply to provide extra stability. Do not let transplants dry out.

CARE AND MAINTENANCE
Keep well watered and weeded. A thick mulch keeps plants from drying out during summer.
Pests and diseases As for kales (see p. 193).

HARVEST
Most of the old open-pollinated varieties tend to produce low yields, and F1 hybrids generally do better in the garden. However, there are a few open-pollinated varieties, including 'Early Half Tall' and 'Seven Hills', which produce a good crop. The first harvests will be available in late summer or early autumn. Pick the lowest sprouts first by cutting them near the stem. The upper sprouts will continue to grow in size. Harvest throughout the autumn and winter. If there is no snow cover in winter, protect the sprouts with hay

'Early Half Tall' is a very early variety which produces a particularly heavy crop all along the stalk, from the top to the bottom.

or harvest the entire plant and hang it in a moist cool location. After harvest, remove the entire plants from the garden to deter soilborne diseases, and add them to the compost. Smashing the stem will speed up decomposition.

VARIETIES
Cavalier Resistant to leaf spot. Prefers poor soils.
Early Half Tall Old open-pollinated variety; early.
Falstaff Decorative red variety.
Seven Hills An old favourite; late open-pollinated variety.
Rubine Decorative red-leaved variety.
Trafalgar High-quality hybrid.

Kohlrabi *Brassica oleracea* Gongylodes Group

Plant types Annual
Nutrition Excellent source of vitamin C. Source of potassium.
Uses The swollen stem or bulb is delicious when eaten raw, but is often served cooked.

SITE AND SOIL
Kohlrabi prefers light soils that are well drained. Work in compost to provide nutrients. Crop rotation is the best defence against diseases.

SOWING
Start sowing outdoors in spring, spaced 20cm/8in apart, or sow indoors two weeks before transplanting. Sow purple varieties directly in the garden in mid-summer. Make a sowing of a quick-maturing variety in early autumn.

CARE AND MAINTENANCE
Kohlrabi is quite drought tolerant. Water occasionally and keep the bed weed free.
Pests and diseases As for kales (see p. 193).

HARVEST
The swollen stems are ready for harvest in as little as forty days. If the stems get wider than 8cm/3in the inside may be woody. Store for two months in moist sand with some leaves attached.

VARIETIES
Azur Star A quick-maturing variety with purple skin. The leaves are edible.
Cindy Early and slow to bolt; not pithy.
Green Delicacy Available since 1880; pale green.
Purple Delicacy Purple version of 'Green Delicacy'.
Quick Star Quick-growing and green-skinned.

Kohlrabi is grown for its swollen stems, called bulbs. The flesh is white and the skin may be pale green or (as in 'Azur Star', left) purple.

MUSTARD
BRASSICACEAE

Calabrese and Broccoli *Brassica oleracea* Italica Group

Plant type Annual or biennial

Nutrition Excellent source of phytochemicals and vitamin C. Good source of folic acid. Significant source of vitamins A, B2, and B6, and phosphorus. Source of fibre, calcium and iron.

Uses Calabrese are typically green or bluish green, while the sprouting broccolis are either purple or white. Calabrese is best when eaten raw or quickly blanched in boiling water. The sprouting broccolis are best eaten cooked.

SITE AND SOIL

These plants need soil with moisture-holding ability. Improve sandy soils by incorporating lots of compost. Plants tolerate frost well.

SOWING

Sow calabrese about every four weeks, starting in early spring, or start indoors four to six weeks before transplanting. If starting indoors, keep soil temperature above 24°C/75°F to speed up germination, then reduce to 16°C/60°F. Plant outside at 30cm/12in spacing. If sowing outdoors, plant three per 30cm and thin to one per 30cm. Sow sprouting broccolis from mid-spring to early summer, transplanting to leave 60cm/24in between plants. They should be planted deeply and may need to be staked in the autumn.

CARE AND MAINTENANCE

Water frequently and keep free of weeds. Broccoli needs about 2.5cm/1in of water every two weeks.

Pests and diseases As for kales (see p. 193).

HARVEST

Calabrese can be harvested from early summer into the autumn. Sprouting broccolis are ready from late winter to late spring. Cut main heads

Broccoli and calabrese are high in nutrients.

when they are tight, before the flowerbuds open. Add compost after the first harvest to encourage side-shoots to form. Chill the cut heads as soon as possible. Cut the side-shoots when they are about 10cm/4in long, before the buds open. To harvest seeds, allow a plant with a central head to bloom, and collect the seeds when they mature.

CALABRESE VARIETIES

De Cicco Produces over a long period.

Autumn Spent An open-pollinated variety.

SPROUTING BROCCOLI VARIETIES

Purple sprouting: There used to be just 'Early' and 'Late' sprouting types, but now there are more named varieties available. 'Rudolph' is an early one, with some plants producing heads in mid-autumn. 'Claret' is a modern hybrid, producing a quality crop.

White sprouting: Two good selections are 'White Eye' and 'White Star', maturing in that order.

Swedes *Brassica napus* Napobrassica Group

Plant type Biennial

Nutrition Good source of vitamin C. Source of potassium.

Uses Grown for their sweet, yellow-fleshed roots used in soups and stews or mashed as a side dish. Young roots are grated for sprinkling on salads and the greens can be cooked like kales.

SITE AND SOIL

Swedes are a cool-season crop and prefer a well-drained soil with low levels of nitrogen. Test the soil to check that it is not deficient in boron. Choose an open site with light, fertile soil. Heavy soils do not produce a good crop.

SOWING

Sow seeds directly in the garden in late spring to early summer. Sow them 1cm/½in deep, spaced at intervals of 8cm/3in. Thin young plants to 23cm/9in spacing, utilizing the greens or any small roots for the table.

PEST PREVENTION

To protect crops from flea beetles, place cloches or floating row covers over the plants.

CARE AND MAINTENANCE

Keep the bed free of weeds and water generously if there is not sufficient rain. Mulching will preserve moisture and discourage weeds.

Pests and diseases As for kales (see p. 193). Consider choosing a variety that is resistant to clubrot and mildew.

HARVEST

Begin harvesting in the autumn. To lift roots, use a garden fork or pull by the tops. They may be left in the ground until needed, but overwintering in the garden may result in woody roots. It is better to harvest the unused portion of the crop before winter and store in dry sand in a shed, or in a clamp outdoors.

VARIETIES

Acme Purple Top Popular standard. Medium size.
Joan Some resistance to clubroot and mildew. Rarely split. Can be sown early for small roots.
Marian Resistant to clubroot and mildew.
Sharpe's Yellow Garden Good garden variety.

Swedes are grown for their sweet-tasting roots. The skin of the root is usually purple and buff, as in 'Acme Purple Top' (left).

Turnips *Brassica rapa* Rapifera Group

Plant type Biennial

Nutrition Roots are a significant source of vitamin C. Greens are an excellent source of vitamin C, a good source of vitamin A and folic acid, and a significant source of calcium.

Uses Roots have a yellow or white flesh that is cooked. The leaves are used in salads or are cooked like spinach.

SITE AND SOIL

Work plenty of compost into the soil and apply a mulch to retain moisture. Choose a sunny location and test for boron deficiency.

SOWING

Sow the first crop in early spring, under cloches or in a tunnel or greenhouse, 0.5cm/¼in deep and 8–10cm/3–4in apart. Choose a bolt-resistant variety. Seeds germinate when the soil reaches 4°C/40°F. Sow successively until late summer, pulling the last crops in late autumn.

CARE AND MAINTENANCE

Ensure that the turnips do not dry out. This will cause them to bolt. Apply mulch to ensure consistent moisture. Water at a rate of 2.5–5cm/ 1–2in a week during dry periods.

Pests and diseases As for kales (see p. 193).

HARVEST

If you leave turnips in the ground for too long they will become woody or bolt. Pull them up after about five weeks. The leaves may be harvested during the growing season, but make sure that you leave enough to keep the roots healthy. Pull up late-sown turnips in late autumn or early winter. Store them in a shed or outdoor clamp, like swedes.

VARIETIES

Atlantic Purple-topped with some bolt resistance.

Golden Ball Round, yellow-fleshed with some bolt resistance.

Green Top Scotch Yellow-fleshed turnip with green shoulders. Keeps well if left in the ground.

Purple Top Milan Flat roots with white flesh.

Snowball Excellent for multi-sown early crop. Eat when young.

Tokyo Cross Quick-growing with buttery flesh.

Veitch Red Globe Red top, white flesh, fast to mature.

Turnips are best harvested young. They store well, and contribute their sweet, mellow flavour to many winter stews and braises.

Radishes *Raphanus sativus*

Plant type Annual or biennial
Nutrition Good source of vitamin C. Source of potassium and fibre.
Uses There are two basic types: small-rooted varieties and large-rooted winter varieties. Young seed pods and leaves are often used in salads. The roots are used fresh in salads or cooked in soups.

SITE AND SOIL
Radishes are generally a cool-season crop. Grow in full sun in a light, well-drained soil.

SOWING
Start sowing the small-rooted varieties in early spring and continue throughout the growing season at two-week intervals. In summer, sow the seeds in partial shade. Sow seeds 1cm/½in apart and thin seedlings. Radishes germinate and mature so quickly that they can be sown in the same row as slow-germinating crops, such as parsnips, to act as handy row-markers. Large-rooted winter radishes should be sown in mid-summer. Try to leave 20cm/8in between plants.

CARE AND MAINTENANCE
Radishes are very fast growing and usually crowd out weeds. Water them regularly in dry weather.
Pests and diseases As for kales (see p. 193).

HARVEST
Start harvesting the small-rooted varieties three weeks after sowing. Harvest promptly, before they become woody. The large winter radishes may need ten to twelve weeks of growth before they can be harvested, and they can be left in the ground longer. After harvesting, the roots may be stored like carrots in buckets of sand. Moisten the sand a little to keep the radishes from drying out.

Tangy crisp-rooted radishes are quick to germinate and can be ready for harvest in as little as twenty-one days. The variety shown here is 'Scarlet Globe'.

SMALL-ROOTED VARIETIES
White Icicle Long white roots.
Cherry Belle Round with red-coloured skin.
French Breakfast Long red roots with white tips.
Scarlet Globe Popular since 1896.
Sparkler Round red roots with white tips.

LARGE-ROOTED VARIETIES
Cherokee Round red-skinned, white-fleshed variety with outstanding flavour.
Muntanghong Round variety with red flesh.
Black Spanish Round Traditional round variety.
China Rose Long, red-skinned roots.
April Cross Long white type that may be more bolt resistant than other varieties. Worth trying an early sowing in May or June.

Watermelons *Citrullus lanatus* var. *lanatus*

Plant type Annual

Nutrition The only food plant commonly grown in gardens which is a significant source of pantothenic acid. It is higher in vitamins B1 and B6 than any other commonly grown plant. Excellent source of vitamin C. Good source of vitamin A. Significant source of magnesium. Source of potassium and fibre.

Uses Eat fresh or use in blended drinks.

SITE AND SOIL

Watermelons are heat-loving and grow best in long-summer areas. In Britain, only quick-maturing varieties will succeed. They need at least 75 frost-free days, or must be grown in a greenhouse. Well-drained sandy soils are best. See site, soil, and sowing advice for melons, page 205.

CARE, MAINTENANCE AND HARVEST

Mulch well to conserve moisture, and water regularly during dry periods. Watermelons take 75–110 days to mature. Ripe watermelons sound hollow when tapped. Cut the stem about 2.5cm/1in from the fruit. They can be stored for two to three weeks at 7°C/45°F.

Pests and diseases High humidity levels cause powdery mildew and mosaic virus. Watch for aphids and fruit flies.

VARIETIES

Charleston Gray Crisp red flesh. Large fruits.

Funbell Very early, with sweet, juicy, pink-red flesh. Skin turns yellow when ripe.

Sugar Baby Matures within eighty days.

Heat-loving watermelons grow best in areas that enjoy long summers. Their large, round or oblong fruits are packed with sweet pink or yellow flesh.

Melons *Cucumis melo*

Plant type Annual

Nutrition Source of fibre. Cantaloupes are an excellent source of vitamins A and C, and a significant source of folic acid. Honeydews are an excellent source of vitamin C, a significant source of vitamin B6, and a source of potassium.

Uses Served as a starter or refreshing dessert.

SITE AND SOIL

Melons thrive in sun and warmth. They need a minimum temperature of 18C°/64°F to germinate and in the early stages of growth, and over 21C°/70°F during the growing season. In cooler climates most varieties will only succeed under glass, with extra warmth provided early in the year. Some can be grown outside in the warmer areas of temperate regions, but should always be planted in the sunniest, most sheltered spot.

Melons prefer a well-drained soil with a pH of 6.6 to 7. Good drainage is particularly important, as in very wet soil they tend to succumb to wilt. For this reason it is a good idea to prepare raised beds in the greenhouse border or in a cold frame. Dig out holes 30cm/12in wide and remove the topsoil. Break up the subsoil at the base of the hole before returning the topsoil well mixed with compost. Leave the soil in a domed mound ready for planting. Alternatively, if you have any spare turf, you can build a turf mound. Fork over the soil, incorporating some compost, and then layer turf upside down over the soil, spreading leaf mould or spent potting compost between layers. Leave a mound about 10cm/4in high at the centre.

SOWING

Sow seeds early in spring in individual 10cm/4in pots, two seeds per pot, and place them in a heated greenhouse. Ideally use a heated bench or

Melons, such as the honeydew 'Helios Yellow' (above), are heavy feeders. To produce the best fruits they need lots of water and plenty of sunshine.

propagator to give them bottom heat. After germination, thin each to the best seedling and grow on with heat. Once the plants have filled the pots, but before they become pot-bound, pot them on into 15cm/6in pots. Remove them from the heated bench or propagator when the ambient daytime temperature in the greenhouse reaches 18C°/65°F, and progressively harden them off. In warmer regions they can be placed outside to acclimatize as soon as all danger of frost has passed. If necessary pot them on again into 23cm/9in pots. Plant them out in the centre of their mounds and water them in well.

CARE AND MAINTENANCE

Melons need careful watering: adequate supplies are essential but overwatering can lead to wilt. It is especially important not to create soggy conditions around the base of the stem. A mulch can be applied in summer but leave a space of at least 20cm/8in around the neck of each plant. They prefer a dry atmosphere, so keep the greenhouse or frame well ventilated once temperatures are adequate.

For best results train the trailing vines as they grow on to strings or pea netting. When at least five true leaves are showing, pinch back to three leaves and allow two long vines to form. Pinch out all other growth. If you are growing in a frame, pinch back again and encourage four vines to grow, laying them out to the corners of the frame to maximize space. When they have filled the space, pinch out the tips.

Fruiting takes place on side-shoots, and male flowers are on the main vine. Melons are insect pollinated, so be sure not to use row covers when flowering. If growing melons in a cold frame, remove the glass during the day and replace at night as necessary. In a greenhouse, you will need to pollinate by hand. Use a small paintbrush to lift pollen from male flowers and brush it on to female flowers on side-shoots. Each vine will produce only three to four melons. In mid- or late summer, pinch off all small fruit and any flowers, leaving just a few large melons to mature. A high-nitrogen liquid organic feed may be applied halfway through the growing season. For greenhouse melons, keep the plants small by pinching the tips regularly. Pinch the main vine at 1.8m/6ft, and laterals after the fifth leaf. In a greenhouse, maintaining a minimum temperature of 24°C/75°F at night will help to produce a good crop of fruits.

Pests and diseases   Aphids, spider mites and whiteflies are the most common pests. Powdery mildew and verticillium wilt may cause problems.

HARVEST

All the work during the growing season pays off at harvest time. Melons are sweet-smelling when mature. If you simply lift the fruit the stems will usually separate from the melon.

CANTALOUPE VARIETIES

Cantaloupes typically have orange flesh with a rough-textured skin. The flesh is very sweet, and the skin is grey to green, with deep grooves.
Sweetheart   Easier to grow than most. Can be grown outside in warm gardens.
Romeo   Suitable for frames, cloches and unheated greenhouses. Good flavour.
Ogen   Small fruits with green flesh. Free fruiting.
Castella (Amber Nectar)   Can be grown outside in warmer areas. Very sweet and juicy. Resistant to powdery mildew and fusarium.

MUSKMELON VARIETIES

Muskmelons are usually smaller than cantaloupes and have smooth, greenish skin with intricate brown or beige markings. Their flesh colour ranges from green to nearly pink.
Blenheim Orange   An orange-fleshed variety that grows well in short seasons.

HONEYDEW VARIETIES

Honeydews have green flesh and generally have light green smooth skin that is rather thin.
Golden Honeydew   Orange-fleshed variety.
Golden Honeymoon   Green-fleshed variety with an orange rind.
Helios Yellow   Popular North American variety.

WINTER MELON VARIETIES

This group includes casaba melons and crenshaws, which have dark green skins. Winter melons are more prone to disease than other melon groups. Stored in a cool place they will keep for up to eight weeks.
Golden Beauty Casaba   A good keeper.
Sungold Casaba   Grown for its sweet, greenish flesh. Stores well.

A green-fleshed honeydew (back) and an orange-fleshed canteloupe (front) ready for the table. In the last days before harvest the sugar content rises.

Cucumbers *Cucumis sativus*

Plant type Annual

Nutrition Source of vitamins A and C and potassium.

Uses Harvested as young fruits and eaten raw or pickled. Occasionally used in soups.

SITE AND SOIL

For outdoor crops, select a sheltered site, and prepare holes about 30cm/12in in diameter and 30cm/12in deep. Space the holes 60cm/24in apart, measuring from the centre. Fill them with compost and mound the soil slightly. Cucumbers also do well in unheated greenhouses and polytunnels.

SOWING

Cucumbers do not transplant well, so sow seed of outdoor crops in prepared mounds after the soil has warmed and all danger of frost has passed.

CARE AND MAINTENANCE

Use trellis or stakes to support outdoor plants, and tie in tendrils as they grow. Bush varieties do not need support. Cut the tips after five leaves have formed to encourage stronger new growth, and again when the tips reach the top of the support. Pinch side-shoots off indoor cucumbers, leaving only the main stem. Train this up a string dangled from the roof of the tunnel or greenhouse. Feed outdoor and indoor plants with a high-potassium organic liquid feed. Regular watering is essential.

Pests and diseases Slugs can be very harmful to young outdoor plants. Watch also for aphids, mildew, cutworms and spider mites. Cucumber mosaic virus causes undersized distorted leaves.

HARVEST

Outdoor cucumbers may be ready for harvest about eight weeks after being transplanted. Indoor cucumbers may be harvested as soon as five to six weeks after transplanting.

VARIETIES

Burpless Tasty Green Mildew-resistant plants producing long slender fruits. Good for indoors or outdoors, though the plants should be trellised.

Crystal Apple Small, round whitish or yellowish fruits that should be picked young. Trailing habit. Good outdoor variety.

Carmen Mildew-resistant indoor variety.

Slice King High-producing indoor variety with good mildew resistance.

Some cucumber varieties have smooth skins; others, such as 'Crystal Apple' (above), are rough or prickly. Outdoor cucumbers should be picked when still young.

Summer Squash *Cucurbita pepo*

Plant type Annual

Nutrition Significant source of vitamin C. Source of vitamin A, calcium, iron and fibre.

Uses Range of fruits, from courgettes to scallops, that are best harvested young and small.

SITE AND SOIL

Pick a sheltered site, and prepare holes about 30cm/12in in diameter and 30cm/12in deep. Measuring from the centre, space the holes 90cm/36in apart for bush types, 1.8m/6ft apart for vines. Fill the holes with compost and mound the soil slightly. Summer squash does not require high nitrogen levels.

SOWING

Summer squash can be sown directly in prepared mounds after the soil has warmed and when all danger of frost has passed. For earlier crops, start seeds indoors in plants or blocks. A thick mulch added after planting will preserve moisture, keep weeds down and prevent the fruits from touching the ground where they will become soiled.

CARE AND MAINTENANCE

Regular watering is essential for summer squash. Feed the plants with a high-potassium organic liquid feed to produce a higher yield. Bush types require no staking, whereas vine types may be trained to grow up a trellis or allowed to grow along the ground. If the plants are not supported by trellis or stakes, gently train the vines clear of any paths so that they do not become damaged. If too many fruits are being produced, leave one or two squashes on the plant past maturity. These remaining fruits will not be edible, but they will slow down the production of new squashes to an acceptable rate.

Summer squash is insect pollinated. If row covers are used to protect plants from pests or if no fruits are setting, you may need to hand pollinate. Firstly, identify the male and the female flowers. The female flower has a tiny bump or thickened section of stem just beneath the flower; the male flower is slightly smaller and lacks this bump. Pick a male flower, remove its petals, and brush it against the centres of the female flowers. Do not damage the female flowers.

Pests and diseases Watch out for slugs, as well as for aphids, which may be carriers of cucumber

Courgettes are easy to grow and bear plenty of fruits. 'De Nice à Fruit Rond' (above) bears round fruits with a good flavour.

mosaic virus. Keep a regular check on the undersides of leaves as this is where bugs commonly lay eggs.

HARVEST

Start harvesting when the fruits are young and small. Cut or twist off the young fruits. The flower may still be attached. Courgettes are at their best when harvested about 10–12cm/4–5in long; yellow squashes can be cut when they reach about 12–15cm/5–6in; harvest scallop types when they are about 8cm/3in in diameter. Harvest regularly to encourage more fruit production. The male flowers are often harvested to be sautéed or stuffed, or used to decorate dishes. Fruits can also be left on the plants and allowed to grow into marrows.

VARIETIES

For spaghetti squash, see Winter squash, p. 211.
All Green Bush Popular, reliable variety. Fruit is long and green.
Ambassador Early to fruit with a long harvesting period. Fruit is long and green and easy to pick.
Clarion Unusual pale green, flask-shaped fruits. Good flavour even if left to develop into marrows.
Custard White A scalloped type, producing many fruits. Bush habit.
Defender Long fruit, green and slightly bulbous.
De Nice à Fruit Rond (Tondo di Nizza) Light green round fruit with a good flavour. Harvest when no larger than 12cm/5in.
Eight Balls Round green fruits.
Gold Rush Brilliant yellow elongated fruits.
Jemmer Bright yellow fruits with good flavour. Excellent for ornamental potagers.
Kojak So named because the plant is free of spiny hairs. Long dark green fruits.
Minipak A bush marrow, cropping heavily.
Leprechaun Dark green round fruits with crisp skin and sweet flavour.

The unusual shapes and bold colours of some summer squash, such as 'Yellow Crookneck', make a striking display in the vegetable plot.

Long Green Trailing Trailing old-fashioned type with long green fruit.
Nero di Milan Excellent new open-pollinated variety with dark green fruits.
Sunburst Bright yellow verion of 'Custard White'. Very productive.
Tiger Cross Resistant to cucumber mosaic virus. Pick young as courgettes or eat as marrows.
Yellow Crookneck Very tasty fruit with a highly textured skin. Harvest young to retain the flavour.

Winter Squash *Cucurbita* spp.

Plant type Annual

Nutrition Excellent source of phytochemicals. Source of potassium and fibre.

Acorn squashes are a good source of vitamin C, and a significant source of vitamin B1 and magnesium.

Pumpkins are a good source of vitamin A, and a significant source of vitamin C.

Hubbards are an excellent source of vitamin A, and a significant source of vitamin C.

Butternuts are an excellent source of vitamins A and C, and a significant source of vitamin B6 and magnesium.

Uses Can be boiled, baked, or made into pies.

SITE AND SOIL

Pick a site that is sheltered from wind and one where the long vines of winter squash will have ample room to grow. Prepare holes about 30cm/12in in diameter and 45cm/18in deep with centres spaced 90cm–1.8m/36in–6ft apart or more, depending on the variety. Fill with compost or well-rotted manure. Mound soil slightly. High nitrogen levels are necessary for a good harvest.

SOWING

Seeds may be soaked in water for a few hours to aid in germination. Seeds may be sown directly in the garden, but since some varieties require a long season to produce mature fruit, starting seeds indoors typically produces a better harvest. If sowing outdoors, plant six seeds in each prepared hill, and thin to three seedlings per hill. For sowing indoors, it is essential that roots are not damaged during transplanting. To this end, start the seeds in 10cm/4in pots. Alternatively, use 5cm/2in soil blocks, which work just as well (except when seeds are started too early and the roots spread into neighbouring soil blocks). Lift the soil blocks with a spatula or other flat device and transplant gently. Sow one seed per soil block, two to three weeks before transplanting in late spring. Harden off plants for a week before planting them outside, two to three seedlings per mound. If using pots, sow four or five seeds in each one, thinning down to three before transplanting.

CARE AND MAINTENANCE

Regular watering is absolutely essential. It is a good idea to feed the plants with a high-potassium

As a group, winter squashes range from inedible ornamental pumpkins to tasty squashes. The fruits may be as small as a cricket ball, or too big to carry.

organic liquid feed to produce a higher yield. Vines may be trained up a trellis if the plant is a variety that produces small fruit; however, vines are typically grown on the ground, and trained so that they are kept clear of nearby paths and do not get trodden on or knocked by passing traffic. Mulch well to preserve moisture and to keep the fruit off the soil.

Squash is insect pollinated. If row covers are being used, or if no fruits are setting, it may be neccessary to hand pollinate (see Summer squash, Care and maintenance, pp. 209–10).

Pests and diseases Watch out for slugs and cucumber mosaic virus. Rot may cause problems for fruits in storage.

Kabocha squash are small fruits with deep-ribbed skins and yellow flesh. The skin is typically dark green but some varieties may range to gold in colour.

HARVEST

In autumn, cut the leaves away from the fruit. This will help them to ripen. Light frosts will kill leaves and make harvest easier. However it may damage the fruit and shorten the time they can be stored. Before a heavy frost, cut the fruit stems with a knife or secateurs about 2.5cm/1in away from the fruit. The stem will be drying and the skin of the fruit hardening. Handle the fruits gently, especially butternuts. Let the squash cure or dry in sunlight for a few days to a week, depending on the type. If frost is expected, cover them with a blanket at night. Store in a low-humidity place with plenty of air circulation between the fruits. A temperature of about 13°C/55°F is ideal. With luck, the fruits may store until mid-winter.

ACORN VARIETIES
Cream of the Crop Fruit with light-coloured flesh and white skin. Bush habit.
Table Ace Dark green fruits on short vines.
Table Gold Bright orange fruits that may need sweetening when cooking. Semi-bush plants.

BUTTERNUT VARIETIES
Butternut Produces tasty dark orange-fleshed fruits that can grow very large and that store well.
Cobnut Good flavour and early ripening. Trailing habit. Quite small fruited, especially when compared to 'Butternut'.
Sprinter Again, relatively small fruits.

DELICATA VARIETIES
Delicata Small orange-fleshed fruits with an extremely sweet flavour.
Sweet Dumpling A round-fruit variety, as sweet as 'Delicata'.

HUBBARD VARIETIES
Blue Ballet A small version of 'Blue Hubbard'.
Blue Hubbard Produces large oblong fruits that store well.

Pumpkins typically have red-orange skin. Most have seeds that are a delicacy when toasted, and some pumpkins make wonderful pies. 'Atlantic Giant' (left) produces massive fruits.

Golden Hubbard A Hubbard with golden fruits.
Red Kuri Smallish, scarlet-coloured fruits.

BUTTERCUP/KABOCHA VARIETIES
Black Forest An old variety that produces small fruits with deep orange flesh.
Buttercup This dark green variety has a small button on the flower end of the fruit.
Delica Green skin and nicely coloured flesh.
Sweet Mama Tasty fruit that is produced on short vines.

SPAGHETTI VARIETIES
Stripetti Spaghetti produced in green-striped fruit.
Tivoli Fruit is borne on a short vine.
Vegetable Spaghetti Long strands of flesh inside oblong fruit.

PUMPKIN VARIETIES
Atlantic Giant A truly giant-fruited plant for winning prizes at shows.
Baby Bear Smallish fruit with long handles and naked seeds.
Jack Be Little Hand-sized fruit with sweet flesh.
Triple Treat Larger than 'Baby Bear', this variety also has naked seeds.

OTHER VARIETIES
Crown Prince Large, flattish grey-blue fruits that are popular in Asian and West Indian cooking.
Gold Nugget Small orange fruit on bushy plants.
Pink Banana Jumbo Its 75cm/30in long fruits look like pink bananas and taste great baked.
Turkish Turban Oddly shaped and coloured fruit that has real decorative value.

Wheat *Triticum aestivum*

Plant type Annual

Nutrition Source of vitamin E and folic acid. Whole wheat is a source of fibre.

Uses Grain can be used for breadmaking. Sow as a cover crop (see pp. 57–61)

Most gardeners do not consider growing wheat because they think of it as a field crop only grown on large acreages. What most do not realize is that with an area of 1.5m/5ft x 1.2m/4ft, enough grain for two loaves of bread can be produced. How many loaves of bread are consumed in a typical household in a year? Between fifty and hundred? A bed measuring between 6m/20ft x 7.5m/25ft and 6m/20ft x 15m/50ft will produce enough wheat to supply a family for a year.

SITE AND SOIL

Many gardeners prefer to spread plantings across different areas of the garden instead of planting wheat in one large block. Cultivate the bed just before sowing.

SOWING

Wheat should be sown directly in the garden, rather than transplanted. Broadcast seeds at the rate of 2kg per 100 sq. m/4lb per 1,000sq. ft. Soil should be very well prepared for an early harvest. Work lots of compost into the soil in order to increase fertility. Wheat can be broadly divided into winter and spring types. The winter types are sown in early to mid-autumn, allowed to overwinter and harvested in mid-summer of the following year. The spring types require less of a commitment, since they are sown and harvested in the same year. They should be sown during late winter or early spring, and if everything goes right, will be harvested later than winter wheat.

CARE AND MAINTENANCE

Keep weeds down in the early stages of crop establishment. Eventually, the leaves of the wheat will shade the ground enough to prevent further weed growth. Water regularly, especially when the grains are filling with starch.

Pests and diseases Wheat is vulnerable to a number of pests and diseases. There is, however, little that can be done to improve the situation, so it is best to just let nature takes its course.

HARVEST

Let the heads dry down on the plants. Then cut off the heads and place them on a flat surface. Walk across them with hard-soled shoes. Separate the seeds from the chaff by tossing up into the air in a light breeze or in front of a fan. The chaff will blow away, leaving behind the seeds for collection. If timely harvests are made, there is still an opportunity to sow an over-wintering crop of peas or broad beans. You can also slip in transplanted spring cabbages, or even a green manure.

VARIETIES

There are very few named wheat varieties available from seed catalogues, but it is not impossible to get appropriate seed. All it takes is a visit to a local organic cereal farmer. Most will be happy to supply your seed needs from a just-harvested crop. Good types to try are *Triticum durum*, a hard wheat used for pasta; and spelt, a nutritious hard wheat used in specialist breads.

Axona A spring wheat for bread.

Hereward A winter wheat popular with organic farmers and bakers.

If you have a generous-sized garden, you might consider growing a crop of wheat to provide you with sufficient grain for a weekly loaf of bread.

Sweetcorn *Zea mays*

Plant type Annual

Nutrition Significant source of vitamin B1.
Source of potassium.

Uses Eaten on the cob when freshly harvested.

SITE AND SOIL

Time the planting carefully because a cold soil
temperature is the most common cause of crop
failure. For direct seeded crops soil temperature
should be 10°C/50°F before sowing, so a sunny
site is important for an early crop. Choose a
location where tall plants will not throw shade
over other areas of the garden. Corn is shallow
rooted and grows best on well-drained soil with a
lot of nitrogen.

SOWING

Sow seeds 2.5cm/2in deep directly in the garden
when the soil is warm. Alternatively, start seeds in
pots, modules or blocks indoors. The corn plant
has two types of flowers: a male tassel at the top
of the plant that produces pollen; and a female ear
that grows from the stalk, bearing many strands
of silk. Each pollinated strand develops into a
single kernel. The wind blows pollen from the
tassels on to the silk of the ear, and the male
gametes travel down the silk into the ear to
pollinate it.

It is best to grow sweetcorn in a block of at
least four rows wide, with plants spaced about
30cm apart in rows spaced 30cm/12in apart.

CARE AND MAINTENANCE

Weed regularly until the corn is established.
Watering is unnecessary except in severe drought.

Pests and diseases Frit flies are the main
problem with sweetcorn. They do not generally
cause any trouble after the seedlings reach the
five-to-six-leaf stage, so transplanting may be a
good control method. Watch out, too, for mice
eating the seeds.

HARVEST

Pick sweetcorn just before cooking to retain
maximum flavour. There are only two worthwhile
methods of storing sweetcorn: either freeze the
cobs or remove the kernels and bottle them.

VARIETIES

Sweetcorn varieties can be divided into three
broad types, based on the amount of sugar in the
kernels and the length of time their sweet taste is
maintained after harvest:

*When sweetcorn is ready for harvest, the plump
kernels will emit a milky-white fluid when
pressed gently.*

Normal sugary These are the least sweet varieties. Sugars are quickly converted to starch.

Sugary-enhanced These tend to be sweeter than the normal sugary types and maintain their sweet taste longer.

Supersweets Some supersweet varieties are the sweetest corns there are. The supersweets also keep their sweet taste the longest.

When growing more than one variety of sweetcorn, it is important to know which types they are. In the majority of cases, the seed catalogues clearly identify their varieties according to type, although there are, unfortunately, vexing exceptions. The significance of the types is based on a corn plant's propensity to cross-pollinate with its neighbour. If, for example, there are crosses between the supersweets and either the normal sugary or sugary-enhanced types, the kernels produced will be tough and starchy.

Strategies can be employed to reduce the chances of crossing, including the separation of types by at least 4.5m/15ft. The problem is not so serious with crosses between normal sugary and sugar-enhanced types, so no such separation is needed.

Sweetcorn must also be distanced from forage maize, and any popcorn and ornamental corn that may also be in the garden. Otherwise you will end up with less-than-sweet corn.

The monotony of the common yellow cobs is broken up by all-white as well as bicolour white and yellow varieties. To add some novelty, blues and reds have also been integrated into sweetcorn's colour scheme.

Though the majority of sweetcorns available in the catalogues are hybrids, there are some notable open-pollinated varieties. Some seeds are organically produced, but most come from conventional sources. When buying conventional seed, be careful, since some varieties are treated with fungicides and insectides.

To enjoy sweetcorn at its best, eat as soon as possible after harvest; otherwise the sugars quickly convert to starch.

NORMAL SUGARY VARIETIES

Country Gentleman Open pollinated, white. Separate from yellow and bicolour varieties to prevent yellow kernels developing in the cob.

Double Standard Open pollinated, bicolour.

Golden Bantam Open pollinated, yellow.

Jubilee Hybrid, yellow.

Kelvedon Glory Hybrid, yellow.

SUGARY-ENHANCED VARIETIES

Ambrosia Middle-maturing bicolour.

Champ Early-maturing yellow.

Incredible Late-maturing yellow.

Tuxedo Middle-maturing yellow.

SUPERSWEET VARIETIES (ALL HYBRIDS)

Dickson Early-maturing yellow.

Fiesta Late-maturing yellow.

Beans (Various)

Plant type Annuals and perennials

Nutrition Excellent source of phytochemicals. Source of vitamins A, B1, B8 and C, calcium, phosphorus and iron.

Fresh beans are a significant source of vitamin C. Dried beans are a source of vitamins B1 and B2, calcium, sulphur and iron.

Uses The seed pods of French or runner beans are used fresh or preserved by freezing or, more rarely, bottling. Other beans are grown for their seeds, which are harvested dry or in the fresh-shelled stage.

SITE AND SOIL

Like other legumes, beans form a symbiotic relationship with soil bacteria that fix atmospheric nitrogen into a form that can be used by the plants. The process begins with the bacteria (called *Rhizobia*) infecting the bean roots. The infection then causes the roots to form nodules, which encapsulate the *Rhizobia* and protect them from the trials and tribulations of the outside world. Once the relationship is established, there is a give and take between the two parties: the beans supply life-sustaining carbohydrates to the bacteria, which then provide essential nitrogen to the beans.

If the relationship between beans and bacteria works out, the nitrogen fertility requirements of the soil will be low. However, you should choose a site with well-cultivated soil that has good drainage. Rotate crops to utilize the bean bed for a nitrogen-loving crop.

SOWING

In an ideal world, all legumes would naturally establish symbiotic relationships with nitrogen-fixing *Rhizobia*. For symbiosis to work, however,

different types of bean need specific types of *Rhizobia*.

For example, fortunately for UK gardeners, the right *Rhizobia* for broad beans are resident in British soils, so root infection, nodulation and nitrogen fixation proceed naturally once the seed is sown in the garden. However, broad bean *Rhizobia* cannot infect other beans, such as the French and runner types. Instead, these beans go symbiotic with their own specific *Rhizobia*, which do not usually live in British soils.

Not all, though, is lost. It seems that the *Rhizobia* can often sneak into the garden on the surface of the seeds, infecting the seedlings during germination and setting them up to fix nitrogen

For climbing beans, construct a framework of canes or horizontal and vertical twines along which the stems can be trained and supported.

Runner beans do very well in a temperate climate and grow on vines that can reach up to 4.2m/14ft and so should be restricted to an easily pickable height. They are usually harvested as the green tender pod, but they can also be harvested as fresh-shelled or even dry beans.

for the benefit of the plant. In older vegetable gardens where beans are grown every year, populations of these exotic *Rhizobia* might even get high enough in the soil to survive from one year to the next, infecting any bean plants that are grown there.

Since nodulation generally occurs early in the life of a bean, the nodules where the *Rhizobia* reside are usually found at the top of the roots. Fastidious gardeners worried about nitrogen fixation can check for the presence of nodules on their bean shoots by simply digging up a few plants and washing the soil from around their roots. To state the obvious, if there are no nodules, there is no nitrogen fixation. On the other hand, the presence of nodules is no guarantee of efficient nitrogen fixation. To check for this, cut the nodules in half. A pink colour means fixation is proceeding nicely, while a white one indicates poor nitrogen fixation.

Most beans are not hardy and will not germinate below 13°C/55°F, although broad beans are frost tolerant. Most types of beans are self-

pollinating. Sow tender types outside after all risk of frost has passed. Sow seeds 5cm/2in deep. For bush varieties, space 10–20cm/4–8in apart. For climbing beans, construct a bamboo teepee, a framework of netting or canes or, especially for runner beans, you can string twine between a brick placed on the ground and a hook placed in the wall on the side of a building. You need to be able to reach all sides of any structure in order to pick the beans. Climbing beans will usually grow to the full height of the support provided – runner beans can reach as high as 3.6–4.2m/12–14ft – so it is wise to keep the structure to a manageable height. Plant two or three seeds at the base of each string.

The flowers of runner beans look particularly attractive against a white or green background. With the right variety, broad beans may be planted in late autumn as long as the winter temperature stays above −12°C/10°F. This will result in a much earlier harvest the next year.

To bring French beans on a little sooner, sow the seeds earlier than you would an outdoor crop,

When trained on a teepee of canes, runner beans form a flowering pyramid that provides an attractive focal point for the vegetable plot.

and grow the plants in an unheated greenhouse or polytunnel. However, avoid the temptation to put runner beans inside: bees are necessary for pollination, and unless a hive is situated just outside the greenhouse or polytunnel you are unlikely to harvest any pods.

CARE AND MAINTENANCE

Consistent moisture is essential for a good harvest. Water regularly and copiously during dry periods. Weed as necessary, and consider applying a mulch around the plants to conserve moisture.
Pests and diseases Watch out for slugs and aphids. Prevention is the best solution to diseases. Rotate crops every year.

HARVEST

Begin harvesting the young tender pods of runner and French beans before they get too tough. Regular harvesting will encourage new pods to form. Some pods may have strings that must be removed before cooking: snap off both ends of the pod and pull the attached string, or cut along the sides with a sharp knife. To save seeds from these beans, leave a plant to mature to the dry seed stage, and harvest the seeds as described below for dry beans.

Fresh-shelled beans may be harvested when the seeds in the pods swell and look plump. Remove the pod from the plant, open it up and remove the soft seeds.

Dry beans are left to mature on the plant. When the pods are dry and brown, harvest dwarf or bush plants by cutting them off just above soil level. It may be necessary to complete drying indoors, in a warm, dry place. Pull up whole plants and hang them upside down, or pick the dried pods of climbing types and hang them in string bags. When they are completely dry, the pods may be opened by hand and the bean seeds removed. Alternatively, place the entire bunch of plants or quantities of pods in a sack, seal it with a tie, and then beat the sack vigorously to extract the seeds from the pods. The seeds will be at the bottom of the bag, the leaves and stems above. Separate out the seeds from the rest.

Soya beans are very easy to shell if you just boil them for a few minutes first. Quickly cool them in water, then pop the seeds out of the pod back into the pot for further cooking. Alternatively, after they have been shelled, they may be preserved by freezing. Some soya beans are grown for their dried beans.

FRENCH BEANS (*Phasaeolus vulgaris*)

Culinarily speaking, French beans are actually three vegetables in one. They can be harvested first as young, tender pods, which, if allowed to mature, will yield fresh-shelled beans that eventually metamorphose into dry beans. Though some varieties can serve in all three capacities, most are relegated to specific culinary roles.

The majority of French bean varieties are grown for their tender, immature pods. The pods vary in length and can be flat, round or oval-shaped in cross section. Colour varies with variety, and may be green, purple, yellow or even green with red streaks. The growth habits of the plants range from dwarf to climbing.

DWARF VARIETIES
Aramis Fine podded type with red flecks.
Arosa Early and heavy cropping, and suitable for greenhouse or outdoor cultivation. Resistant to mosaic virus.

Although the pods of dry beans are too fibrous to eat, the seeds are delicious. The seeds store well and are often made into wonderful soups.

Cropper Teepee Very heavy cropper which carries its pods high and proud.
Maxi Long pods with fine flavour. Grows well in poorer soils. Some resistance to mosaic virus.
Mont d'Or Broad, waxy golden pods.
Purple Queen (**Royalty**) Wonderful purple colour which unfortunately reverts to green when beans are cooked. Good flavour.
Sungold (formerly **Golden Sands**) Yellow waxy pod. Early and stringless.

CLIMBING VARIETIES
Blue Lake Probably the most popular climbing French bean. Very productive. Pods can be eaten green or seeds harvested for drying.
Farba Long round beans. Resistant to bean mosaic virus and happy in cooler situations.
Fortex Round green beans with good flavour.
Marvel of Venice Flat golden pods. Originates from Italy and prefers warmer situations.
Viola Cornetti Very pretty climbing bean with small purple flowers and purple pods.

FRESH SHELLING VARIETIES
Some varieties are particularly good for fresh shelling, and deserve a place in the garden. The pods can, of course, be left on the plant for harvesting as dried beans.
Pea Bean A climbing variety with delicious bi-coloured beans.
Chevrier Vert Dwarf plants producing mild-flavoured pale green beans.
Barlotto Lingua di Fuoco Climbing plants producing tasty white beans streaked with red.

DRYING VARIETIES
The following varieties are all dwarf, and are probably worth harvesting first as fresh shelled beans.
Brown Dutch Golden brown beans.
Canadian Wonder Though the pods can be eaten, the dry red beans may be better.

French beans, such as 'Purple Queen' (top) and pale yellow 'Mont d'Or' (bottom), are usually harvested young and eaten lightly cooked.

Horsehead Dark red beans.

Stop Red beans that retain their colour in the pot.

RUNNER BEANS (*Phaseolus coccineus*)

Runner beans are perennials that are grown as annuals, and do well in the British climate. The vines can grow to 4.2m/14ft so need to be trained on a manageable structure. They also tolerate some shade. Like French beans, runner beans can be harvested as green beans (the immature pod), as a fresh-shelled bean and finally as a dry bean. If the green pods are not continually picked, production will dwindle, and the remaining pods will quickly begin to mature. Runner beans are also admired for their attractive flowers, which are edible. Though not as popular as climbing types, dwarf varieties are available.

Czar An older white-seeded variety with excellent fresh shelling quality.

Desirée White flowers. Bears a heavy crop of handsome stringless beans with exceptionally good flavour.

Hammond Dwarf Scarlet A dwarf, bush type that needs no staking.

Hestia A dwarf variety with red and white flowers.

Kelvedon Marvel An early short-podded variety.

Painted Lady A Victorian variety with red-and-white flowers and beautifully coloured seeds. Very attractive, but perhaps not the best choice for flavour.

Red Knight Heavy crop of stringless beans. They have a good flavour and freeze well.

Scarlet Emperor Probably the best-known variety, dating from 1906. Red flowers and beans with good flavour.

Sunset An unusual variety with salmon-coloured flowers.

BROAD BEANS (*Vicia faba*)

These cool-season plants produce pods that can be eaten when very immature, but are more commonly picked at the fresh-shelled stage. They can also be harvested dry. Some varieties are very cold hardy and most can tolerate frost. Many varieties are quite venerable.

Aquadulce Claudia A very old variety and still the best for overwintering.

Bunyard's Exhibition A fine-flavoured long-pod variety, dating from 1884.

Futura An early variety with compact pods. Disease-resistant and suitable for overwintering.

Imperial Green Longpod Tall plants producing long pods.

Stereo A variety with small beans.

The Sutton Just about the only dwarf broad bean, growing to a mere 30cm/12in. Very hardy.

White Windsor A good variety, dating from 1895. Not hardy, so sow a little later than other varieties.

Hyacinth bean (*Lablab purpureus*)

This heat-loving climbing perennial, treated as an annual, may reach 6m/20ft, and has edible immature pods. The seeds are most often dried and cooked, or used for sprouting. Choosing a daylight-neutral type is important for this sub-tropical bean. Its attractive flowers add ornamental interest in the garden. Hyacinth beans may be started inside and transplanted. They may be listed in the catalogues as either 'lablab bean' or '*Dolichus lablab*'. If you cannot find them in the vegetable section of the seed catalogues, try looking in the flower section.

Ruby Moon A variety with decorative properties.

Soya bean (*Glycine max*)

Soya beans are often grown as fresh-shelling beans. Dried beans are also made into tofu. The young tender pods are often boiled and can be served as a delicious appetizer, with the beans being taken out and eaten. They are high in protein and provide good yields. They can be stored or frozen in the pods or shelled.

Envy A fresh-shelling variety that may be adapted to cool climates.

Blackjet A variety normally grown for its dried beans.

Yard-long beans (*Vigna sesquipedalis*)

This sub-tropical Oriental type has long pods that sometimes reach 75cm/30in long. Yields will be small in colder climate areas, so they are better grown in tall tunnels or greenhouses. The seed pods are harvested young and are blanched or stir fried.

Asparagus pea (*Tetragonolobus purpureus*)

The asparagus pea is not a pea at all. Rather, it is a four-sided bean sometimes known as the 'winged' bean because of the wings or fins that run lengthwise along the pods.

The whole pod is eaten, preferably when about 2.5cm/1in long. It really does taste quite similar to asparagus, and, like asparagus, is best steamed and served with butter so that its delicate flavour is not lost.

The plants grow well outside, although they are frost-sensitive.

Soya bean seeds (those of 'Blackjet', often grown for its dried beans, are shown above) are high in protein and provide good yields.

Peas *Pisum sativum*

Plant type Annual

Nutrition Excellent source of phytochemicals and vitamin C. Significant source of vitamin B1 and folic acid. Source of vitamin K, potassium and fibre.

Uses Peas can be eaten fresh or cooked. They are suitable for drying and are easy to freeze. Mangetouts and snap peas also have edible seed pods. Others are grown for their green shoots.

SITE AND SOIL

Peas do not require a high-nitrogen soil. Like beans, they form associations with specialized bacteria that collect atmospheric nitrogen and pass it on to the plants. As with broad beans, the correct type of bacteria exists in British soil. Peas are a cool-weather crop. They are usually sown in spring, but there are also varieties that can be sown in the autumn and overwintered for an early harvest. They should be protected with cloches if the weather turns cold. Choose a sunny site that has been deeply cultivated with a lot of low-nitrogen compost worked in. Peas will not tolerate either drought or wet soil, so while the soil should be kept moist, good drainage is essential. Peas, like beans, should be rotated every year. Prepare the site further by providing a fence or trellis for the peas to climb. Many gardeners use stakes, but it is better to build a simple frame of bamboo and tie twine across.

SOWING

As soon as the soil can be cultivated in early spring, sow in a wide band (twenty-four seeds per 30cm/12in), 2cm/¾in deep at the foot of the trellis.

The shelling pea 'Hurst Greenshaft' (right) has a good flavour and freezes well.

Germination will be poor until the soil has reached 10°C/50°F. Peas that are to be over-wintered can be sown in mid- or late autumn.

CARE AND MAINTENANCE

Peas, especially the taller varieties, need to be supported so they do not trail on the ground. Unless there is a lot of rain, you will need to water regularly. Mulch plants as they mature, to keep roots cool, retain moisture and control weeds.

Pests and diseases Prone to attack from birds, mice and slugs. Mildew and the pea moth can also cause problems.

HARVEST

Pea shoots may be harvested as needed. Harvest shelling types and open the pods to reveal lush green seeds, which may be used fresh or frozen. Spring-sown varieties are ready any time from eleven to sixteen weeks after sowing, depending on variety and the weather. The entire plant may also be harvested and hung in a warm place to dry for dried peas. Snap peas are typically harvested fresh and used immediately. They may also be shelled or they can be frozen in the pods. Mangetouts are used fresh or quickly blanched or sautéed; they do not keep well.

SHELLING PEA VARIETIES

Shelling peas are hardy. Some varieties can be sown in the autumn and overwintered for the earliest possible pea crop; however, these are less sweet than the spring-sown varieties.

Early Onward A spring-sown variety that matures early. Has medium-length stems.

Feltham First An autumn-sown variety, with short to medium-length stems.

Hurst Greenshaft A spring-sown variety with medium to long stems.

Meteor An autumn-sown variety. Short stems.

Pilot Very hardy, early with an extended cropping period.

Mangetout peas, such as 'Norli' (above), are best eaten raw or very lightly cooked. They may be a delicious addition to salads or stir-fries.

SNAP PEA VARIETIES

These have edible pods and big seeds. When cooking snap peas, remove strings first.

Sugar Rae Dwarfer habit than 'Sugar Snap', but yields less.

Sugar Snap High-yielding, tall-growing variety.

MANGETOUT VARIETIES

Also known as snow peas, these are harvested for their edible pods when the seeds are very small. Remove the strings before eating.

Carouby de Mausanne Tall, needing good support. Purple flowers and large broad pods.

Norli (Sugar Dwarf Sweet Green) Small pods and a dwarf habit. The genuine mangetout.

Oregon Sugar Pod Superb flavour.

Onions *Allium cepa*

Plant type Biennial

Nutrition Excellent source of phytochemicals. Significant source of vitamin C. Source of vitamin A, calcium, iron, potassium and fibre. Shallots are an excellent source of phytochemicals, and a source of vitamins A and C, calcium and iron.

Uses May be eaten raw or cooked.

SITE AND SOIL

Onions prefer a well-drained rich soil with lots of compost worked in, a pH over 6.5 and an open sunny site. They have low nitrogen requirements, so do not plant on freshly manured ground.

SOWING

Onions are cool-weather plants that grow best below 24°C/75°F. They require a long growing season to produce large bulbs for storage, but most may be harvested in an immature state. While sets are planted directly in the garden as soon as the soil can be worked, it is best to start sowing indoors to achieve good results with seed.

One method that works particularly well is to plant three or four seeds in each soil block. As the bulbs mature, they push each other aside gently without getting damaged. By this method, four times more onions can be started from seed indoors without taking up any more space or requiring any additional effort. All the onions planted together should be harvested together. Sow in late winter to early spring indoors, and transplant out as soon as the soil can be worked.

Plant the seedling groups 15cm/6in apart. In long-season areas, sow directly in the garden, 1cm/½in apart and 0.5cm/¼in deep, as soon as the soil can be worked. Thin to 8cm/3in spacing by harvesting some of the seedlings.

Some varieties grow best when sown in late summer for an early harvest the next year.

CARE AND MAINTENANCE

Water regularly. Onions have shallow roots and require well-drained soil. They need a lot of water, either by rain or by irrigation. Keep them well weeded, especially just after transplanting.

Pests and diseases Onion fly maggots, downy mildew, thrips, and onion white rot are the most common problems. If maggots attack the onions, practise companion planting (see pp. 118–19). (If you introduce a few onion plants randomly throughout the garden, they will also deter pests from affecting other plants.)

HARVEST

Start harvesting for immediate use as they mature. Storage varieties should be left in the ground until

Once they have been harvested, dry onions in the sun for about ten days, ensuring good ventilation by laying them on a raised wire screen.

the leaves die in the autumn. Pull or lift the onions using a garden fork. Dry, preferably in the sun, until the leaves rustle and become papery. When drying inside, make sure there is good ventilation. Do not let dried onions come into contact with wet soil or water. Store onions at 0–5°C/32–42°F at low humidity. A cool upstairs room or attic or a garden shed makes a good choice. Check stored onions regularly for neck rot; use affected onions immediately.

RED-SKINNED BULBING VARIETIES
Long Red Florence Mild flavour. Its long torpedo shape makes for easy slicing.
Red Baron Usually available as sets. It has an excellent flavour.
Red Brunswick Mild flavour, good for salads. Sow in mid-spring to avoid bolting.

YELLOW- AND BROWN-SKINNED BULBING VARIETIES
Buffalo Hybrid that works for both a spring and a late summer sowing.
Golden Bear Very early to mature. Highly tolerant of downy mildew, botrytis and white rot.
Robusta A reliable cropper of good quality. Stores well.
Senshyu Yellow An open-pollinated variety for late summer sowing.

PICKLING ONION VARIETIES
Some cultivars are best when harvested at about 2.5cm/1in in diameter. Preserve these onions by freezing or pickling. Sow directly in the garden at high density.
Paris Silverskin Tiny white onions ideal for cooking whole or pickling. They ripen early.
Purplette Red skin, white flesh. Young bulbs are delicious in salads.

CHIVES (*A. schoenoprasum*)
These perennials are grown for their round

Onion tops are bent over in the autumn to help cure them before harvesting and storage. If you store onions properly, you can be sure of a year-round supply.

hollow grass-like tops. They have pinkish-purple blossoms that also make them a good choice for the ornamental garden. Soil requirements are the same as for storage onions. Chives can be grown from seed or divided from an existing patch. Once planted, chives generally spread and make an edible attraction in the garden. Once harvested, they can be cut up with scissors and used in salads or as a garnish.

EGYPTIAN TOP ONION
These perennial onions produce a small bulb at the tip of their stems, above ground, where a flower might typically form. They are usually

sown in the autumn directly in the garden. They may be harvested as salad onions in the spring, but starting in mid-summer and extending well into autumn, the bulbs can be harvested. Pick when the tops begin to dry. Store by freezing. Cultivate in the same way as onions.

SALAD ONIONS/SPRING ONIONS/SCALLIONS
(*A. cepa* and *A. fistulosum*)
Many of these are bulb onions sown close together and harvested before the bulbs get too big. Some salad onions, however, are perennials grown only for their greens – the Welsh onion (*A. fistulosum*) is a common example. Cultivation is identical to that of onions, above.

Guardsman Tender, with a slightly sweet flavour.

Ishikura A perennial type producing stems with very little, if any, bulbing. Left to their own devices, individual plants will keep on growing to form multi-stemmed clumps.

Redmate Normally grown for its bulbs, but excellent as a salad onion when young.

White Lisbon Very popular and widely used. Can be grown successionally.

White Lisbon Winter Hardy Sow in autumn for a very early crop. Very hardy.

SHALLOTS
Individual plants of this distinctively flavoured vegetable may form multiple bulbs attached to each other at the base. They are eaten raw or cooked and add a flavour that is much milder and more delicate than that of standard onions. The greens may also be harvested as spring onions for salads. The multi-bulbs can be broken apart into separate 'sets' and planted in the spring to produce next year's crop. Some varieties can also be started from seed.

Ambition A good hybrid produced from seed.

Longer Elongated bulbs produced from sets.

Matador A white-fleshed hybrid produced from seed.

Mikor Somewhat elongated bulbs started from sets.

Shallots are eaten raw or used in cooking to add a distinctive garlic-onion flavour that is much milder than that of standard onions.

Leeks *Allium porrum*

Plant type Biennial
Nutrition Significant source of vitamin C.
Uses Leeks have a delicate onion flavour and are particularly good in soups for a creamy texture.

SITE AND SOIL

Choose an open site and work compost into the soil to increase its moisture-holding ability. A deeply cultivated soil with high nitrogen levels is required. Work fresh manure into the soil three weeks before transplanting. Do not let leeks dry out in high temperatures.

SOWING

Leeks can be sown outdoors from early to late spring. A preferable alternative is to start seeds indoors in late winter. Sow two to four seeds in each module of a module tray or in 5cm/2in soil blocks, and space the blocks 5cm/2in apart. Transplant when the seedlings reach 20cm/8in high; allow 18cm/9in between transplanted modules or soil blocks. Place each module or soil block in a 15cm/6in deep hole in the bed and gently fill soil around the stem, leaving about 5cm/2in of the plant visible above the soil.

CARE AND MAINTENANCE

Water around the seedlings and firm the soil against them gently after transplanting outdoors. This will help to blanch the stems. Leeks need regular and thorough watering until they are well established. Do not let the soil dry out during summer droughts, and keep the bed free of weeds by weeding regularly. Mulch to discourage weeds and retain moisture.
Pests and diseases Onion fly maggots, white rot and rust can be problems, as can leek moths, and a range of soil-borne mildew and fungus diseases.

HARVEST

Leeks taste best after a light frost, but may be harvested as baby leeks within a couple of months of sowing.

VARIETIES

Alvito Late. Highly resistant to bolting and rust.
Bleu de Solaise French heirloom with blue leaves that stores well through the winter in the ground.
King Richard Large, long plant of superb quality.
Monstruoso di Carentan Fat early leek for havesting until mid-winter.
Musselburgh A hardy variety.

Leek stems can be blanched by planting the seedlings deeply and ridging up the soil during the growing season. 'Monstruoso de Carentan' is shown above.

Garlic *Allium sativum*

Plant type Perennial

Nutrition Excellent source of phytochemicals. Source of vitamins A and C, calcium and iron.

Uses Grown for its bulb-like root. The green chive-like stems are tasty eaten fresh.

SITE AND SOIL

Choose a site with full sun and dig in compost. Good drainage is essential. Garlic tolerates a wide range of temperatures, but requires a cool period below 10°C/50°F for at least one month.

PLANTING

Separate the head into cloves. Either during the late autumn or in late winter to early spring, plant cloves with the pointed end up, and the root (flat base end) down, 15cm/6in apart and 5cm/2in deep.

CARE AND MAINTENANCE

Little attention is needed in the growing season. If a plant attempts to flower, pinch off the shoot. Water during the bulb-forming stage if rain is in short supply. As the bulb grows, it will push upwards and out of the ground. Weed the bed regularly.

Pests and diseases Garlic is very hardy, with few diseases and pests. Watch for onion maggots, downy mildew and onion white rot.

HARVEST

Bulbs should be ready for harvesting about midsummer. When the leaves start to die back and turn brown, lift the bulbs with a garden fork. Be careful not to damage the outer wrapping around the cloves. You can leave the plants in the ground for longer to increase size, but do not let them start sprouting. Dry bulbs well in a dark, dry place with good air circulation. Trim the roots after drying. The necks can be braided and hung for storage or decoration. Garlic stores best at 4°–10°C/40–50°F.

VARIETIES

Christo A popular variety that produces good yields.

Elephant Garlic Actually a type of leek producing large, mild-flavoured cloves. Worth a try.

Moraluz Produces attractive red-skinned cloves. It will send out flower stalks, which should be pinched out.

Printanor Suitable for later plantings.

Russian Red A very hardy and flavourful type. A favourite of garlic connoisseurs.

Thermidrome Early and reliable. Suitable for cooler climates.

When you find a variety of garlic that you like and that grows well in your garden, separate the heads and replant the cloves.

Asparagus *Asparagus officinalis*

Plant type Perennial

Nutrition Excellent source of phytochemicals and folic acid. Significant source of vitamins B1, B6 and C. Source of potassium, fibre, calcium and iron.

Uses Tasty, tender shoots are eaten cooked.

SITE AND SOIL

Choose a sunny or partially shaded spot with good drainage. Dig a trench 30–45cm/12–18in wide and 30cm/12in deep. Using a garden fork, loosen the soil at the bottom of the hole. Add 5–8cm/2–3in of leaf mould, then 2.5–5cm/1–2in of the topsoil. Dust heavily with rock phosphate. With the fork, mix the compost, leaf mould and rock phosphate. Then add 2.5cm/1in of compost and the same of topsoil and mix again. Every 45cm/18in, mound up the soil 5cm/2in high.

SOWING AND PLANTING

Though some varieties are available as seed, it is generally easier to start asparagus from crowns. Prune any damaged roots, and soak the crowns in warm (35°C/95°F) water. Place a crown on each mound of soil and spread the roots evenly around. Cover with 5–8cm/2–3in of compost and gently pack down. Fill in with some of the remaining soil. Leave the remainder piled next to the trench.

CARE AND MAINTENANCE

During the first year, leave the asparagus to develop its root system. Weed carefully around the growing stems, but do not harvest any. As the shoots grow, fill around them carefully, using all the soil from the pile next to the trench, until the soil is slightly mounded. Water regularly and mulch well. Cut back the ferns in the autumn.

Pests and Diseases Rust, slugs, asparagus beetles.

Asparagus is prized for the tender shoots that appear in spring. Male and female plants are available, but the male plants are more productive.

HARVEST

Starting in the second or third year, cut small shoots in mid- to late spring. Always leave a few shoots to mature, and do not overharvest in the first three years. To harvest, bend a spear until it snaps, or use an asparagus knife to cut off the shoot below soil level.

VARIETIES

Connover's Colossal Available as seed and crowns. An old variety with a long life expectancy.

Franklin Also available as seed and crowns. Early cropping and good quality.

Buckwheat *Fagopyrum esculentum*

Plant type Annual

Uses Grain is cooked or ground. Good for use as a green manure. Buckwheat attracts bees and other beneficial insects to the garden.

To grow as a green manure (see pp. 57–61), turn the earth just before sowing. Doing this disturbs weed seeds so that they do not have a competitive advantage over the buckwheat. Sow the buckwheat on the surface of the soil during the spring, summer and early autumn.

Buckwheat will not tolerate frost and needs thirty days to reach a useful state for green manure. Sowing may be accomplished by hand or with a simple hand-powered broadcast seeder, depending on the size of the plot. Rake gently over the plot if it is small or, if large, drag a dead tree branch over it to slightly cover the seed. If there is no rain forecast for the next week, irrigate copiously from an overhead sprinkler. Otherwise, do not weed or water (unless absolutely necessary); simply watch it grow. After the white or pink flowers form, turn the greens under and cultivate the soil.

To grow for a crop of grain, follow the instructions given above, but rather than turn the greens into the soil let the flowers go to seed. The seed should be hard and dry, but not so dry that it falls off the plants when touched. Harvest the entire plant.

The grain may be thrashed with a flail the traditional way, or small harvests may be placed in a pillowcase or sack and beaten to separate the chaff from the seed. Leave the seed in a warm place to finish drying. It may then be stored for a very long time at room temperature. Grind or cook buckwheat according to use.

Buckwheat matures so quickly that three successive crops can be grown in a season to increase soil fertility. It attracts bees and other beneficial insects to the garden.

Rhubarb *Rheum x hybridum*

Plant type Perennial
Nutrition Source of vitamin C, calcium and fibre.
Uses The stems are eaten cooked.

SITE AND SOIL

Choose a site that is sunny and has good drainage. It is essential to spend a lot of time preparing the soil so that the rhubarb will produce a good harvest for the next twenty to forty years. The extra effort spent now will pay off with many years of bountiful harvests. Dig holes 90cm/36in apart. The holes should be very large, up to 90cm/36in in diameter. This may seem excessive but it is worthwhile. The removed soil should be mixed with compost at a ratio of two parts soil to one part compost. Backfill the hole, leaving a 30cm/12in diameter hole that is 5cm/2in deep. Rhubarb is hard to grow in very warm climates.

SOWING

Instead of buying rhubarb seed, it is much better to buy crowns. Plant one crown in each prepared hole and fill around it with soil. Press gently to ensure good contact between the soil and the roots. Water generously after planting.

CARE AND MAINTENANCE

After the plants begin growing, apply a thick mulch to conserve moisture and discourage weeds. Over the years, adding a little compost followed by mulch will continue to feed the rhubarb and ensure a good harvest. The soil must not dry out, even when the plants are dormant. When flower stalks appear, remove them before bloom to encourage leaf stalk production. If a plant should become crowded with many small stalks, dig up the plant and divide it into two or three plants and replant as described above.

Rhubarb (including 'Champagne Early', above) is among the earliest of crops. Its tasty stems may be harvested from late winter through to summer.

Pests and diseases Rhubarb is not much afflicted by either pests or diseases, though if either verticillum or crown should occur, you should destroy the entire patch and start again elsewhere in the garden. The biggest problem will be perennial weeds, which can overwhelm a patch.

HARVEST

Starting the second year, harvest the stems from late winter through to summer. Twist and pull the stems when the leaves are fully developed.

VARIETIES

Champagne Early Very early with good flavour.
Glaskin's Perpetual Reliable. Quick to establish – allows cutting in first year.
Victoria An excellent variety. The stems never become woody.

Peppers *Capsicum* spp.

Plant type Perennial, grown as annual
Nutrition Sweet peppers are an excellent source of phytochemicals and vitamin C. Hot peppers are also an excellent source of phytochemicals. Both types are sources of vitamin A, potassium and iron.
Uses Hot peppers add spiciness to dishes; sweet peppers are eaten fresh or cooked.

SITE AND SOIL

Unless you have a very sheltered, sunny site, grow peppers in a greenhouse or polythene tunnel. Do not rotate with other members of this family. Work a lot of compost into the soil and ensure good drainage.

SOWING

Start seeds indoors six to eight weeks before transplanting. Some chilli peppers can be started earlier, about twelve weeks before transplanting in mid-spring. Pepper seedlings are very sensitive to their roots being disturbed. They may also suffer from damping off; therefore it is best to bottom-water them. Start seedlings in 5cm/2in soil blocks. Seeds germinate best at 24°C/75°F. Sow two seeds to each block and cut the stem of the weaker seedling when two leaves develop. Reduce the temperature to below 21°C/70°F after germination. Transfer the seedlings into 10cm/4in pots if necessary before transplanting into a tunnel or greenhouse in mid- to late spring. Space the plants 45–60cm/18–24in apart, depending on variety.

CARE AND MAINTENANCE

It is essential to make sure the plants are shielded from wind. All peppers grow as bushes, and small varieties do not need staking. However, most of those grown in temperate climates need support as the weight of the fruit may snap the brittle branches. Consistent moisture is essential to produce good sweet peppers. Hot peppers generally require more water, but any dry spells will usually result in much a hotter flavour. Water generously if there is insufficient rainfall. Weed as necessary. Apply a medium-strength nitrogen organic liquid fertilizer if the plants show little growth.

Pests and diseases Aphids, whiteflies, caterpillars and spider mites may cause problems.

Available in a wide range of bold colours and shapes, the fruits of sweet peppers are grown for their crisp, mild-tasting flesh.

If the site does not have good drainage, root rot may also be a problem. Calcium deficiency may result in blossom end rot. Cutworms may be a problem for seedlings. Be on the alert and if you come across them, destroy them.

HARVEST

There are numerous variables affecting the time of the first harvest, including weather, personal preference and variety. Hot peppers may be stored by drying, or making them into a liquid sauce. They do not store well fresh. Both sweet and hot peppers are best used fresh but may be refrigerated for up to three weeks. They can be frozen as well as bottled.

You can save seeds from ripe fruits; when saving sweet pepper seeds be sure to choose fruits from plants that were not grown near hotter varieties; otherwise, there is a danger of cross-pollination, which could make the next generation of sweet peppers hotter.

HOT PEPPER VARIETIES

These are the most ornamental types of pepper.

Anaheim Mildly hot pepper with long fruits.

Early Jalapeno Popular in Mexican dishes.

Habanero An ultra-hot pepper that dries well and is commonly used in Jamaican 'jerk' sauces.

Heatwave Fruits in red, yellow and orange. Pretty plants that pack a hefty punch in flavour.

Hero Virus-resistant and tolerant of lower temperatures. Thick fleshed.

Hungarian Yellow Wax Produces fairly hot yellow banana-shaped fruits.

Long Slim Cayenne type. Best variety for drying and grinding into a red pepper powder.

Prairie Fire Definitely hot, producing a prolific crop of tiny attractive fruits.

SWEET PEPPER VARIETIES

Big Bertha Very large tapered fruits up to 25cm/10in long. Very early.

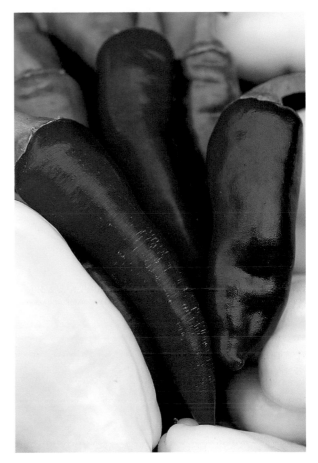

Hot peppers such as 'Long Slim' (above) are also ornamental, so even if you find them too hot to eat you could grow them for their decorative qualities.

Carnival Multicoloured fruits with fleshy walls.

Corno di Toro Red and yellow varieties with a long curved shape.

Gypsy Very heavy crops of good-sized red fruits. Resistant to tobacco mosaic virus.

Islander Excellent lavender pepper that grows well under adverse conditions.

Jingle Bells A bright red diminutive variety.

Long Yellow Ringo Long tapered fruits, coloured yellow when ripe.

Mandy Fruits green turning red. Early to mature. Resistant to mosaic virus.

Redskin Compact and early. Suitable for a sunny windowsill or patio plot.

Tomatoes *Lycopersicon esculentum*

Plant type Perennial grown as annual

Nutrition Excellent source of phytochemicals and vitamin C. Significant source of vitamin A. Source of potassium and iron.

Uses Fruits are eaten fresh in salads, or used for sauces, soups and casseroles. Leaves are toxic.

SITE AND SOIL

Tomatoes prefer a very sunny site with rich fertile soil. They are best grown in the same site every year, fed with a compost made mostly of tomato vines and leaves. Do not plant tomatoes near any black walnut trees, the roots of which release a chemical that retards the growth of tomato plants.

SOWING

Sow seeds indoors no earlier than six to eight weeks before transplanting; otherwise the seedlings will be rootbound and leggy. They are also prone to damping off, so water them from the bottom only. Using modular trays or 5cm/2in soil blocks, sow two seeds to each block and cut the stem of the weaker seedling when they develop two leaves. Seeds germinate best at 27°C/80°F. After germination, reduce the temperature to below 21°C/70°F. Transfer the seedlings to 10cm/4in pots if necessary.

Tomatoes can be grown either in the open or indoors. Outdoors types should be hardened off and then transplanted in late spring or early summer, spaced 30–60cm/12–24in apart, depending on the variety, and shielded from the wind. Indoor ones can go into cold tunnels or greenhouses in late spring.

Tomatoes vary greatly in shape and colour. This mixed basket includes 'Auriga', 'Sweet Million', 'Sungold' and green-striped 'Zebra'.

CARE AND MAINTENANCE

Tomato varieties display extremes in growth habit, from tall indeterminate giants to determinate, bush-like dwarves. Tall varieties, which can reach heights of 2m/7ft, need to be trained off the ground (cordoned) by staking, trellising or growing up strings. The side-shoots or suckers growing between the main stem and the leaves need to be pinched out or pruned. The best time to do this is when the suckers are 5–8cm/2–3in long. In late summer, prune back the top of the main stem to stop new growth and help mature any unripe fruit before cold weather sets in. The smaller bush varieties need neither pinching out nor staking up. They are ideal for the laid-back gardener, though yields may be lower than they are for their taller counterparts.

Tomatoes are perennials in very warm climates but are grown as annuals elsewhere. Varieties range from large beefsteaks to the small cherry types shown here.

To avoid diseases indoors, water the root area only and do not irrigate from above. Apply a thick mulch to both indoor and outdoor crops to retain moisture and suppress weeds. Overwatering after a period of water deprivation can cause the fruit to split, so a constant moisture supply is essential. **Pests and diseases** Aphids, whitefly and red spider mites can be infrequent problems. Late blight, which also affects potatoes, can infect the leaves, stems and fruits. It can be controlled with traditional copper-based fungicides, though the fruits may be left with a blue tinge. Blossom end rot, caused by a calcium deficiency results in blackened depressions on the fruit. More prevalent in varieties of processing tomatoes, it does not appear in later maturing fruit.

HARVEST

Pick tomatoes as they ripen. Indoor cherry tomatoes are the first to bear fruit, whereas long-vine types take longer. Tomatoes do not refrigerate well. Use fresh or store them by drying. In the autumn, green tomatoes may be harvested for use straightaway, or the entire plant may be removed and hung in a warm place to encourage the green fruit to ripen.

CORDON (INDETERMINATE) VARIETIES

Ailsa Craig Scottish variety of excellent flavour.
Alicante Early, reliable and good flavour.
Auriga Well-flavoured variety, high in carotene.
Black Krym Grown for its dramatic appearance.
Gardener's Delight An old favourite cherry tomato with long trusses of sweet red tomatoes.
Green Grape Tiny cherry tomatoes in long trusses. Very sweet. Ripens to green-yellow colour.
Sungold F1 hybrid with very good flavour. For indoor or outdoor growing.
Sweet Million Good climbing cherry variety.
Wonder Light Bears lemon-shaped fruit.
Zebra Productive beefsteak variety.

BUSH (DETERMINATE) VARIETIES

Carefree Very long season of cropping, needing little management. Copious crops of little fruits.
Red Alert Early to mature and heavy cropping.
Tornado Crops over a long period.
Tumbler Trailing; suitable for container growing.

The shapes and forms of tomatoes vary greatly. 'Black Krym' (back of picture) is as spectacular in appearance as it is mild in flavour. 'Wonder Light' (foreground) has curious lemon-shaped fruit.

Aubergines *Solanum melongena*

Plant type Perennial grown as annual
Nutrition Source of vitamin C, iron, potassium and fibre.
Uses Colourful fruits provide ornamental interest. Serve cooked.

SITE AND SOIL
Aubergines do best indoors, producing excellent crops in cold greenhouses and tunnels. Add lots of compost to the soil.

SOWING
Soak the seeds in water for twenty-four hours to encourage germination. Start seeds in a slightly acidic compost (pH 6.0). Transplant to 8–10cm/3–4in pots when they get large. Plant them 45cm/18in apart in late spring.

CARE AND MAINTENANCE
Mulch and keep well watered. Weed as necessary until plants are established. For large fruits, limit the number of fruits to six per plant.

Pests and diseases Aphids and red spider mites are the worst enemies.

HARVEST
Begin harvesting in mid-summer. Using pruners, remove fruit from the stem. Picking regularly will encourage production. Storage is possible for a few weeks at high humidity around 13°C/55°F.

VARIETIES
Bonica Oval purple-skinned variety with good flavour and chewy texture.
Kermit Round variety with green and white fruit.
Louisiana Long Green Beautiful long green fruit.
Machian Long thin pinkish fruits that are tender and delicious.
Moneymaker Large purple variety that dependably produces in cold tunnels and greenhouses.
Snowy Elongated white fruit.

The white and light purple varieties of aubergine tend to be less bitter than the dark purple varieties.

Potatoes *Solanum tuberosum*

Plant type Perennial

Nutrition Excellent source of vitamin C. Significant source of vitamins B3 and B6, and iodine. Source of potassium and fibre. The only commonly available source of B3 and iodine.

Uses Cooked in a variety of ways, eaten hot or cold. Suitable for storing during winter.

SITE AND SOIL

Potatoes need fertile well-drained soil. Choose a sunny spot and work plenty of compost into the soil. Potatoes will tolerate a wide range of soils but they grow best where the soil is cultivated deeply and has a pH of 5–6. Potatoes are subject to soilborne diseases so it is essential to rotate them each year.

PLANTING

It is possible to grow potatoes from seed, but the results are most often unsatisfactory. The best way is to buy 'double certified' seed potatoes. This means that they are certified to be organically grown as well as disease and virus free. After the first year's crop, save some in a cool dark frost-free place to plant out the next spring.

To help the crop along, the seed potatoes (which are actually small tubers) should be chitted, or pre-sprouted before planting. This is done by standing the seeds in trays in a cool dry place that is light; avoid placing the trays in direct sunlight. Make sure the seeds are upright, putting on top that end of the tuber with the highest concentration of buds. The buds will sprout in a month or so and the potatoes will be ready for planting.

Potatoes are divided into first early, second early and maincrop varieties. First earlies can go into the ground in mid-spring, while second early and maincrop plantings should be delayed until late spring. The sprouted end of the tuber should be upright, while the planting should be deep enough to cover both the tuber and sprouts with about 2.5cm/1in of soil. Plant early varieties about 40cm/16in apart. Main croppers can be planted 40cm/16in apart in rows 75cm/30in apart.

CARE AND MAINTENANCE

If you think the early potatoes may be hit by frost, try throwing a little soil over the new growth. As the potatoes grow, weed as necessary. When the plants reach about 30cm/12in, hoe up the soil around the bases of the plants to a height of 15cm/

Potato cultivars range in colour from red and pink, as in 'Red Duke of York' (above), through white to blue. A mixture will make a striking display at your table.

6in. Do this very gently so as not to disturb the roots or any tubers that may be forming. After earthing up, apply a 2.5cm/1in mulch of straw or hay to deter weeds and conserve moisture. If the soil is not earthed up around the bases of the plants, the potatoes may become visible and exposed to daylight. When this happens, the potatoes develop a greenish tinge; this area is toxic and the tuber should be discarded. During dry spells, water at a rate of 5cm/2in a week.

Pests and diseases There are many diseases that affect potatoes and rotation is the best solution. Ensure the bed has well-drained soil and plant only certified disease- and virus-free seed potatoes. Diseases to watch out for are blackleg, potato blight, virus and scab. Pests that may affect potatoes are slugs and eelworms.

Hollow areas in tubers are caused by excessively rapid growth. To combat this, reduce watering and do not feed with any high nitrogen fertilizers.

HARVEST

First and second early varieties can be harvested as 'new' potatoes, before the skins have set. Second earlies can also be left to mature and then stored. Maincrop potatoes are ready for harvest in September to October. Cut the stems off above the ground and let the potatoes remain in the soil for a week or two before lifting them with a garden fork. This will harden the skins of the potatoes and make it much easier for you to harvest them without damaging the skins.

Harvest potatoes on a dry sunny day. Let them rest in the sun for an hour or two before storing them in a cool frost-free place. It is essential that they do not freeze while in storage; otherwise they will spoil. Save some of the potatoes from the harvest to use in next year's planting. To avoid ring rot, which may attack stored crops, only store good healthy tubers. Make sure the storage place is clean.

FIRST EARLY VARIETIES
Arran Pilot Good flavour and disease resistance.
Duke of York Good quality, but prone to blight.
Red Duke of York Attractive red version of above.

SECOND EARLY VARIETIES
Estima High-yielding, good blight resistance.
Wilja Good yield, versatile cooking qualities.

MAINCROP VARIETIES
Desiree High-yielding, pink-skinned variety.
King Edward Moderate yields, high-quality tubers.
Pink Fir Apple The ideal salad potato.
Sante A choice variety for the organic gardener.

Choose 'double certified' seed potatoes, which are guaranteed to be both organic and free from viruses and diseases.

Celery *Apium graveolens*

Plant type Biennial

Nutrition Significant source of vitamin C and folic acid. Source of potassium and fibre.

Uses The stalks are usually eaten fresh or used in soups and stews. The leaves are typically used to flavour broth or are composted.

SITE AND SOIL

Choose a site that is not near parsnips as both crops may be attacked by celery flies. Rotating celery in the garden will discourage diseases and pests. Improve the soil's moisture-retaining ability by working in plenty of organic compost. Some varieties of celery need to be planted in trenches to blanch the stems. Prepare a trench measuring 28cm/11in deep and slightly more than 30cm/12in wide. Fill the bottom of the trench with a 5cm/2in layer of compost.

SOWING

Sow indoors in late winter with heat in seedtrays. Do not allow any checks to growth or plants will bolt. Plant out after all danger of frost is over, as the plants are likely to bolt if temperatures drop below 10°C/50°F. To blanch traditional celery, either plant in trenches (see opposite), or wrap the stems loosely with heavy paper, such as corrugated cardboard or brown parcel paper or several layers of newspaper.

CARE AND MAINTENANCE

Celery requires constant moisture. Water the plants regularly during drought at a rate of 2.5cm/1in per week. An organic liquid fertilizer applied one month after germination will be beneficial. Self-blanching varieties should be mulched with a thick layer of straw which will help to retain moisture in the soil.

Traditional celery has white, pink or red stems that are blanched. Typical American varieties have green stems and are not blanched.

Pests and diseases Celery flies and slugs may affect the crop. Fungal leaf spots may occur in younger plants. Remove all infected leaves immediately, including those that are on the ground, and compost them.

HARVEST

Using a garden fork, lift self-blanching varieties

and paper-wrapped varieties before the first frosts. Store in a high-humidity location that is cool but protected from freezing. If the celery is planted in a trench, its harvest season is extended well into the winter. To store for harvest through the winter and spring, build a straw or hay bale house over the trenched plants. Put a bale at each end of the row, and bales along both sides. Fill the gap above the plants with loose hay or straw, cover with boards and sit bales on top of the boards. Celery may be stored in the refrigerator for five weeks if kept slightly moist.

TRENCH VARIETIES

Traditional celery has white, pink or red stems that are blanched. The red stem varieties have the best taste and hardiness, but require blanching to ensure protection from sunlight. Planting in a trench works best, but is the most labour intensive. Tie together the stems loosely with twine and fill in the trench gradually as the plants grow. When the trench is filled with earth, you may need to add a collar of paper, or better yet heap up the soil to form a mound around the growing plants.

Giant Red Stalks have a pinkish tinge.

Giant White Creamy white stalks.

Hopkin's Fenlander Good-flavoured white variety.

Solid Pink An 1894 variety which will stand the early frosts but not survive over winter.

Solid White Even older than 'Solid Pink' and still a fine variety.

SELF-BLANCHING VARIETIES

Typical North American varieties have green stems and are not blanched.

Celebrity Vigorous and bolt-resistant; one of the least stringy varieties.

Gigante Dorato 2 (Golden Self-blanching) Matures early and is popular with gardeners.

Latham (Latham Self-blanching) A wonderfully tasty variety with yellow stems.

Tall Utah Flavoursome variety.

Victoria Green sticks of good flavour. Earlier than most.

HOW TO BLANCH CELERY

1 Dig a trench one spade deep and 30cm/12in wide. Line the bottom with 5cm/2in of compost. Plant seedlings 23–30cm/9–12in apart, or sow seeds directly.

2 In mid-summer, bundle plants together, wrap with thick paper and fill soil around stalks to the bottom of the leaves. This is done to blanch most varieties.

3 As the plants grow, mound up the soil every few weeks. Always leave the foliage visible above the soil. Slope the soil away from the plants to drain off rain.

Carrots *Daucus carota*

Plant type Biennial grown as an annual
Nutrition Excellent source of phytochemicals and vitamin A. Source of vitamins C, D, E and K, and B vitamins and potassium.
Uses Roots are eaten fresh in salads or cooked.

SITE AND SOIL
Carrots prefer deeply cultivated soil that is loose and sandy. Heavy soils may create oddly shaped roots that are more difficult to harvest, though you may be able to get round this problem if you choose the right variety.

SOWING
Directly sow in garden beds in closely spaced rows about 2.5cm/1in apart. You can begin sowing in early spring, as soon as the soil has warmed and is workable, and continue through mid-summer. However, it is easier to control carrot root flies if you delay sowing maincrop varieties until late spring or early summer.

CARE AND MAINTENANCE
Weed regularly until the carrots are well established; the tops will discourage weed growth.
Pests and diseases Carrot root flies are attracted by the scent of the foliage, so be sure to compost harvested tops. You can also erect 45cm/18in high barriers of polythene sheeting around the crop or, alternatively, cover the plot with fine netting or mesh anchored around the edges.

HARVEST
Once the carrots display a good bright colour, they may be harvested: lift with a fork or pull by the tops. Store, with the tops removed, in cool dry conditions in buckets of sand, or leave in the garden. Baby carrots may be harvested to thin out the bed.

VARIETIES
Chantenay Red-cored Good for storage.
Guérande (Oxheart) Thick-rooted, stores well.
Thumbelina Small, round apple-shaped roots.

The taste of organically grown carrots is notably superior to those not grown organically. 'Chantenay Red-cored' (left) stores well.

Parsnips *Pastinaca sativa*

Plant type Biennial grown as annual
Nutrition Significant source of vitamin C and folic acid. Source of potassium and fibre.
Uses Roots are boiled or added to soups, stews and casseroles.

SITE AND SOIL

Parsnips like a loose and deeply cultivated soil. Heavy soils should be mixed with liberal amounts of leaf mould. Small and deformed roots are likely to occur in heavy soils.

SOWING

Sow seeds in mid- or late spring, spaced 2.5cm/1in apart, sown 1cm/½in deep in rows closely spaced (20–30cm/8–12in apart depending on variety). Mark the row well for easier weeding before germination. The seed is very slow to germinate, taking about three weeks. Ensure the seeds you sow are fresh because germination rates of seeds stored for more than a year are very low. Thin seedlings to 5–8cm/2–3in. Do not allow soil to dry out during the germination period.

CARE AND MAINTENANCE

Weed as necessary until established. Take care not to overwater the plants.
Pests and diseases Choose a canker-resistant variety. Carrot root fly can be a problem.

HARVEST

Parsnips are ready to harvest in autumn. To harvest, cut off the tops and lift with a garden fork. Following a heavy frost in the autumn, roots may be harvested and stored in a garden shed. They keep best near freezing with high humidity. If you wish, you can freeze the young roots. Better still, leave roots in the garden over winter and harvest as you need them. If growth begins, the centre of the root will be woody. To save seeds, leave a few parsnips in the ground during winter, and let them grow the next spring. Parsnips are pollinated by insects and the seeds can be harvested in the autumn.

VARIETIES

Gladiator A modern hybrid with excellent resistance to canker. Very white and hefty root.
Hollow Crown Smooth, slender root with white flesh that keeps its texture in stews.
Tender and True Old but good, with resistance to canker.

Parsnips, such as 'Hollow Crown' (above), become sweet when stored in the ground during winter because sugars start to form as fuel for spring growth.

Minor Salad Vegetables

Amaranthus (*Amaranthus* spp.) Grown for its light green oval leaves, which are especially popular in Indian, African and West Indian cooking, amaranthus is also known as Indian or African spinach. This plant prefers to grow in warm locations. Not cold hardy.

Orach (*Atriplex hortensis*) A colourful salad ingredient, which may have green, yellow-green or red leaves, depending on variety. Orach tolerates hot weather but suffers damage from frost. Direct seed 5cm/2in apart, thinning to 15cm/6in. Harvest in forty days when plants reach 30cm/12in tall.

Tolerant of a wide range of soils, lamb's lettuce is invaluable during autumn and winter for providing tasty green leaves for salads.

Indian mustard (*Brassica juncea*) Grown for its spicy seedling leaves and beautiful yellow flowers. This cool-season crop bolts quickly in warm weather. Sow seeds 2.5cm/1in apart and harvest in as little as three weeks. Indian mustard makes a wonderful cover crop, adding green manure to the soil quickly. Be sure to turn it under before it goes to seed or there will be a weed problem.

Rocket (*Eruca vesicaria* var. *sativa*) Also known as argula, rucola or roquette, this plant is of Mediterranean origin. The spicy leaves are used in salads. Rocket prefers cool climates and grows well in a cold frame or greenhouse in winter.

Shungiku (*Glebionis coronaria*) Also known as edible chrysanthemum. Delicious in salads, this green is sown 1cm/½in apart. Harvest when the leaves are 10–18cm/4–8in tall.

Cress (*Lepidium sativum*) A fast-growing plant that runs to seed quickly in hot weather. Its seedling leaves are harvested for salads. Grow it in a cold frame in winter and use it to fill spaces between larger vegetables like beans or tomatoes before they mature. Harvest ten days after sowing by cutting the leaves. The stumps of the stems will regrow for additional cuttings.

Winter purslane (*Montia perfoliata*) A cold-hardy plant with heart-shaped leaves that can be eaten fresh in salads or cooked like spinach. Can be grown all winter in mild climates or in cold frames. Direct seed 5cm/2in apart and harvest leaves continually. Miner's lettuce can self-seed. Harvest leaves after forty days.

Buck's-horn plantain (*Plantago coronopus*) This is the most cold-hardy salad plant for winter.

Flowerbuds are also edible. Sow 1cm/½in apart and begin harvesting in fifty days. Will regrow after cutting.

Purslane (*Portulaca oleracea*) The yellowish green leaves are used fresh in salads or cooked. Sow 2.5cm/1in apart during spring after any risk of frost has passed, and begin harvesting in fifty days. Always leave a few leaves in the ground when harvesting so that the plant can grow and produce another crop. Check regularly for slugs, which can cause severe damage.

Watercress (*Rorippa nasturtium-aquaticum*) A spicy-leaved perennial used in salads and soups. Prefers a moist well-watered part of the garden. Place stems of leaves in water to root, then plant outside. May be grown in a pot sitting in a dish of water. Harvest leaves as needed.

Sorrel (*Rumex acetosa*) Early spring greens that add a lemon flavour to salads or soups. Direct seed in the garden in early spring.

Dandelion (*Taraxacum officinale*) The tender young leaves are used raw in salads. Blanching can prevent bitterness. The flowers and roots are also edible. Harvest from your lawn.

New Zealand spinach (*Tetragonia tetragonioides*) A 60cm/24in high, spreading plant with pointed leaves that may be cooked or used raw in salads. It tolerates heat but is sensitive to frost. To assist germination, soak in warm water for twenty-four hours before planting.

Lamb's lettuce/Mache (*Valerianella locusta*) This hardy annual grows in a wide range of soils to provide greens in autumn and winter. Sow in the garden 2.5cm/1in apart and keep moist. Harvest leaves as needed and the plants will produce a second crop. Grows well indoors in winter.

Salsify (*Tragopogon porrifolius*) A hardy biennial grown for its roots, which are similar to scorzonera. The roots, young leaves and flowerbuds are eaten cooked. Cultivation is the same as for carrots. Salsify roots are best stored at high humidity. Alternatively, leave in the ground and consume during the first winter.

Scorzonera (*Scorzonera hispanica*) A hardy perennial grown as an annual with black-skinned, slender roots. The cultivation is the same as for carrots, but store roots at high humidity. Scorzonera also needs a longer season to produce good-sized roots. They may be overwintered in the ground in mild climates

The dark-fleshed roots of scorzonera are prepared in the same way as potatoes. Their edible yellow flowers can also be used to decorate dishes.

Figs *Ficus carica*

Plant type Deciduous bush

Nutrition Good source of calcium. Significant source of iron and phosphorus. Source of vitamins A and C, potassium and fibre.

Uses Fruits are often made into jams and jellies as well as having many uses fresh in the kitchen.

SITE AND SOIL

Choose a protected site and be prepared for the tops to die back. In cold climates, figs can be grown under glass or against a protected sunny wall. They dislike soil that is high in nitrogen, as fruiting will be poor. If growing against a wall or under glass, plant into a pit with brick or block walls to restrict root growth.

CARE AND MAINTENANCE

Apply mulch in late spring. Thin fruits to encourage a crop of good-sized fruits. Prune in spring just before growth begins. Figs are one of the rare fruits that do not need pollination to set fruit.

Pests and diseases Figs are rarely affected by pests and diseases. Cover ripening fruits with close-woven netting to keep birds away. Wasps may be a nuisance.

HARVEST

In warm climates, figs can bear two crops in a growing season. Hand-pick the fruits just as they start to droop on the stem. Preserve figs by drying.

VARIETIES

Black Ischia Early, excellent flavour. For warm gardens or indoor use.

Brown Turkey Tolerates cold climates.

Desert King Suitable for areas with cool winters.

White Marseilles White flesh. Grows indoors or out.

MULBERRY
MORACEAE

The large, sweet fruits of the fig are a good source of calcium. Except where the climate is very warm, fig trees need to be grown under glass or trained against a protected sunny wall.

Quinces *Cydonia oblonga*

Plant type Deciduous tree or bush
Nutrition Reliable scientific data unavailable.
Uses Raw quinces are usually unpalatable. Jellies and jams are often made from the fruits and the juice can be added to apple cider.

SITE AND SOIL

Quinces are hardy in a wide range of climates and soil types. They grow particularly well on the bank of a pond or stream. Plant quinces in a spot that is protected from cold winds.

CARE AND MAINTENANCE

Mulch well to conserve moisture. A seaweed solution may be used as a foliar feed. Prune dead wood in winter. Many varieties sucker from the roots, creating a bush; it is better to prune them to maintain a tree shape. The fruits are self-fertile.

Pests and diseases Quinces are rarely affected by pests and diseases. If you notice fireblight in time, prune off the affected branches at once: it spreads very quickly and you may lose the whole tree.

HARVEST

Harvest in the autumn and store apart from other fruits. They prefer to be stored in a cool place with good air circulation.

VARIETIES

Meeches Prolific Reliable cropping and early. Self-fertile. Yellow when ripe.
Vranja Serbian variety introduced in 1800. Self-fertile. Greeny-yellow when ripe.

Valued in the flower garden as ornamental small bushes or trees, quinces are delicious when cooked. The raw fruits are usually unpalatable.

ROSE
ROSACEAE

Apples *Malus domestica*

Plant type Deciduous tree

Nutrition Excellent source of phytochemicals. Significant source of vitamin C. Source of vitamin A, iron and fibre.

Uses Some apples are best eaten fresh; others are best cooked or pressed for cider or juice.

SITE AND SOIL

Apples will grow in a wide range of soils and climates. Be sure to choose a variety that is hardy in your climate and a rootstock that is compatible with your soil type. Apples need to experience cold weather in winter or they will not bear fruit. Some dwarf varieties may be grown in containers. There are hundreds if not thousands of varieties and two (or in some cases three) are needed for cross-pollination. In the small garden it may be wise to have only one tree and graft several varieties on to different branches. In this way they can cross-pollinate each other and the gardener can have several varieties without using too much space.

CARE AND MAINTENANCE

Weed in the early spring, apply organic fertilizers if necessary, and then mulch around the base of the tree. During the first four years after transplanting, supplemental water may be

Apple trees are easy to grow and their fruits offer a wonderful source of nutrition. The blossoms provide floral interest in spring.

necessary. Consistent moisture during the four years after transplanting will result in an earlier crop by up to three years. Water is usually the limiting growth factor in fruit trees. Protect the trunks from rodent damage before winter. Prune trees during winter or early spring (see pp. 164–7).

Pests and diseases Apple sawfly maggots or codling moths bore holes in the fruits. Aphids, winter moths and capsid bugs, mildews, canker, tortrix rust and scab may affect the trees.

HARVEST

Early varieties do not generally keep well and should be used immediately. Mid-season and late varieties can be stored or eaten fresh. Leave late varieties on the tree as long as possible before storing and take great care not to bruise them.

COOKING VARIETIES

Bramley's Seedling Long history of use. Vigorous; needs two pollinators.

Golden Noble A wonderful eighteenth-century cooker with beautiful golden skin. Generally free of scab and mildew.

DESSERT VARIETIES: EARLY

Beauty of Bath Yellow with a red flush. Sweet and full of juice.

Epicure Small tasty fruits; a heavy cropper.

DESSERT VARIETIES: MID-SEASON

Charles Ross Large yellow apple, scab resistant.

Ellison's Orange Resistant to scab and powdery mildew; slight aniseed aftertaste; delicious.

Lord Lambourne Quite sweet and very reliable. Aromatic. Generally disease free.

DESSERT VARIETIES: LATE

Cox's Orange Pippin An excellent keeper with good flavour.

Kidd's Orange Red Resistant to scab. Sweet, aromatic apple of distinction with flavour not

'Charles Ross' (above) is a dual-purpose variety, used both in cooking and as a dessert apple.

dissimilar to Cox's Orange Pippin.

Saturn New late apple which develops good flavour in store. Very resistant to scab and mildew.

Red Devil An excellent late selection for garden use. Resistant to scab and mildew; self-fertile.

ROOTSTOCK VARIETIES

M9 Dwarfing to 2.5m/8ft. Best on fertile clay; needs permanent staking.

M26 Dwarfing to 3m/10ft. Suits most soils.

M27 Very dwarfing, producing trees no higher than 1.8m/6ft. Suited to heavy fertile soil but will also perform well on lighter soil.

MM106 Semi-dwarfing, growing to 3.6–4.5m/ 12–15ft. Commonly available and generally trouble free. Suits all soil types.

MM111 Vigorous. Produces 4.5–6m/15–20ft trees; suited to traditional orchard sites or single large trees. Also useful on very poor soils, where the effect is more dwarfing.

ROSE
ROSACEAE

251

Apricots *Prunus armeniaca*

Plant type Deciduous tree

Nutrition Excellent source of vitamin A. Significant source of vitamin C. Source of potassium, calcium and iron.

Uses Apricots are wonderful eaten fresh; they also taste good when dried. They make delicious jam.

SITE AND SOIL

This early season fruit usually grows on small trees, which are suitable for compact city gardens. Apricots need to be well-protected from frost because they flower early, from late winter onwards. In the UK, they only grow if trained on to a sheltered, very warm wall, or under glass. Plant in a sheltered site with good drainage and a light loam soil. Heavy soils will need to have plenty of compost incorporated.

CARE AND MAINTENANCE

Weed the site in the early spring, and feed with an organic fertilizer if necessary. Apply a thick layer of mulch around the base of the tree. It may be necessary to thin fruits to produce a better crop. Prune any dead wood in winter. Apricots are generally self-fertile but will bear more heavily with cross-pollination. In the UK, cold wet winters often lead to die-back.

Pests and diseases Birds are the worst pest, attacking fruit early on, as it is ripening. Use netting to protect the fruits from birds and wasps. Aphids and scale may be a problem. Canker and borers affect apricots.

HARVEST

Apricots are enjoyed at their best when picked ripe and eaten immediately. They can also be dried to make delicious treats that store well for use all year round.

VARIETIES

Alfred Hardy variety from the United States; popular for mid-season planting.

Early Moorpark Very juicy; red-orange flesh.

Golden Glow Very hardy variety of UK origin, suitable in warmer areas for growing as a free-standing tree rather than wall-trained.

Apricots are an excellent source of vitamin A. They are ideal for fan-training or espaliering against a warm sunny wall.

ROSE
ROSACEAE

Cherries *Prunus avium/Prunus cerasus*

Plant type Deciduous tree
Nutrition Excellent source of phytochemicals.
Good source of vitamin C and fibre.
Source of vitamins A and B2, iron and calcium.
Uses Sweet cherries are for eating fresh. Sour
cherries are most often used in cooking.

SITE AND SOIL

Cherries need well-drained soil, high in nutrients
with good moisture retention, as the fruits need
plenty of water. Open up heavy soils by
incorporating plenty of compost before planting.
Cherries prefer warm dry climates; however, they
need to experience cold weather in winter to bear
fruit. Sour cherries tend to be more cold hardy.
Some cherry trees have a large spread (up to
9m/30ft). If your garden is small, opt for a dwarf
variety.

CARE AND MAINTENANCE

Weed in early spring and apply organic fertilizers
if necessary. Mulch around the base of the tree.
Prune from late spring to early autumn to avoid
silver leaf, removing dead or diseased wood. Use
netting to protect the fruits from birds. Few
cherries are self-fertile, and two varieties may be
needed to set fruit.
Pests and diseases Birds can plunder the fruits a
few days before harvest. Silver leaf, bacterial
canker and viruses may also affect trees.

HARVEST

Ensure that the tree has consistent moisture in the
last few weeks before harvest. Too much moisture
can result in fruit that splits from swelling, while
too little may result in shrivelled fruit and reduced
storage time. Harvest the cherry clusters by hand,
detaching them by the stalks.

*Protect cherries from birds with nets or bird scarers to
ensure that you get to enjoy the crop of ripe fruit.*

ROOTSTOCK VARIETIES
Gisela 5 Dwarf variety.
Hexaploid Colt New version of the semi-dwarf
Colt, reducing growth by about 25 per cent.

SWEET CHERRY VARIETIES
Early Rivers Produces large red-black fruits.
Not self-fertile. Compatible with 'Stella'.
Stella Self-fertile, popular variety.
Sunburst Self-fertile. Wonderful flavour.

ACID VARIETIES
Morello Hardy, self-fertile.
Nabella Large fruits; reliable cropping. Self-fertile.

ROSE
ROSACEAE

Plums *Prunus* CVS

Plant type Deciduous tree
Nutrition Significant source of vitamin C.
Source of vitamin A, potassium and fibre.
Uses Plums are eaten fresh or dried, made into
jams and jellies, and used in cooking. Prunes are
the dried plums, in which the nutrients and flavour
are concentrated.

SITE AND SOIL

Plums are hardy in a wide range of climates. Some
varieties are able to withstand very cold winters.
They grow well in heavy soils and can tolerate
damp, clay soils. Plums should be planted in a
sheltered site that will protect the spring blossoms
from damage by frost. Alternatively, fan-train the
tree against a warm wall.

CARE AND MAINTENANCE

Plums require little care yet produce a large crop.
Weed in the early spring, fertilize if needed, then
mulch around the base of the tree. Prune as
necessary in late spring to early autumn to avoid
silver leaf. Some plums are not self-fertile; two
varieties may be required for cross-pollination.

Pests and diseases Plums are affected by many
diseases and the best defence is to supply optimal
growing conditions and to practise good hygiene
by removing any windfalls during the autumn and
by harvesting all remaining fruits on the tree
before winter. This helps to deter brown rot and
grey mould. Bacterial leafspot and apple maggots
may be a problem. Hang up a sticky red ball that
looks like an apple to attract and trap them.

HARVEST

Plums do not store well. Pick them when ripe and
use immediately. Or, if your climate is dry, you can
leave late-maturing plums to dry on the tree.

ROOTSTOCK VARIETIES

Pixy Dwarf. Suited to most soils.
St Julien A Semi-vigorous.

PLUM VARIETIES

Belle de Louvain Large purple fruits for eating
fresh or cooking. Self-fertile.
Kirke's Blue Good flavour. Large fruits.
Marjorie's Seedling Large, late, self-fertile. Good
flavour. Ripens late.
Old Greengage Rich sweet flavour.
Opal Excellent flavour. Early. Self-fertile.

*Plum varieties come in a variety of sizes and range
in colour from green through red and purple to
almost black.*

ROSE
ROSACEAE

Peaches *Prunus persica*

Plant type Deciduous tree
Nutrition Significant source of vitamin C.
Source of vitamin A and fibre.
Uses Fruits are usually eaten fresh.

SITE AND SOIL
Peaches need well-drained, moist soil that is high in nutrients. Open up heavy soils by incorporating lots of compost. In cool temperate climates, grow under glass or as wall-trained fans outdoors, choosing a sheltered site that will protect the blossoms from damage by late spring frosts.

CARE AND MAINTENANCE
Weed in the early spring and apply an organic fertilizer if necessary. Apply a layer of mulch around the base of the tree. Some varieties are self-fertile, others require cross-pollination. Hand pollination may be required. Thin the peaches to encourage a crop of good-sized fruits. Protect trunks from rodent damage before winter. Prune trees from late spring to early autumn to avoid silver leaf.
Pests and diseases Peach leaf curl is the most common problem. It defoliates and kills trees. Keep rain off by protecting with a frame from mid-winter to late spring. Cover small trees or individual fruits with a net to protect fruit from birds and wasps. Earwigs may also attack fruit.

HARVEST
Let the fruit ripen completely before harvesting. Peaches do not keep well and should be used immediately or preserved in a light syrup.

ROOTSTOCK VARIETIES
St Julien A A semi-vigorous plum rootstock, suited to most soils.

Nectarines require almost the same growing conditions as peaches but need more protection from cold. Unlike peaches, nectarines are always fuzzless.

CULTIVATED PEACH VARIETIES
Garden Lady A natural dwarf, suitable for pots or planting out. In pots, bring indoors during winter to avoid damage and eliminate leaf curl.
Peregrine Popular white-fleshed variety. Heavy crops in a warm, sheltered spot.
Red Haven Grows well in short seasons if there is sufficient warmth.
Rochester Yellow flesh with excellent flavour.

NECTARINE VARIETIES
Close relatives of peaches, nectarines have the same cultural requirements, but are less hardy.
Humboldt Orange flesh, rich flavour.
Lord Napier Early, with large white fruits.
Nectarella Natural dwarf. Orange-red flesh; good flavour.

ROSE
ROSACEAE

Pears *Pyrus communis*

Plant type Deciduous tree
Nutrition Significant source of vitamin C.
Source of calcium, potassium and fibre.
Uses Eaten fresh or used in pies and desserts.

SITE AND SOIL

Pears are easy to grow and will tolerate a wide range of soils. The European type tends to be more hardy than Asian types (*Pyrus pyrifolia*) and matures in a shorter season. Look for a variety that is hardy in your climate. Plant trees in a location that protects the early blossoms from frost. The graft unions may be planted below the soil level for a full-sized tree growing up to 12–15m/40–50ft.

There are two basic types of pear – European, such as 'Williams' Bon Chrétien' (above), and the rounded Asian, which generally requires warmer climates.

CARE AND MAINTENANCE

Weed in the early spring, apply organic fertilizers if necessary and then mulch around the base of the tree. For a crop of good-size fruits, thin the shoots in spring. Prune dead branches during winter. Pears can be pruned in summer if necessary, but late season pruning can result in lots of vegetative growth that may die back in a harsh winter. Pears usually require cross-pollination but some varieties are self-fertile.

Pests and diseases Mealy fruit arises when fruits ripen in very warm or cold weather. Open-centre pruning can help to avoid fireblight and scab. Pear decline is a disease that causes the leaves to wilt; trees dry out and can die within a season. Protect trees from rodent damage before winter.

HARVEST

Handpick the fruits before they are fully ripe, just as soon as they will easily detach from the tree. If left on the tree, the flavour becomes unpalatable. Pears keep well in a cool frost-free place, often until late winter. Store them apart from apples.

ROOTSTOCK VARIETIES

Pear rootstocks produce huge, very vigorous trees, so quince roots are commonly used.
Quince A Semi-dwarf, reaching about 3m/10ft.
Quince C Semi-dwarf, reaching over 3.6m/12ft.

PEAR VARIETIES

Beth Small, well-flavoured fruits. Early.
Catillac Large fruits, good for cooking. Late.
Conference Excellent mid-season pear. Hardy, reliable and self-fertile.
Glou Morceau Fine-flavoured pear for store.
Glow Red Williams A red form of the famous 'Williams' Bon Chrétien'. Less disease-prone.
Jargonelle Very early. Reliable and hardy.

Walnuts *Juglans* spp.

Plant type Deciduous tree

Nutrition Walnuts are an excellent source of phytochemicals and a significant source of vitamin E. Source of vitamin C, folic acid, iron, copper, potassium, phosphorus and fibre.

Uses Nuts are eaten fresh, baked in cakes, or used as crunchy toppings. They are also ground for flour.

SITE AND SOIL

Walnut trees may reach maturity at 18–45m/ 60–150ft depending on variety. They grow best in heavy soils. Light soils should be improved with lots of compost. Keep the soil moist but not waterlogged. Walnuts usually require cross-pollination to produce well.

CARE AND MAINTENANCE

Walnut trees require very little care. Prune any dead branches in winter.

Pests and diseases Watch out for squirrels stealing nuts at harvest time.

HARVEST

Collect the nuts as soon as they drop in the autumn. The green covering over the nut is sticky and stains; remove it before drying the nuts.

WALNUT VARIETIES

Broadview The most commonly grown walnut. It fruits early in its life and is self-fertile.

Buccaneer Similar to 'Broadview' but not quite so quick to come into bearing.

Franquette Late season, large fruited. Needs a pollinator.

OTHER TYPES OF WALNUT

Juglans ailantifolia The Heartnut, a walnut species from Japan. The tree has attractive purple flowers and large handsome leaves. The heart-shaped nuts are borne on long strings. Trees will eventually reach over 15–18m/50–60ft in height, with similar spread.

***Juglans nigra* 'Thomas'** Named cultivar of the black walnut, originating from Pennsylvania in America. This tree is very large, reaching over 18m/60ft. The nuts are larger than those of the species and have thinner shells.

Juglans cinerea The Butternut, a very large, spreading and fast-growing tree, reaching up to 24m/80ft high and 20m/65ft wide. Heavy clusters of round nuts in autumn.

When stored in a dry place, walnuts will keep for more than a year, ensuring that you have a steady supply to enjoy at the table.

WALNUT
JUGLANDACEAE

Hazelnuts *Corylus* spp. **and Chestnuts** *Castanea* spp.

Plant type Deciduous tree or bush

Nutrition Source of vitamins A, C and E, folic acid, potassium, calcium, magnesium and phosphorus.

Uses The nuts can be eaten fresh, dried or ground.

SITE AND SOIL

The term hazelnuts covers both cobnuts and filberts. Hazelnuts tolerate poor soil conditions and grow in most climates. They suit hedgerows and wet areas. Hazels are small trees, forming bushes with a height/spread of 4.5–6m/ 15–20ft, and producing nuts within three to four years.

CARE AND MAINTENANCE

Many hazels have bush form unless they are kept pruned to tree shape. Remove any dead branches. Hazels require cross-pollination.

Pests and diseases Canker, big bud mite and nut weevil may affect trees, and mice and squirrels can be a nuisance.

HARVEST

When nuts are ready for harvest they drop from the tree. If squirrels start to steal nuts, harvest them early.

VARIETIES

Butler Vigorous and heavy cropping; mid- to late season. Susceptible to big bud mite but resistant to canker. Pollinated by 'Ennis'.

Cosford Excellent flavour but a shy cropper. Pollinated by 'Gunslebert' and 'Kentish Cob'.

Ennis Can be biennial in bearing but the flavour is excellent. Pollinated by 'Butler'.

Gunslebert Moderate resistance to big bud mite

and canker. Vigorous and heavy in cropping; late. Pollinated by 'Cosford' and 'Kentish Cob'.

Kentish Cob (Longue d'Espagne) Popular commercial variety with excellent flavour. Pollinated by 'Cosford' and 'Gunslebert'.

CHESTNUTS

Chestnut trees produce tasty nuts that are good roasted or made into soup.

Chinese Chestnut (*Castanea mollissima*) Reaches 7.6m/25ft and is resistant to blight.

Sweet Chestnut/European Chestnut (*Castanea dentata*) Has been in cultivation for 2,000 years.

Grown as an informal hedge or small tree, hazelnuts produce a reliable harvest. Their catkins provide welcome colour and decoration in late winter.

Blueberries *Vaccinium* spp.

Plant type Deciduous bush
Nutrition Excellent source of phytochemicals.
Good source of vitamin C. Source of iron
and fibre.
Uses Berries are used fresh or frozen, and made
into jellies, jams or preserves. They are a fine
addition to many baked goods.

SITE AND SOIL

Blueberries prefer acidic soils (pH 4.0–5.0) that
are very moist. They are often found growing wild
along the edges of rivers or lakes. Although they
are self-fertile, blueberries produce better when
more than one variety is grown. They are very cold
hardy and will tolerate a wide range of climates.
Highbush varieties range in height from 45cm/
18in to 1.8m/6ft. Lowbush varieties are 15cm/6in
to 45cm/18in.

CARE AND MAINTENANCE

During the first year after planting, remove all
flowers to encourage bushes to establish quickly.
Do not over-fertilize blueberries. Prune bushes
when planting. Remove any dead wood in winter.
Highbush blueberries should be pruned to remove
older wood and branches that intertwine. Bushes
that are crowded produce a smaller crop. Mulch
well to conserve water. If you irrigate blueberries,
be aware that they tolerate lime-free water only.
Pests and diseases Yellow leaves are often caused
by iron deficiency or a soil pH that is too high. Use
floating row covers over lowbush varieties and
nets over taller varieties to protect the fruits from
attack by birds.

HARVEST

Pick the berries when they are fully ripe and use or
preserve them immediately.

*Blueberries can play a succulent part in almost any
fruit recipe and are excellent in jellies and jams.*

EARLY VARIETIES
Bluecrop Large fruits, good flavour. Ripens by
late summer. Good autumn colours.
Patriot Cold-hardy variety that bears large fruits.

MID-SEASON VARIETIES
Berkeley Vigorous and very productive with large
light blue fruits of excellent flavour.
Goldtraube Good crops of dark blue fruits.
Ivanhoe Dark berries of good flavour on upright
bushes. Good autumn colour.

LATE VARIETIES
Coville Very late productive variety. Leave to
ripen fully on the bushes.
Jersey Easy-to-grow variety.

HEATH
ERICACEAE

Cranberries *Vaccinium macrocarpon*

Plant type Evergreen bush

Nutrition Significant source of vitamin C. Source of fibre.

Uses Berries used in desserts and for sauces.

SITE AND SOIL

Cranberries prefer wet and boggy, very acidic soils, so choose a wet site that is enriched with plenty of acidic compost. Cranberries are self-fertile and range in size from 15cm/6in to 60cm/24in.

CARE AND MAINTENANCE

Weed cranberries well in the spring. Apply a heavy mulch to preserve moisture. If you live in a dry climate, set up a drip irrigation system fitted with a timer for good results. Like blueberries, cranberries dislike alkaline tap water.

Pests and diseases A high pH causes most problems with cranberries.

HARVEST

Pick the berries before the first frost, or their flavour will be affected. Cranberries store extremely well: you can freeze them or make them into jams or jellies.

VARIETIES

Edible cranberries should not be confused with American (highbush) cranberries (*Viburnum trilobum*) which are used for ornamental purposes or as wildlife feed.

Olson's Honkers Very large fruits and a heavy yield.

Pilgrim A fast-growing bush with tasty berries.

A close relative of blueberries, cranberries are grown for their firm red berries, which are a significant source of vitamin C.

HEATH
ERICACEAE

Strawberries *Fragaria* spp.

Plant type Perennial
Nutrition Excellent source of phytochemicals and vitamin C. Source of calcium, iron, fibre and potassium.
Uses Eaten fresh and used in desserts and jams.

SITE AND SOIL

Strawberries will grow in a wide variety of climates and can be grown under glass (with heat) in winter. They need a soil rich in organic matter to fruit well. Most cultivated varieties are bought as plants, not seeds, and are asexually propagated by collecting and replanting runners. The dainty-looking alpine strawberries are grown from seed. Their small, delicious fruits look similar to wild strawberries.

CARE AND MAINTENANCE

The plants have shallow roots, which makes weeding difficult. Mulch them with a thick layer of straw to suppress weeds and space the plants widely to ease weeding. Reapply straw mulch as necessary throughout the season. It may be helpful to run over the straw with a lawnmower before mulching. Runners will drain the plant's energy away from producing fruits. Root some runners for future use in other beds and remove the rest. Remove debris from the bed in the autumn to discourage diseases.
Pests and diseases Use floating row covers to protect the crop from birds. Moulds can be a problem, so remove any rotting fruit immediately.

HARVEST

Some varieties bear early, others late, and alpine and perpetual strawberries bear from early summer to early autumn. Hand-pick the fruits as they ripen and use immediately. They do not store

One of the most nutritious fruits, packed with beneficial phytochemicals, strawberries can be grown in containers where space is limited.

well unless made into jams, jellies or syrups.

VARIETIES

Alexandria The best red alpine strawberry.
Baron Solemacher Non-runnering; alpine, good flavour.
Bolero A new perpetual, producing good-quality fruit in quantity. Good flavour.
Cambridge Late Pine Many regard this as the finest-flavoured strawberry of all. Mid-season.
Emily Very early. Resists powdery mildew and other leaf diseases.
Honeyoye Early, sweet flavour. Less susceptible to botrytis than most strawberries.
Mara de Bois Large berries with 'alpine' flavour. A perpetual used for late cropping.
Pegasus Mid-season variety with some disease resistance. Large good-flavoured fruits.

ROSE
ROSACEAE

SOFT FRUITS

Raspberries *Rubus idaeus*

Plant type Deciduous bush
Nutrition Excellent source of vitamin C and phytochemicals. Source of calcium, iron, fibre, and potassium.
Uses Eaten fresh or used in desserts, jams and jellies.

SITE AND SOIL
Raspberries need sun and acid soil. A planting should last at least twelve years. With a pH over 7 they tend to develop iron deficiency and decline.

CARE AND MAINTENANCE
Water well. Weed in spring and follow with a thick mulch. Cut, hoe or pull off all new emerging canes (spawn) that grow away from the rows. Summer-fruiting raspberries produce new canes while the old canes are fruiting. Thin well-placed, strong canes to about 8 to 10 per square metre/yard and tie in to supporting wires. After cropping, cut down old canes. Tip back new canes in late winter to just above the top wire (about 1.5m/5ft) at a bud. Autumn-fruiting varieties grow canes which fruit in the same year. Prune back all growth in late winter to the ground. Tie in new growth as it develops.
Pests and diseases Net against birds. Other pests include raspberry aphids, raspberry beetle and cane midge. The canes are prone to viruses. Remove and burn affected plants. Do not re-plant raspberries or strawberries on virus-infected land. Other diseases include cane blight, cane spot, spur blight and botrytis.

HARVEST
When fruit comes off easily, hand-pick carefully and gently, as pressure damages the fruit. Harvest when it is cool and not wet. Raspberries freeze well, but are at their best freshly picked.

To expand the soft fruit season, plant a variety of raspberry such as 'Autumn Bliss' (above) which produces fruit in late summer and early autumn.

VARIETIES
All Gold Autumn-fruiting variety. Sweet but crumbly yellow fruits that need careful picking.
Autumn Bliss Autumn-fruiting variety. Good quality and produces a good crop.
Glen Clova Early, good flavour.
Leo Vigorous and resistant to one raspberry aphid.
Malling Jewel Early to mid-season variety; virus tolerant.

OTHER BERRY VARIETIES
Laganberry LY59 A raspberry-blackberry cross. Reliable and richly juicy.
Loganberry L654 Thornless version of LY59.
Tayberry A raspberry-blackberry cross.

Blackberries *Rubus fruticosus*

Plant type Deciduous bush or vine
Nutrition Excellent source of phytochemicals. Source of calcium, iron and fibre.
Uses Eaten fresh or cooked with apples for flavour and colour or made into jams and jellies.

SITE AND SOIL

Blackberries do well in most conditions, but prefer very rich moist soils. They are hardy in all but the coldest locations. Check that the variety you choose is hardy in your climate; those that grow best in very cold climates often do not fruit well. They are self-fertile. Choose a site with care because some varieties can be invasive.

CARE AND MAINTENANCE

In spring, weed and mulch the plants. Generally blackberries need little care. Blackberries bear on the previous year's growth, and should be pruned like summer-fruiting raspberries. Head back canes (to about 13cm/5in) the first summer after planting to encourage formation of laterals.

Pests and diseases Blackberries may be affected by the same pests and diseases as raspberries. Birds do not usually attack the crop.

HARVEST

Blackberries should be harvested when they fall off the plant at the gentlest touch. The fruits spoil quickly and should be used immediately.

THORNLESS VARIETIES

These are not as hardy as thorned varieties.
Merton Thornless Much less vigorous than other varieties, so suited to small gardens.
Thornfree Reliable but less decorative than Oregon Thornless.

Blackberries can be very thorny and this makes their cultivation a prickly and often painful task. Opt for a thornless variety to make harvesting easier.

ROSE
ROSACEAE

Gooseberries *Ribes uva-crispa* var. *reclinatum*

Plant type Deciduous bush
Nutrition Source of vitamins A and C, calcium, phosphorus and iron.
Uses The dessert varieties are delicious eaten fresh; the small green varieties are most often made into jam and preserves.

SITE AND SOIL
Gooseberries are very cold hardy and tolerate a wide range of soils, except for sandy dry soils. They thrive in cool climates. Gooseberry bushes reach up to 1.2m/4ft; they are self-fertile.

CARE AND MAINTENANCE
Weed and mulch in spring; prune the bushes in winter. Gooseberries produce best when pruned to a single stem. They can also be trained as a cordon. Stems will bear for about five years, after which they should be removed. New shoots will quickly replace them. Pruning can make it easier to pick fruits from between the thorns.

Pests and diseases Gooseberry sawfly. Birds may attack ripe fruit. Gooseberries are prone to moulds and mildews in humid areas. Prune to ensure good air circulation.

HARVEST
Hand-pick as the fruits approach ripeness for use in jams and preserves; harvest ripe fruits for eating fresh. Protect your hands with lightweight gloves.

VARIETIES
Black Velvet Smaller, dark purple berries.
Greenfinch Cooking variety, green berries.
Hinnomaki Red Good disease-free dessert variety. Red berries.
Invicta White berries, usually used for cooking. Very mildew resistant.
Whitesmith Large, yellowish and sweet fruits.

'Whitesmith' gooseberries (left) are grown for their sweet, juicy fruits, which ripen from pale green to yellowish. They are eaten fresh and can also be cooked in pies or made into jams, jellies and preserves.

SAXIFRAGE
SAXIFRAGACEAE

Currants *Ribes* spp.

Plant type Deciduous bush
Nutrition Source of vitamins A, B1, B2, B3 and C, calcium, phosphorus and iron.
Uses The tart fruits are usually made into jelly, jam, preserves and juices, or used in cooking.

SITE AND SOIL
Currants are very cold tolerant and grow best in cool soils. Blackcurrants like rich soil with plenty of compost worked in. Red and white currants generally do not require rich soil. Currants are self-fertile and form a 1.2–2m/4–7ft tall bush.

CARE AND MAINTENANCE
Weed and mulch in spring. Prune in winter. Blackcurrants need hard pruning: cut out whole branches of older wood, removing up to a quarter of the branches each year. Treat white and red currants like gooseberries.

Pests and diseases Birds are a major pest, eating red currants as soon as they are ripe. Prune well to avoid moulds and mildews.

HARVEST
Hand-pick currants beginning in summer as they turn the appropriate colour for that variety. The harvest season extends well into autumn.

BLACKCURRANT VARIETIES
Ben Lomond Large berries, heavy cropper. Some resistance to mildew.
Ben Sarek Very compact. Resists mildew, leaf spot and leaf midge.

RED- AND WHITE-CURRANT VARIETIES
Jonkheer van Tets Very popular early red variety.
Red Lake Very reliable cropper. Good flavour.
White Versailles Sweet berries that have a high pectin content.

Blackcurrants, unlike white and red currants, demand a rich soil with plenty of compost worked in. 'Ben Lomond' is shown right.

Kiwi Fruits *Actinidia* spp.

Plant type Deciduous vine
Nutrition Excellent source of vitamin C.
Significant source of vitamin E. Source of vitamin
A, calcium, iron, potassium and fibre.
Uses Eaten raw and used in desserts.

SITE AND SOIL

Kiwi fruits, also known as Chinese gooseberries,
are only hardy in warm winter areas. Most
varieties are not self-fertile; one male plant must
be planted along with as many females as are
desired. They require full sun and fertile soil to

*Hairy outer skins protect the tasty lime-green flesh and
slender black seeds of kiwi fruits. The fruits are ripe if
they indent slightly when gently pressed.*

crop heavily. The vines reach about 7.5m/25ft in
length and need to be supported with trellis.

CARE AND MAINTENANCE

Kiwis grow quickly and need to be pruned back
hard in late winter or early spring. It may be
necessary to tie the vines to the trellis. Head back
the side-shoots in summer and autumn, to control
the size of the vine and to encourage the plant to
devote energy to ripening fruit. Kiwi fruits will
probably need watering during dry periods in the
summer months.
Pests and diseases Kiwi fruits are generally not
affected by pests or diseases.

HARVEST

In autumn, harvest the fruits before first frost. If
picked before fully ripe, they will keep for two to
three months in the refrigerator or any cool dry
location – leave them out to soften before use.

ARGUTA/TARA VINE VARIETIES

Arguta kiwis have hairless skins; they are hardy in
moderately cold climates.
Jenny Self-fertile with rather small fruits.

KIWI FRUIT VARIETIES

Hayward A commonly available female variety.
Tomuri A male variety that will not carry fruit;
needed to pollinate the females.

KOLOMIKTA VARIETIES

Kolomikta kiwis are quite cold hardy and the
males have foliage tinted from green to pink to
white. In warmer climates kolomiktas grow better
in partial shade than in direct sunlight.
Sentyabraskaya (September Sun) A female
variety that has attractive coloured foliage similar
to that of male kolomiktas.

Grapes *Vitis* cvs

Plant type Deciduous vine

Nutrition Grapes are a significant source of vitamin C. Source of vitamin A, calcium and iron. Raisins are a significant source of vitamin B6, iron, phosphorus, magnesium and copper. Source of calcium, potassium and fibre.

Uses Wine grapes are mostly used for wine. Table grapes are eaten fresh, juiced or used in cooking.

SITE AND SOIL

Grapes will grow in a wide variety of soils. Dessert grapes produce juicier grapes in rich soils; wine grapes dislike rich soils. The vines need to be pruned and trained on a support or wall. If not pruned, grape vines tend to grow very long and produce small hard berries that never ripen.

CARE AND MAINTENANCE

Train vines to ensure good air circulation, which discourages moulds and diseases, and to keep the fruits off the ground. Grapes are produced on new growth. Prune back the shoots to about eight buds in the spring. After fruiting, prune back the side-shoot (in the next spring), leaving a stub with a bud to produce a shoot for the next year's crop.

Pests and diseases Viruses can be a problem and have no cure. Moulds and mildews can be prevented with care but may be a problem in humid areas. Watch for bird and rodent damage.

HARVEST

Using pruners, cut the bunches of fruit when ripe. Most varieties ripen all at once.

WINE GRAPE VARIETIES

In temperate climates, early varieties are the most likely to ripen outdoors. Late varieties are likely to

'Red Flame' (left) is one of the few dessert grapes that may succeed outdoors in temperate climates. 'Thompson Seedless' (right) needs a greenhouse.

need the extended season of a greenhouse to guarantee success. Good varieties include 'Madeleine Sylvaner', 'Muller Thurgau', 'Seibel 13053' and 'Seyval Blanc' (late).

DESSERT GRAPE VARIETIES

These varieties will usually need greenhouse protection.

Black Hamburg Also suitable for wine-making. A quality black grape, widely available.

Buckland Sweetwater Early, sweet white grape.

Muscat of Alexandria Definitely one for the greenhouse; a late Muscat of fine flavour. White.

Red Flame Sweet, seedless dark red grape.

Thompson Seedless Late-maturing sweet white grape.

Herb Selection

Dill (*Anethum graveolens*) Annual, full sun, 90cm/36in tall. Sow directly with 10cm/4in spacing, in spring. A herb used in cooking and for flavouring foods. Use both seeds and greens.

Tarragon (*Artemisia dracunculus*) Perennial, full sun, 45cm/18in tall, hardy to −9°C/15°F. Transplant (15cm/6in spacing) in spring. The dried leaves are used in sauces or to flavour meat.

Caraway (*Carum carvi*) Biennial, full sun, 60cm/24in tall, hardy to −7°C/20°F. Transplant (2.5cm/1in spacing) in spring. The seeds (which only form in the second year) are used in baking and to flavour stews. The leaves may be added to salads or chopped into soups.

Coriander (*Coriandrum sativum*)
Annual, full sun (partial sun in very warm climates), 30–45cm/12–18in tall. Sow directly with 8cm/3in spacing in spring. The greens are very often used in Mexican cuisine. The seeds, which are both sweet and spicy, are used in sausages, chutney and baking.

Florence fennel/Sweet fennel (*Foeniculum vulgare* var. *dulce*) Perennial, full sun, 60–90cm/24–36in tall, hardy to −12°C/10°F. Sow directly or transplant (13cm/5in spacing), in spring. Fennel is often grown as an annual in cold climates for its feathery leaves, which are used for flavouring. Florence fennel is grown as a herb and as a vegetable. The leaf stem (bulb) can be eaten raw or cooked.

Bay (*Laurus nobilis*) Tree, full sun, hardy to −12°C/10°F. Bay trees may be grown in pots and brought indoors in winter in cold climates. The leaves are used to flavour soups and sauces.

Lavender (*Lavandula angustifolia*) Perennial, full sun to partial shade, 45cm/18in tall, transplant (2.5cm/1in spacing) in late spring, hardy to 0°C/32°F. Lavender flowers are added to jams, breads, and vinegars. The scent is popular in soaps and potpourri sachets.

German chamomile/Scented mayweed (*Matricaria recutita*) Annual, full sun, 15–75cm/6–30in tall. Transplant (15cm/6in spacing) in spring. Chamomile is generally used as an infusion to aid insomnia and digestion. The leaves have antiseptic qualities.

Mint (*Mentha* spp.) Perennial, full sun, 30–90cm/12–36in tall, hardy to 4°C/40°F. Transplant seedlings (30cm/12in spacing) in spring or autumn. Mints are best propagated by cuttings that are rooted in the spring or autumn, or by

Basil is an ideal plant to grow in a pot on a kitchen windowsill. Its aromatic leaves make a valuable contribution to many dishes.

division of an existing plant. Mint can be invasive, so consider growing it in a pot. Be sure to pick leaves before the plant goes to flower.

Basil (*Ocimum basilicum*) Annual, full sun, 30–60cm/12–24in tall. Sow in trays or modules with heat and transplant or prick out into pots as soon as they are large enough. Except in very warm gardens it is best to grow basil in pots that can then be moved indoors or out as the weather dictates; it is not hardy.

Marjoram (*Origanum majorana*) Perennial, treated as an annual in temperate climates, full sun, 30–60cm/12–24in tall. Sow directly or transplant with 15cm/6in spacing, in late spring. Good in salads and vegetable dishes.

Greek oregano (*Origanum vulgare* var. *hirtum*)/ Mexican oregano (*Lippia graveolens*) Perennial, full sun, 2.5–15cm/1–6in tall, cold hardy to –13˚C/ 9˚F (Greek), –12˚C/10˚F (Mexican). Mexican oregano can be grown as an annual. Transplant seedlings with 2.5–5cm/1–2in spacing, in late spring. Oregano is a popular flavouring for meat, cheese and tomato dishes.

Parsley (*Petroselinum* spp.) Biennial, full sun, 35–60cm/15–24in. Parsley takes four to six weeks to germinate. Soak parsley seeds in warm water for several hours before sowing indoors in late winter. Transplant (15cm/6in spacing) in spring. Pinch out flowers on parsley overwintered outside. Grow in pots indoors during the winter for a fresh supply. The flat-leaf variety has more flavour than the curled-leaf variety.

Rosemary (*Rosmarinus officinalis*) Shrub, full sun, 30cm–1.2m/12in–4ft tall, hardy to –18˚C/0˚F (or colder depending on variety). Transplant with 45cm/18in spacing, after last frost. This evergreen produces foliage that is used to flavour meat. Its

A vigorous grower that can overtake a bed if not restrained, Moroccan spearmint produces lilac, white or pink flowers in summer.

upright or trailing spikes of pale blue or pink flowers are a valuable addition to flowerbeds.

Sage (*Salvia officinalis*) Perennial, full sun or part shade, 30–90cm/12–36in tall, hardy to –1˚C/30˚F. Transplant (30cm/12in spacing) in spring. Sage is used to flavour meats and sauces, and is popular in stuffing.

Stevia (*Stevia rebaudiana*) Perennial, partial shade in warm climates, 2.5–5cm/1–2in tall, transplant (2.5cm/1in spacing) in spring, hardy to 0˚C/32˚F. Stevia is propagated by cuttings. Its leaves are extremely sweet yet contain almost no calories. Dry the leaves and grind them for use as a sugar replacement.

Thyme (*Thymus vulgaris*) Perennial, full sun to partial shade, 30cm/12in tall, hardy to –7˚C/20˚F. Transplant (15cm/6in spacing) after last frost. The greens are used in French and Italian cooking to flavour soups and sauces.

APPENDIX I: TOOLS

BASIC TOOLCARE

It is important to keep your gardening tools and equipment in the best possible condition, so that they perform the task required and remain serviceable for a long time. Tools should be cleaned immediately after use and put away in a clean, dry storage area. More gardening tools are damaged by rain than by use.

Use a stiff brush to remove any dirt and residue that has become attached, then wipe the tool dry with a soft cloth or rag. Store the tool away from moisture to reduce any chance of it rusting. Try to hang your tools on wall hooks, especially if your shed is prone to damp during winter. Have a place for every tool and put each one away after use. Wooden handles benefit from a seasonal coating of preserving oil, such as linseed oil. This prevents the wood from becoming too dry and brittle.

Any tools that have come into contact with diseased plant material need to be cleaned thoroughly to avoid spreading infection to other plants. A dip in a bleach/water solution will usually suffice. Sterilize your seed-starting trays and supplies before use in spring by washing them in hot, soapy water.

SHARPENING

Many tools have cutting blades which need to be sharpened regularly for them to make good,

Tools for grass care (from top): long-handled edger, scythe, wide wooden rake, garden rake, garden shears and spring-tine lawn rake.

clean cuts (see pruning advice on pp. 164–7). Blunt or rusted blades can tear or snag a plant stem, leaving a wound that will be prone to infection.

If you sharpen your cutting tools regularly with a file or sharpening stone, they will always be a joy to use. However, if you let the blades become hopelessly dull, they will probably need to be sent to a professional sharpening service.

Left to right: a rake, round-nosed shovel, hoe, fork, pruning shears, spade, and (behind) secateurs and pruning saw are the basics of a gardener's tool kit. A scoop may be useful for seed and compost, a pitchfork for turning hay.

LONG-HANDLED TOOLS

Spade For digging, chopping roots, prying out rocks, dividing perennials and cutting straight edges. You are

Left to right: Dutch hoe, three-tine cultivator, draw hoe and other hoeing tools.

likely to use a spade more than any other garden tool, so be sure to choose one that suits your height and strength. The standard size for spades is about 95cm/38in, but tall gardeners should opt for a 107cm/43in long model. Shorter or less strong gardeners may prefer a 'border' spade, which has a small head. A companion border fork is also available.

Many gardeners prefer a stainless steel head over traditional hand-forged steel because wet soil does not stick to the surface. Although their price may be tempting, avoid buying cheap ones as they are made of thin steel that bends and breaks easily.

Fork For loosening subsoil and lifting root crops, such as potatoes and parsnips. A companion to the spade, a fork cuts into soil more easily. The strong tines can be used to mix compost and additives into the soil. A fork with good thin, square tines is a general-purpose tool. Forks with broad, flat tines are better for lifting potatoes. Choose a fork that suits your height and strength; see the sizes recommended above for spades. A fork made of hand-forged steel is best because it is strong and unlikely to bend in normal use.

Broadfork For single digging and aerating the soil. The broadfork is a two-handled, deep cultivation tool. It is used to renovate existing beds that are starting to show signs of compaction. As you work from the edges of the bed, drive the long tines deep into the soil, right through the surface of the bed. The long handles enable even small gardeners to use

their weight to loosen the soil. The purpose is not to turn the soil, but just to loosen it. Work your way across the bed, then finish it as described in Chapter 4 (see Renovating existing beds, pp. 132–3).

Garden rake For smoothing the soil, working in compost and removing stones and debris from beds. The rake is also useful for covering seeds with soil and for working broadcast seeds into the top layer of the bed. Using the back of the rake, you can create a fine, level tilth. Choose a forged steel rake with twelve tines.

Lawn rake For removing leaves from the lawn. A spring-tine rake has flexible metal tines; a fan rake has stiff bamboo tines.

Round-nosed long-handled shovel For digging in heavy or rocky soil. This shovel is quite well suited to digging deep round holes for transplanted trees and bushes. Choose a model with a heavy steel head and a long handle. The typical overall length is about 1.5m/5ft.

Shovel For scooping up compost or other material and transferring it to another location. It is not used for digging. A shovel is larger than a garden spade with angled sides that contain the material on the blade.

Three-tine cultivator or claw hoe For dislodging large weeds and loosening the surface of the soil.

Draw hoe For cutting off weeds just below the surface (as illustrated on p. 146). It is used by holding its long handle in both hands with your thumbs pointing upwards. Your back should be comfortably straight and the blade of the hoe should be parallel to the ground.

HANDTOOLS

Trowel/hand fork For working in garden beds. These are simply smaller versions of shovels and forks.

Three-tine cultivator For delicate weeding in beds.

Bricklayer's trowel For transplanting seedlings into the soil. Hold the tool with the blade facing down and your thumb facing up. Drive the trowel into the soil and pull it towards you, leaving a hole for a soil block. Use the trowel to lift a soil block out of the tray and lower it into the hole.

CUTTING TOOLS

Pruning shears or secateurs For cutting back woody growth and removing dead, diseased or damaged branches. Do not skimp on getting good pruners; left-handed versions are available. Cutting branches that are too large for the tool's bite will damage the pruners.

Pruning saw For removing branches and cutting down trees. A 'turbo saw' is an indispensable cutting tool.

Garden knife A simple pocket knife is very useful if kept sharp. Use a budding knife for grafting. The hooked end of an asparagus knife is used for cutting off asparagus spears below the soil level.

Hedge trimmers or shears For trimming and shaping hedges. Manual trimmers are safer and easier to use than the electric models. Also useful for cutting small or awkward areas of grass. Be sure to sharpen them regularly.

Half-moon edger For cutting a straight edge where the bed meets the turf.

Long-handled edger For cutting grass that grows over the edge of a bed. These look like hedge trimmers with long handles.

OTHER EQUIPMENT

Wheelbarrow For mixing soil with compost, and transporting soil and sundries around the garden. A garden cart with inflatable tyres is suitable for carrying heavy loads and does not tip like a wheelbarrow.

This well-used equipment – hoe, spades, fork, half-moon edger and wheelbarrow – shows that tools will last a lifetime if they receive proper care.

From top: trowel, light pruning shears, scythe, dibber (for planting and sowing), pruning saw and secateurs.

Buckets and baskets For collecting produce in your garden. Choose plastic buckets, as metal ones tend to rust and plastic ones break easily. Baskets that attach to your belt are useful when picking small fruits.

Strimmer For edging grass around beds and paving, and for removing weeds between pavers and around tree trunks. Take care not to girdle trees by hitting their bark with the strimmer; keep the exposed nylon line facing away from the tree. Wear protective goggles to shield your eyes from debris thrown up by the trimmer.

WATERING EQUIPMENT

Watering can A well-balanced watering can is indispensable in the garden. A removable brass rose allows you to water newly planted seedlings without causing erosion.

Garden hose Choose a good-quality hose that is resistant to kinks and has heavy brass fittings. The most useful lengths of hose are 15m/50ft and 30m/100ft.

Sprinkler For irrigating newly seeded lawns or large green manure beds. Both racheting types and oscillating ones are common.

Watering wand For watering container plants, hanging baskets, window troughs and beds without wetting the foliage. The wand attaches to a hose and has a shut-off control fitted on the handle.

Soaker hose For delivering water to the roots of plants without wetting the foliage. Water is released slowly so that it seeps into the ground instead of forming puddles on the surface of the soil. Choose a high-quality soaker model as cheap ones form kinks and clog up easily. Drip irrigation tape is a flattened tube with precise, evenly spaced holes. It works like a soaker hose, but without clogging. Since dirt particles can ruin a soaker hose, filter the water with a 20micron filter beforehand. (See pp. 144–5.)

From top: metal and plastic watering cans, pulse-jet (left) and rotating sprinklers, watering wand and hose.

APPENDIX II: PRESERVING

PRESERVING PRODUCE

Many fruits and vegetables are only available for a short time during the growing season, but with proper storage and harvest extension techniques, they can be made available throughout the year. It is best to store food by methods that retain the maximum amount of vitamins, minerals, phytochemicals and other nutrients. Bottling and freezing are the most common methods of preservation used today, although traditional techniques are experiencing a revival because they preserve nutrients more efficiently and generally use less energy to preserve.

WHY FOOD SPOILS

Fruits and vegetables spoil because of microbial action. Bacteria, yeast and moulds are everywhere. Unlike bottling and freezing, traditional preserving methods, such as lactic fermentation, do not necessarily kill bacteria; they simply prevent them from multiplying by slowing down or stopping their growth. For example, pickling creates an acidic environment that prevents the growth and spread of micro-organisms.

CHOOSING A STORAGE METHOD

First consider the fruit or vegetable that you wish to store and your intended use of the food. Before the invention of bottling and freezing, live storage, drying and lactic fermentation were the most common

Glass jars with tightly sealed lids are ideal for pickling and preserving foods.

methods of storage. Everything that could be kept fresh in a cool, moist place was stored in that way. However, some fruits and vegetables do not store for long periods by this method. Fruits keep particularly well by drying and vegetables tend to store well by lactic fermentation. Other methods of live storage are less useful because they alter the flavour significantly.

BOTTLING AND FREEZING

Both bottling and freezing are forms of dead storage (see *Keeping Food Fresh* by The Gardeners and Farmers of Terre Vivante). Bottling requires lots of heat and pressure to process foods over long periods of time, killing bacteria and moulds that cause food

to spoil. During the heating process, many vitamins are destroyed and phytochemicals are often broken down. Freezing, like bottling, kills or slows the growth of bacteria and moulds. It requires significant energy too, from the time of storage until the time of usage. With most fruits and vegetables, the vitamin content decreases the longer the food is frozen. However, bottling and freezing remain good methods of preservation for some fruits and vegetables. Frozen peas, for example, retain almost all their nutritive value.

LIVE STORAGE

Live storage is the preferred method of winter storage because more

Some vegetables can be preserved in oil, making attractive ornaments. The flavoured oil can also be used.

phytochemicals and vitamins are retained. The easiest method takes a laid-back, passive approach. The vegetables are simply left to stand in the garden until needed. Good examples of this 'garden' storage are the winter cabbages that are ready to harvest in mid-autumn, but remain in good condition until the following spring. The variety 'Tundra' has particularly good standing ability, and will keep until mid-spring. The kales, too, stand well throughout the winter months without showing obvious signs of deterioration.

Leeks and root crops such as beetroots, parsnips and swedes can also be kept outside during the winter, but should be given extra protection by having soil piled up around them. Carrots can be treated the same way; the 'Autumn King' types are best for this type of storage.

Extra insulation can be provided to root crops by covering them with a bulky material such as straw – preferably from an organic source – or leaves. After the last roots are harvested, the covering can then go on to the compost heap.

The system of live storage in the garden is, unfortunately, not a perfect one. Mice, for example, may be a problem, especially with the root crops. Given the amount of rain that falls during the winter, the chances of success are dramatically improved if the crops are grown on a well-drained soil formed into raised beds.

CLAMPING

For the more ambitious gardener with enough time, root crops can be stored in clamps. The clamp is made by piling up the vegetables in a pyramid shape directly on the ground. The roots are then covered by a layer of straw, over which a layer of soil is put. However, the effort is really a wasted one, since the roots will probably store just as well *in situ* in the garden.

ROOT CELLARING

In areas where winter temperatures are near or below freezing, a root cellar can be built to preserve food. The cellar can be as simple as a container of vegetables partially buried in the ground and then covered with soil, or an insulating layer of hay or straw. At the other extreme, it can resemble a small room below ground level. It can be built inside or outside the home, and is insulated and ventilated.

The goal of a root cellar is to keep food between 0°C/32°F and 5°C/40°F with very high humidity (80–90 per cent). Failure to achieve high humidity can result in evaporation that causes food to shrivel and spoil. Moulds can be a problem in high humidity, so make sure there is good ventilation in the cellar. The old adage about one rotten apple spoiling the barrel holds true. Remove immediately any foods that start to spoil. Vegetables and fruits should be stored apart. Generally, different vegetables can be stored in the same container without causing any problems.

For decorative effect, store dried beans in alternating layers of colour.

GARDEN SHEDS AND GARAGES

If they are well ventilated and allow for some air movement, garden sheds and garages can make good stores for your garden produce. Onions and shallots can be woven into ropes or put into nets, and hung from the ceiling where they will be kept dry. Potatoes can be stored on the floor in heavy paper sacks, and covered with blankets if temperatures in the store get too low.

Even root crops can be stored in a shed or garage. The roots should be kept inside wooden boxes, where they are laid down in single layers. Cover each layer with enough moist sand to prevent the roots from touching each other. This reduces the chances of diseases spreading in store.

Fruit and vegetables do not mix in store, so find another place for any apples and pears you want to keep.

LACTIC FERMENTATION

The process of lactic fermentation has fallen out of favour; *sauerkraut* remains the only notable exception. Lactic fermentation preserves without heat or cold and allows the vegetables to retain their nutritional value. The process is simple but only works on vegetables.

Grate or slice vegetables into small pieces and season them with herbs before adding salt or a mild salt water solution. Without salt, the process will not work. The amount of salt added depends on the quantity of vegetables. Weigh the vegetables and add the salt at a rate of 1.5–2.0 per cent of the weight.

Let the vegetables soak in their own juices (or brine solution if salt water was added). Micro-organisms develop in the solution and convert the sugars in the vegetables into lactic acid. When the vegetables and solution become acidic enough, the bacteria that cause food to rot and spoil will be unable to survive.

Bottling jars can be used for this process. Allow 1–3 tablespoons of salt per 1qt/l jar. Leave the jars without their lids on in the kitchen for a week or so, covered with a cloth to keep out contaminants. Be sure the liquid stays above the level of the vegetables – evaporation may lower the level. Then cover the jars loosely with the lids and move them to a cool place. Tighten the lids after five weeks, when the gas given off during the fermentation process will have died down. Some cooks prefer to loosely fasten the lids for the first week of fermentation.

Vegetables preserved in this way are acidic and tend to be only palatable in small quantities unless they are prepared by cooking. They are a good supplement to vegetables stored in a garden shed or garage. Many people choose to cook vegetables preserved in this way to reduce their acidity, but this destroys nutrients and affects texture. You can rinse the vegetables to reduce the salt content and acidity. If you add water, be sure that it is not chlorinated, as this will prevent fermentation.

DRYING

Fruits and herbs can be stored effectively by drying, but most vegetables lose their flavour and vitamins when dried. Dried tomatoes, dried beans, sweetcorn and popcorn are notable exceptions. Drying in the kitchen can be easily accomplished in any climate. Fruits are simply placed on trays or non-metallic screens and left in a warm oven or a hot dry place until 80–90 per cent of the moisture is removed from the food. The lack of moisture stops the growth of microbes that spoil food. As the fruit dries, the sugar becomes concentrated and the flavour is much sweeter. If the food is not dried in excessive heat, most of the nutrients are preserved. Food stored in this way can be kept for long periods of time without spoiling.

Some fruits may lose their colour and nutrient content when dried. This is caused by the action of certain enzymes. In some fruits, blanching for a few minutes before drying destroys these enzymes and prevents colour and vitamin loss. For specific details on drying fruits, consult a cookery book. Slice the fruit thinly, and peel the fruit if desired, before oven or sun drying.

SUN DRYING

Make a drying rack from a simple wooden frame covered with a non-metallic or fibreglass screen, or a very thin non-absorbent cloth. Allow plenty of air space between the sliced fruit when it is placed on the screen. Low humidity, air circulation and hot days are the key to success when drying outdoors. Set up the screen on a stand that allows air to flow over and under the fruit. Make sure it cannot be upset by the wind or attacked by pests. Cover the tray with another screen or thin cloth to protect from insects.

OVEN DRYING

Preheat the oven to 66°C/150°F and use a good-quality kitchen thermometer to ensure accuracy. Place the fruit on baking trays in a single layer, spaced widely apart and position them several rows apart on the oven shelves. Open the door to lower the oven temperature to 49°C/120°F. Rearrange the baking trays from top to bottom, turning them so that

Onions should be dried before storing. When drying indoors, ensure they have good ventilation.

the fruit dries evenly. Return the heat to about 60°C/140°F for half of the drying time. The overall drying time varies from 6 to 48 hours, depending on the size of the pieces and the fruit being dried.

Test the fruit for dryness by squeezing it to see whether any moisture is released. Fruit should appear leathery and vegetables should be dry and brittle. The weight of each piece will be reduced by one-half to two-thirds.

OTHER METHODS OF LIVE STORAGE

There are many other methods of preserving food that do not destroy nutrients. Most produce food that has distinctive flavour for specialized use. An example of this is making grapes, blueberries or apples into wine.

Preserving in vinegar or pickling This is similar to lactic fermentation. Vegetables, such as cucumbers

and beets, are stored in a vinegar/water solution to create an acidic environment to prevent food spoilage.

Preserving with sugar Jellies and jams are typical examples. Avoid adding more sugar than is necessary to preserve the food – this makes the jam sweeter and raises the calorie content too.

Preserving in oil Used to preserve garlic and other flavoursome vegetables, the oil that remains is almost as valuable as the vegetable itself because of its flavour. Many vegetables and fruits can be kept in oil for a long time and used as needed in the kitchen. They make attractive ornaments when stored in coloured or shaped glass bottles.

Preserving in alcohol A traditional method of preserving medicinal plants. Fruits are often made into wine or simply placed in alcohol to prevent them from spoiling.

USEFUL ADDRESSES

ORGANIC ORGANIZATIONS

Garden Organic (formerly HDRA)
Ryton Organic Gardens
Coventry CV8 3LG
Tel: 024 7630 3517
Fax: 024 7663 9229
www.gardenorganic.org.uk

The Soil Association
Bristol House
40–56 Victoria Street
Bristol BS1 6BY
Tel: 0117 929 0661
Fax: 0117 925 2504
info@soilassociation.org.uk
www.soilassociation.org.uk

Biodynamic Agricultural Association
Painswick Inn Project
Gloucester Street
Stroud
Gloucestershire GL5 1QG
Tel/fax: 01453 759501
bdaa@biodynamic.freeserve.co.uk
www.anth.org.uk/biodynamic

Permaculture Association (Britain)
BCM Permaculture Association
London WC1N 3XX
Tel: 07041 390170
office@permaculture.org.uk
www.permaculture.org.uk

Centre for Alternative Technology
Machynlleth
Powys SY20 9AZ
Tel: 01654 702400
Fax: 01654 702782
info@cat.org.uk
www.cat.org.uk

ORGANIC SEEDS

Organic Gardening Catalogue
Riverdene
Molesey Road
Hersham
Surrey KT12 4RG
Tel: 01932 253666
Fax: 01932 252707
www.organiccatalog.co.uk

Heritage Seed Library (see Garden Organic)
A collection of heirloom open-pollinated varieties accessed by separate membership.

Tamar Organics
Unit 5a West Bridge Industrial Estate
Tavistock
Devon PL19 8DE
tamarorganics@compuserve.com
www.tamarorganics.co.uk

Terre de Semences
Ripple Farm
Crundale, Canterbury
Kent CT4 7EB
Tel: 01966 448379
www.terredesemences.com

Edwin Tucker and Sons
Brewery Meadow
Stonepark, Ashburton
Newton Abbot
Devon TQ13 7DG
Tel: 01364 652403
Fax: 01364 654300

Unwins Seeds Ltd
Mail Order Dept
Histon, Cambridge
CB4 9ZZ
Tel: 01945 588522
Fax: 01945 475255

Mr Fothergill's Seeds
Mail Order Dept
Kentford, Newmarket
Suffolk CB8 7QB
Tel: 01638 750468
Fax: 01638 552512
mailorder@mr-fothergills.co.uk

E.W. King and Co. Ltd
Monks Farm
Coggleshall Road
Kelvedon
Essex CO5 9PG
Tel: 01376 570000
Fax: 01376 571189
(Also **Suffolk Herbs** at same address)
suffolkherbs@internet.com

C.N. Seeds
Denmark House
Pymoor, Ely
Cambridgeshire CB6 2EG
Tel: 01353 699413
Fax: 01353 698806
chris@cnseeds.demon.co.uk
www.cnseeds.demon.co.uk

NURSERIES

Blooming Things
Dept HD
Y Bwthyn, Cymerau
Glandyfi, Machynlleth
Powys SY20 8SS
Tel/Fax: 01654 781256

Butterworth's Organic Nursery
Garden Cottage
Auchinleck Estate
Cumnock
Ayrshire KA18 2LR
Tel: 01290 551088
Organic fruit trees.

Jekka's Herb Farm
Rose Cottage
Shellards Lane
Alverston, Bristol
Avon BS35 3SY
Tel: 01454 418878
Fax: 01454 411988
Organic herb plants.

Welsh Fruit Stocks
Brygwyn
Kington
Hereford HR5 5SQ
www.welshfruitstocks.co.uk
Organic soft fruit plants.

Waterland Organics
Quaystone Cottage
The Hythe
Reach
Cambridgeshire CB5 OJQ
Tel: 01638 742178
Organic soft fruit plants.

Leaving an area unmown provides a habitat for beneficial insects and animals.

INDEX

Bold figures refer to main entries.
Italic figures refer to information
given in boxes or picture captions.

peppers 88, *88*, 135, **234–5**,
234, 235
  chilli peppers 171, *171*, 234,
    235
  hot peppers 235, *235*
  sweet peppers 235
perennials 75, 108
  feeding 149
  mulching 149
pesticides and fungicides 12, 13,
  14, 30, 82, 169, 171
  organic forms 168, 169, 171
  resistance to 69–70
pests and diseases 8, 12, 15, 23,
  64, 65, 80, **168–77**
  animal pests 23, 157, 159,
    171, 175
  barriers and traps *153*, 169, 175
  biological controls 8, 169, 172
  companion planting and 64–5,
    118–19
  disease resistance 64, 150
  diseases and ailments 176–7
  fruit 150, *153*, 159, 176, 177
  in greenhouses 98, 169, 172
  natural predators 12, 15, 23,
    65, 121, 123, 169, 173–4
  non-native pests 12
  pest types 174–5
  prevention and control 168–72
pH 26, 34, 38, 39, 42
  adjusting 37, 54–5, 133
  testing 34, 129
Phasmarhabditis hermaphrodita 172
pheronomes 8
phosphate deficiency 177
phosphorus 53, 55, 56, 87
phytochemicals 9, 64, *82, 84, 86,*
88–9, 180
Phytoseiulus persimilis 172, 175
pickling 279
pine needles 54, 55, 148
pine nuts 104
pineapples 89
planning the garden
  companion planting 64–5,
    118–19
  edible landscaping 16, 65,
    100–101
  food consumption 64, 92
  hazards 102
  landscaping 65
  locating trees, bushes and
    perennials 105–6, 109–10
  nutritional needs 64, 82–3

screening 101, *110*, 113
views 102, 105
winter colour and interest 101, 110
year-round harvest 90–92
see also choosing plants; crop
  protection; crop rotation; garden plans and planting ideas;
  herb gardens; wildlife
plant hardiness 64, 66, 83, 90,
105
planting distances 134–5
plate seeders 137, *137*
plums 88, 151, **254**, *254*
pollen beetles 174
pollination 65
  cross-pollination 75–6, 153
  fruit 153
  open pollination 17, 24, 64, 68,
    72, 73, 74
  self-pollination 75
  wind-pollination 70, 76
pollution 12, 13, 16
polytunnels 90, 92, 98, 169, 173
potassium 42, 53, 55, 56, 87,
149
  deficiency 177
potato blight 176–7
potatoes 25, 73, 80, 81, 89, *109,*
119, *148*, 169, **240–41**, *240,*
241, 278
  varieties 241
potting on 143
poultry manure *40, 41*
powdery mildew 171, 176
preserving produce 25, 82, 90,
276–9
  in alcohol 279
  bottling and freezing 25, 82, 83,
    276
  clamping 277
  dead storage 82
  drying 278–9
  in garden sheds and garages 278
  lactic fermentation 82, 276, 278
  live storage 82, 92, 276–9
  in oil 82, 279
  pickling 279
  root cellaring 82, 277
  with sugar 279
propagation
  asexual 73, 74, 75
  from seed 75
pruning
  basic cuts 165
  callus formation 165

fruit 155, **164–7**
  guidelines 164–5
  heading back 165, *165*, 166,
    167
  large branches, removing 165–6
  purpose 164
  thinning out 165, *165*, 167
  timing 165
  training trees into shapes 164,
    167, 167
pruning saw 273, *275*
pruning shears 273, *275*
prunings
  soft prunings 42
  woody prunings 42–3
pumpkins 213, *213*
purslane 247
pyrethrins 171
pyrethrum 119, 171

Q
quinces 151, **249**, *249*

R
rabbits 23, *157*, 159, 175, *175*
radishes 80, 91, 92, **203**, *203*
rainfall, excessive 168
rainwater collection system 144
raised beds *38*, 98, **99**, *99*
rakes *270, 272*
rape 58
raspberries 88, 100, 103, 104,
109, 122, 151, **262**, *262*
  varieties 262
raw vegetables and fruits 83, 89
red spider mites 98, 172
Rhizobium 60, 218
rhubarb 233, *233*
rock dust 56, 133
rock phosphate (colloidal phosphate)
56
rocket 246
root cellaring 82, 277
root crops 80, 81, 92
rootstocks 153, 162
Rosa rugosa 100, 122
rosehips 100, *100*, 101, 122
rosemary 110, 114, 269
runner beans 219, *219*, 220, *220,*
221, 222
rust 176

S
sage 110, 121, 269
salad onions 228

ACKNOWLEDGMENTS

Many thanks to my family – especially David, Helen, Charlie, Stella and William – for their inspiration and support. I also wish to thank everyone at Frances Lincoln, especially Jo Christian, Jo Grey, and Carey Smith. Special thanks to my friends Stella, John, Lavinia, and Francis. For her work on the organization of the book in the early days, I'm indebted to Susan Berry. There is no way to express my gratitude to Steven Wooster for his spectacular photography. I also thank John Ferguson for introducing me to Frances Lincoln. David deserves so much appreciation for being my own personal horticultural expert in his proofreading of the 110,000 word manuscript. And finally I'd like to thank everyone who allowed photos to be taken in their gardens.